IEG WORLD BAI
INDEPENDENT EVALUATION GROUP

Evaluative Lessons from World Bank Group Experience

Growth and Productivity in Agriculture and Agribusiness

2011
The World Bank
Washington, D.C.

Cover photo: Women are harvesting vegetables in the Kathmandu Valley, Nepal. © Jorgen Schytte/Specialist Stock.

ISBN: 978-0-8213-8606-4
eISBN: 978-0-8213-8646-0
DOI: 10.1596/978-0-8213-8606-4

Library of Congress Cataloging-in-Publication data.

Growth and productivity in agriculture and agribusiness : evaluative lessons from World Bank Group experience.
    p. cm.
ISBN 978-0-8213-8606-4 -- ISBN 978-0-8213-8646-0
1. World Bank. 2. International Finance Corporation. 3. Agricultural assistance—Developing countries. 4. Agricultural industries—Developing countries—Finance. 5. Agriculture—Economic aspects—Developing countries. I. World Bank.
HD1431.G76 2011
338.109172'4--dc22

2011000434

World Bank InfoShop
E-mail: pic@worldbank.org
Telephone: 202-458-5454
Facsimile: 202-522-1500

Independent Evaluation Group
Communications, Learning, and Strategy
E-mail: ieg@worldbank.org
Telephone: 202-458-4497
Facsimile: 202-522-3125

 Printed on Recycled Paper

Table of Contents

Appendixes

Boxes

Figures

Tables

Abbreviations

AAA	Analytic and advisory activities
ARD	Agriculture and Rural Development (Department, World Bank)
ATMA	Agricultural Technology Management Agency (India)
CAE	Country Assistance Evaluation
CAG	Agribusiness Department, IFC
CAS	Country Assistance Strategy
CBO	Community-based organization
CDD	Community-driven development
CGIAR	Consultative Group on International Agricultural Research
CGS	Competitive Grant Scheme
CPIA	Country Policy and Institutional Assessment
DFID	Department for International Development (U.K.)
DO	Development outcome (IFC)
DPL	Development policy loan/lending
EBRD	European Bank for Reconstruction and Development
ESW	Economic and sector work
EU	European Union
F&A	Food and Agriculture (Sector, IFC)
FAO	Food and Agriculture Organization of the United Nations
FDI	Foreign direct investment
FIAS	Foreign Investment Advisory Service
GDP	Gross domestic product
GNI	Gross national income
IBRD	International Bank for Reconstruction and Development
ICR	Implementation Completion Report
IDA	International Development Association
IEG	Independent Evaluation Group
IFC	International Finance Corporation
IFPRI	International Food Policy Research Institute
IO	Investment outcome (IFC)
M&E	Monitoring and evaluation
MDG	Millennium Development Goal
NGO	Nongovernmental organization
ODA	Official development assistance
OECD	Organisation for Economic Co-operation and Development
OPCS	Operations Policy and Country Services
PRSC	Poverty Reduction Support Credit
PRSP	Poverty Reduction Strategy Paper
QAE	Quality at entry
QAG	Quality Assurance Group
QSA	Quality of Supervision Assessment
R&D	Research and development
SME	Small and medium-size enterprise
WDR	World Development Report
WUA	Water users association
XPSR	Expanded Project Supervision Report (IFC)

Acknowledgments

This report was prepared by a core team consisting of Nalini Kumar (Task Manager, IEG-World Bank), Miguel Angel Rebolledo Dellepiane (Task Manager, IEG-IFC), Jock Anderson, Rex Bosson, April Connelly, Jouni Eerikainen, Flora Nankhuni, Victoria Viray-Mendoza, and Hassan Wally under the guidance of Cheryl Gray, Monika Huppi, and Stoyan Tenev. In addition, valuable input was received from (alphabetically) Anna Amato, Malcolm Bale, Regina Birner, Debora Brakarz, Richard Burcroff, Tarik Chafdi, Zhigang Chen, Carlos Cuevas, Gayatri Datar, Ximena Del Carpio, Kutlay Ebiri, Victoria Elliott, Peter Gaff, Jorge Garcia-Garcia, Joy Hecht, Narpat Jodha, Shashi Kolavalli, Lisa Moorman, Ridley Nelson, Mark Newman, Keith Oblitas, Nethra Palaniswamy, Katharina Raabe, Neeru Sharma, Shampa Sinha, Xingwen Wang, and Xiaobo Zhang. Other IEG colleagues and consultants who provided input included Alemayehu Ambel, Lopamudra Chakraborti, Sophia Flores Cruz, Gita Gopal, Fareed Hassan, John Heath, Silke Heuser, Ramachandra Jammi, Kavita Mathur, Keith Pitman, and Helena Tang. William Hurlbut and Caroline McEuen edited the report. Marie Charles, Janice Joshi, Richard Kraus, Rosemarie Pena, and Svetlana Raykova provided research and administrative support.

James Bond, Denis Carpio, John Eriksson, Gershon Feder, Albert Stocker, and Décio Zylbersztajn provided valuable contributions as peer reviewers. The report has also benefitted tremendously from the council of an external expert advisory panel comprised of Michel Debatisse, P. K. Joshi, Ramatu Mahama, and C. Peter Timmer.

The report benefited from guidance provided by Martha Ainsworth, Soniya Carvalho, Ken Chomitz, Shahrokh Fardoust, Daniela Gressani, Mark Sundberg, Marvin Taylor-Dormond, and Vinod Thomas.

Colleagues inside the World Bank and IFC also provided valuable comments and support at various stages: Gokhan Akinci, Imoni Akpofure, Nabil Chaherli, Oscar Chemerinski, Sanjiva Cooke, Marc Tristant De Laney, Yolande Duhem, Sushma Ganguli, Usaid El-Hanbaly, Richard Henry, Willem Janssen, Renate Kloeppinger-Todd, Patrick Labaste, John Lamb, Julian Lampietti, Amelia Laya, Paolo Martelli, Patricia Miller, Stephen Mink, Osaretin Odaro, Mary Porter Peschka, Solomon Quaynor, Chris Richards, Pierre Rondot, Tijan Salah, Ethel Sennhauser, Ahmad Shawky, Nada Shousha, Anil Sinha, Maki Tsumagari, John Underwood, German Vegarra, Juergen Voegele, Peter White, and J. W. Van Holst Pellekaan.

This review was greatly enhanced by the generous support of the Swiss Agency for Development and Cooperation and the Norwegian Agency for Development Cooperation.

Director-General, Evaluation: *Vinod Thomas*
Director, IEG-World Bank: *Cheryl Gray*
Director, IEG-IFC: *Marvin Taylor-Dormond*
Manager, IEG, Sector Evaluation: *Monica Huppi*
Head, Macro Evaluation, IEG-IFC: *Stoyan Tenev*
Task Manager, IEG-World Bank: *Nalini Kumar*
Task Manager, IEG-IFC: *Miguel Rebolledo Dellepiane*

Foreword

One billion people worldwide still live in extreme poverty. Agricultural growth remains central to poverty reduction, particularly in the poorest countries, where a large share of the population relies on agriculture for their livelihood. At the same time, global demand for some of the major agricultural product groups is growing due to the growth in population and incomes, dietary shifts, and demand for biofuels.

In these circumstances, a steady increase in agricultural production driven by greater productivity is needed. But growth in agricultural productivity has been held back in recent years by a number of factors—land and water constraints, underinvestment in rural infrastructure and agricultural innovation, lack of access to inputs, and weather disruptions. Climate change is already adding to the severe stress on the environment for agriculture.

The recent food and financial crises have added momentum to an emerging renewal of financing for agriculture and agribusi-

committed $23.7 billion in financing agricultural activities in addition to analytical work and advisory services. This was less than half of the commitments in the agricultural portfolio (and an even lower share in Sub-Saharan Africa), with the rest being directed to other rural activities.

Second, special attention is warranted for the agriculture-based economies, particularly those of Sub-Saharan Africa, where the needs are greatest and the success has been lowest. IFC, which has made an important entry into the Region, has nevertheless had limited engagement in this period. All Regions have important needs that the Bank Group should continue to support, given the increased demand for food. Yet greater effectiveness in the poorest countries is the most crucial challenge.

A third encompassing opportunity lies in exploiting synergies for which the Bank Group is uniquely positioned. Expanded public investments, be they in research or infrastructure, will pay off only if linked to private business—for example, in its

Photo courtesy of Julio Pantoja/World Bank.

ness at the World Bank Group and other international financial agencies. This augmented engagement is timely and welcome, but the crucial question concerns what steps would lead to greater effectiveness than in the past. This evaluation of World Bank Group support for agriculture aims to inform this issue.

A first overarching lesson concerns the needed focus of action. While broader rural and social development contributes to agricultural development, increase in productivity requires focused attention to the availability of improved crop production techniques, supply of water and agrochemicals, market access for farmers, and a favorable legal and policy environment. During 1998–2008 the World Bank and IFC together

marketing or financing aspects. The World Bank and IFC can partner more effectively than in the past, linking public and private investments, national and global initiatives, and financing and knowledge programs. Concerted efforts can also be channeled toward enhancing capacity for the clients as well as for staff as the Bank Group seeks to match the increase in financing with its own know-how.

The World Bank Group can help make a vital difference as countries confront old problems of improving agricultural yields and new challenges of the environment and climate change. Lessons learned both from the past and in real time provide precious avenues for a lasting impact.

Vinod Thomas

Vinod Thomas
Director-General, Evaluation

Executive Summary

Enhanced agricultural growth and productivity are essential if we are to meet the world-wide demand for food and reduce poverty, particularly in the poorest developing countries. Between 1998 and 2008, the period covered by this evaluation, the World Bank Group provided $23.7 billion in financing for agriculture and agribusiness in 108 countries (roughly 8 percent of total World Bank Group financing), spanning areas from irrigation and marketing to research and extension. This was, however, a time of declining focus on agricultural growth and productivity by both countries and donors.

The cost of inadequate attention to agriculture, especially in agriculture-based economies, came into focus with the food crisis of 2007–08. The crisis added momentum to an emerging renewal of attention and stepped-up financing to agriculture and agribusiness at the World Bank and International Finance Corporation (IFC), as well as at several multilateral and bilateral agencies. World Bank financing rose two and a half times from 2008 to 2009, although this increased lending seems to have been accompanied by a decline in analytical work, which this review finds valuable in achieving results. This evaluation seeks to provide lessons from successes and failures in the Bank Group's activities in the sector to help improve the development impact of the renewed attention.

Ratings against the World Bank's stated objectives and IFC's market-based benchmarks for agriculture and agribusiness projects have equaled or surpassed portfolio averages in East Asia, Latin America, and the transition economies in Europe,

with notable successes over a long period in China and India. But performance of World Bank Group interventions has been well below average in Sub-Saharan Africa, where IFC has had little engagement in agribusiness. Inconsistent client commitment and weak capacity have limited the effectiveness of Bank Group support in agriculture-based economies, particularly in Sub-Saharan Africa, and constraints on staffing and internal coordination within the Bank Group have also hurt outcomes. Financial sustainability has been constrained by insufficient government funding and the difficulty of maintaining agricultural services and infrastructure.

The World Bank Group has a unique opportunity to match the increases in financing for agriculture with a sharper focus on improving agricultural growth and productivity in agriculture-based economies, notably in Sub-Saharan Africa. Greater effort will be needed to connect sectoral interventions and achieve synergies from public and private sec-

tor interventions; to build capacity and knowledge exchange; to take stock of experience in rain-fed agriculture; to ensure attention to financial sustainability and to cross-cutting issues of gender, environmental, and social impacts and climate; and to better integrate World Bank Group support at the global and regional levels with that at the country level.

One billion people around the world are still chronically poor and undernourished. These people are concentrated in rural areas, and the donor community recognizes that without improved agricultural growth and productivity, it is unlikely that poverty will be reduced, and the Millennium Development Goals will not be achieved. Moreover, increased agricultural production will be necessary to meet the expected doubling of worldwide demand for food by 2050 as population, incomes, and consumption of animal products grow. However, any increase in production will have to be brought about in an environment where natural resources are scarce and promoting efficiency is critical.

This evaluation uses the typology of economies developed by the *Agriculture for Development: World Development Report 2008* as one classification in its analysis. In the agriculture-based category, which includes most of Sub-Saharan Africa, development of the agriculture sector is essential to growth and poverty reduction, yet productivity is low, constrained by limited access to modern inputs, irrigation, communication, and transport. World Bank Group support focused on alleviating these constraints is important to help achieve poverty reduction.

In the transforming category—mainly countries in South and East Asia and the Middle East and North Africa—the sector's contribution to economic growth is comparatively less important, and land and labor productivity are much higher, but poverty is still predominantly a rural phenomenon. In these economies Bank Group support for growth in agriculture is needed to reduce poverty and narrow the urban-rural divide.

In the urbanized category—mainly countries in Latin America and Europe and Central Asia—poverty is no longer primarily rural and agriculture contributes relatively little to growth. But even in this last category, Bank Group support in the sector can contribute to economic development and to the adoption of new technologies to sustainably increase productivity.

Growing demand for both animal products and biofuels provides increased opportunities for the private sector to invest profitably to grow grains for livestock feed and sugarcane and non-food crops for biofuels. But water availability will be an increasing constraint. Climate change is likely to make water sources more variable, and increased droughts and floods will further stress agricultural systems.

World Bank Group Financing

Between 1998 and 2008, the World Bank Group provided about $23.7 billion in financing for agriculture and agribusiness activities in 108 countries. Seventy-six percent, or $18.1 billion, of this support came from the World Bank and 24 percent, or $5.6 billion, from IFC. An additional $3.8 billion was committed by the World Bank and $1.6 billion by IFC in 2009. Both the World Bank and IFC also provided nonlending services to their clients, and the World Bank supported several global and regional programs and partnerships in the agriculture sector.

Only a share of World Bank interventions that included support for agricultural activities focused on improving agricultural growth and productivity in poor, agriculture-based economies. The Bank's strategic focus shifted in the early 1990s from a narrower focus on agriculture to a broader focus on poverty and rural development; this led to Bank-supported projects focusing beyond agricultural production in the rural sector. Many rural projects, for example, adopted community-driven development (CDD) approaches in which agricultural development was one of many priorities. This trend was particularly pronounced in Sub-Saharan Africa, which had one of the smallest shares among Bank Regions of rural projects focused explicitly on improving agricultural growth and productivity. IFC investments, although focused on agribusiness growth and development, were concentrated primarily in urbanized and transforming economies in Latin America and Europe and Central Asia.

Project ratings against stated objectives in World Bank lending for agriculture have been on a par with lending in other sectors, with Europe and Central Asia achieving higher results than the Bank-wide average, and Sub-Saharan Africa notably lower results. Not only is the environment for agricultural development less favorable in Sub-Saharan Africa's agriculture-based economies—with poor road and market infrastructure, underdeveloped financial sectors, and higher weather-related and disease risks—but country capacity and governance are weaker as well. The relatively poor project performance, problems in governance, and limited counterpart interest in agriculture in many countries help to explain why the Bank has looked for alternative ways to engage these borrowers, including CDD interventions, among others.

Similarly, IFC investments in agribusiness had above-average development outcome ratings in Latin America and the Caribbean and Europe and Central Asia but have been weak in Sub-Saharan Africa. In Latin America and the Caribbean and Europe and Central Asia, successful outcomes resulted from effective support to the integrated trader-processor model, and some of IFC's clients have become local and regional enterprises and south-south investors. Difficult business environments, a shortage of indigenous entrepreneurs, the small size of the potential investments, lack of access to markets, and the discouraging experience of working directly with small-scale sponsors have constrained IFC engagement and performance in Sub-Saharan Africa and pushed it toward a focus on foreign sponsors and export-oriented or niche local or regional businesses, such as palm oil and rubber.

The evaluation assesses the Bank Group's contribution in six areas—irrigation and drainage, research and extension, access to credit, access to land and formalization of land rights, roads and marketing infrastructure, and markets and agribusiness—with a goal of identifying lessons for the future.

In **irrigation and drainage**, World Bank Group support for physical infrastructure has helped provide farmers with access to water, and thus has contributed to increased agricultural productivity, but lack of reliable funding for operation and maintenance has made sustainability an issue. The World Bank Group needs to devote more attention and resources to helping governments design and implement politically and institutionally feasible mechanisms for cost recovery, to facilitate a larger role for the private sector by helping clients foster an environment in which public-private partnerships can succeed, and to monitor results more diligently. Greater attention to water use efficiency and its monitoring is also needed. The recent IEG evaluation of the Bank's water-related activities (IEG 2010f) also highlighted the above issues for greater focus. Further, the Bank needs to separately track its water management activities in rain-fed areas to allow the institution to take stock of what works in addressing water management issues in these areas and to contribute strategically to their development.

Both the Bank and IFC have supported **research and extension**, the Bank through support to global programs (most notably the Consultative Group on International Agricultural Research, CGIAR), to public systems in client countries, and to partnership arrangements with other stakeholders, and IFC through financing and advisory services to agribusiness trader-processors, who in turn assist their contract farmers. Previous reviews have noted that links between CGIAR centers and national programs are weak; research results from CGIAR institutions need to be mainstreamed consistently in country-level Bank projects. Sustainability has been an issue in the Bank's support for research and extension because of insufficient government funding and limited cost recovery, whereas IFC's trader-processors can recover costs through the prices paid for farmers' crops.

The World Bank Group can also help governments create the conditions for nascent agribusiness technology companies to thrive, both on their own and in partnership with public research institutions. The outcomes of World Bank Group in-

terventions have been better when interventions combined investment and knowledge services and built on partnerships. Better monitoring and evaluation (M&E) is needed in projects, because there is limited evidence on the extent to which improved technologies have been created or adopted as a result of Bank interventions.

Access to credit, whether for buying inputs in the short term or for investing in land improvements in the long term, is a major constraint to investments to improve agricultural productivity, and the Bank and IFC are both important for expanding credit supply and efficiency. In response to a disappointing experience with support to rural credit, the Bank shifted from directed agricultural credit to a broader rural finance approach focused on strengthening the capacity of financial institutions to operate in rural areas. The broader approach appears to be benefiting the agriculture sector, although it is difficult to ascertain how much support has been provided specifically for agricultural credit. Sustainability beyond project duration remains a challenge, and greater synergy is needed between financial sector interventions and agriculture lending. Addressing risks related to weather and prices in the agriculture sector also requires synergies among agriculture, financial sector, and disaster and risk-management lending.

IFC has used investments in trader-processors, trade finance, private equity, wholesaling through banks, and index insurance products to promote access to credit. Some of these approaches have demonstrated effectiveness in improving the livelihood of small-scale farmers; for example, providing small amounts to thousands of individual farmers through large trader-processors can make a big difference, sometimes involving commercial lenders and buy-back arrangements.

Access to land and formalization of land rights are thought to contribute to both poverty reduction and improvements in agricultural production and productivity, and the Bank and IFC have been quite active in both—most notably land administration—in recent years. Evidence of the impacts of these efforts on agricultural productivity is sparse, however, particularly for land administration, because these projects do not typically have agricultural productivity as a core objective to be monitored. Greater emphasis is needed on measurement of these impacts to reflect the increasing focus on production and productivity in the Bank's agricultural portfolio. Given the multifaceted nature of agricultural development, in some settings it may be important to combine land administration with other support services to achieve productivity gains.

The Bank has been engaged extensively in building **roads and marketing infrastructure**, including rural roads, and both the Bank and IFC have invested in other market infrastructure and logistics, such as storage, ports, forwarders, and trading platforms. Available data point to high average success rates in these projects, although this is less so in Sub-Saharan Africa. Given the low rates of market access in Sub-Saharan Africa, the World Bank and IFC need to continue to seek innovative ways to support the development and maintenance of transport and market infrastructure in the Region through both public and private investments.

Finally, the World Bank Group has provided extensive support to clients to improve the **broader enabling environment,** including through World Bank development policy lending and access to input and output markets, including through the development of agribusiness linked to small-scale producers. Where the Bank has done this effectively, it has often used analytic and advisory activities as an entry point. Appropriate policies and a supportive business environment are critical to agricultural development, and although much progress has been made through liberalization and globalization in the past two to three decades, challenges remain. The complementary roles of the Bank and IFC should be recognized and coordinated much more thoroughly.

Institutional Factors

Institutional issues in countries—including commitment, capacity, and governance—strongly influence the level and effectiveness of World Bank Group activities in agriculture. Commitment to agricultural development has been strong for decades in some transforming and urbanized economies, such as China and India (which dramatically increased their investments in the agriculture sector from the 1950s to the 1980s), and rose rapidly with the economic transition in the early 1990s in some Central and Eastern European countries. However, it has been relatively weak until recently in many agriculture-based economies, in part due to a greater emphasis on industrialization and urbanization in postwar development thinking. In addition, serious capacity and governance constraints make it difficult for projects to achieve desired objectives in many settings.

Institutional limitations within the World Bank Group have also inhibited its contribution to agricultural development, particularly in Sub-Saharan Africa and the agriculture-based economies. Until recently the Bank and IFC lacked a focused strategy that prioritized agricultural growth and productivity. Potential synergies among sectors such as transport, finance, and agriculture have sometimes been missed within the World Bank and IFC, and synergies between the complementary public-private sector roles of the World Bank and IFC have not yet been fully exploited. Though farming is essentially a private sector activity, a minimum level of public capacity is needed for the private sector to work effectively, and ideally the World Bank Group entities can work synergistically to support both the public and private sectors.

Though data are incomplete, quantitative and qualitative evidence points to a decline in agriculture-related skills over the past decade (including skills in policy analysis and client dialogue) among World Bank staff, most notably in Sub-Saharan Africa. There is also a shortage of agribusiness specialists in IFC relative to the need.

These factors may all have contributed to the recognized weaknesses in World Bank project outcomes and project quality at entry and supervision in Sub-Saharan Africa. They may also constrain implementation of the recent Agriculture Action Plan 2010–12 (World Bank 2009e) and a stronger IFC agribusiness presence in Sub-Saharan Africa in the future. Recent IFC decentralization efforts run the risk of exacerbating this situation by further stretching scarce industry expertise.

M&E continues to be weak in both investment and development policy lending, and the Bank's data and coding systems do not effectively track all agriculture activities. Reporting on outcomes and results—such as improvement in water-use efficiency, adoption of technologies, and agricultural productivity—is incomplete in both the Bank and IFC, and this constrains assessment of project effectiveness and inhibits institutional learning.

The World Bank Group's analytic work has made important contributions and needs to be supported and linked to lending where possible, particularly in poorer countries. Analytic work is critical in identifying issues and informing both policy advice and financing. The Bank's agriculture analytic and advisory activities (AAA) have generally been of sound quality, and the lending these activities informed had better outcomes than lending that was not. However, in some of the poorer International Development Association (IDA) countries, such as Ethiopia, Ghana, Guinea, and Nepal, little AAA was done in the agriculture sector over several years.

IFC advisory services have been largely supply-driven and have lacked a focus on relevant agribusiness subsectors. Few advisory services leveraged outcomes by linking with investments.

Gender and environment are cross-cutting World Bank Group priorities, and agriculture and agribusiness could make a strong contribution to gender empowerment and environmental sustainability. In the Bank, greater attention has been paid to gender issues during the design of projects than in their implementation, and both need to be stepped up. In IFC, the tracking of gender in agribusiness is limited to the number of women employed, and a richer set of indicators is needed.

With regard to environment, Bank-supported projects appear to be generally in compliance with the Bank's environmental safeguards, but supervision and reporting related to safeguards and environmental outcomes are weak. In addition, Bank projects have the potential to improve the readiness of countries to deal with the effects of climate change, and focused analytical work can be important in helping clients identify the direct links between agricultural production and climate change, a rising priority across countries.

IFC's Performance Standards have been viewed as a key component of IFC's additionality in the sector, but their implementation needs a more robust approach for identifying and addressing environmental and social risks along the supply chain. Inadequate management of agribusiness supply-chain issues has been evident in four pre–Performance Standards and in two post–Performance Standards projects based on complaints submitted to the compliance advisor and ombudsman, reflecting the concerns of individuals or communities affected by various IFC investments. Addressing the environmental impacts of agribusiness remains a crucial challenge, especially in light of today's heightened concerns about environmental destruction where regulations are weak.

Although IFC has been an early supporter, commodity roundtables have not yet developed internationally accepted standards for supply-chain certification, and more attention is needed in this area. Commodity roundtables need to develop rigorous certification systems to provide sustainability for food and agribusiness production along the entire supply chain. Once they are developed, IFC could refer to roundtable certification in project-specific environmental and social requirements and promote their use as global standards.

Recommendations

The overarching recommendation of this review is:

To get the most from recent increases in financing for agriculture and agribusiness, the World Bank Group needs to increase the effectiveness of its support for agricultural growth and productivity in agriculture-based economies, notably Sub-Saharan Africa.

It is in the agriculture-based economies, particularly those of Sub-Saharan Africa, that the needs are greatest and success has been the most elusive. Other countries and regions also have important needs that the World Bank Group should continue to support, given that the increased demand for global food production also has to be met. However, greater effectiveness in the poorest countries is the most critical challenge.

The findings of this evaluation point to specific recommendations in three areas.

1. Synergies and complementarities

In the areas that drive productivity, such as irrigation and drainage, agricultural research and extension, access to credit, access to land, transport infrastructure, and the policy environment, complementarities and synergies are key drivers of effectiveness. To take better advantage of these complementarities:

- Step up *IFC's engagement in Sub-Saharan Africa*, including support for public-private partnerships and adapting the integrated trader-processor model for more effective use with small-to-midsize indigenous companies in the agriculture-based economies.

- Set up a *knowledge network* that links agriculture and agribusiness supply-chain specialists across the World Bank Group to strengthen communication and collaboration among sector departments within the Bank and IFC, as well as across the World Bank Group.

- Work with partners to ensure that CGIAR research and other *global and regional efforts* are translated into benefits in client countries, and facilitate partnerships among countries to encourage south-south knowledge exchange.

2. Knowledge and capacity building

Experience points to the importance of capacity and how analytical work can highlight issues and raise awareness—particularly when capacity is weak:

- Ensure sufficient quantity and quality of *Bank AAA and IFC advisory services in agriculture-based economies*, link them closely to lending, and use them to build counterpart commitment and to address constraints along the production chain.

- Establish mechanisms to confirm ex ante if *project M&E frameworks* are adequate, with clear, relevant, and realistic objectives; thorough cost-benefit analysis; appropriate indicators; and adequate baseline data.

- Review the *human resource base and skill gaps* (also in light of the increased lending) and develop and implement a strategic plan to enhance the technical and policy skills of Bank and IFC staff working in the agriculture sector, particularly in agriculture-based economies.

3. Efficiency and sustainability

The impact of increased resource flows into agriculture will depend on the efficiency of resource use and the financial, social, and environmental sustainability of investments:

- Increase World Bank Group support to *medium-term expenditure planning* to help ensure the adequacy of funding for operations and maintenance, and work with clients to ensure *sustainable financing*—including cost recovery where appropriate—for irrigation, transport, and research and extension services.

- Take stock of experience in water management and crop technologies in *rain-fed areas* to inform future World Bank Group support.

- Ensure that *gender concerns* are adequately mainstreamed and monitored in World Bank and IFC agriculture operations.

- Expand the application of *IFC Performance Standards* to material biodiversity and other environmental and social aspects along the supply chain for primary suppliers (and for secondary suppliers to the extent the client has leverage), and enhance IFC support to the development and application of internationally accepted commodity certification systems.

Management Response

I. Introduction

Management welcomes this evaluation of the World Bank Group's support for agriculture and agribusiness, covering the period 1998 through 2008, by the Independent Evaluation Group (IEG). In particular, the evaluation reconfirms actions already undertaken in the context of the Bank Group's Agriculture Action Plan 2010–2012, "Implementing Agriculture for Development.[1]" A major contribution of this report is to combine an assessment of Bank and IFC activities in the sector, placing the two organizations comparative advantages in a value chain framework, and indicating areas of collaboration.

Much of the report resonates with management's earlier analyses, in particular the recognition of the low level of resourcing in the decade covered by the report, the importance of increasing investment in agriculture, the value of and need to strengthen: (a) cross-sector linkages; (b) Bank Group collaboration and donor coordination; (c) gender mainstreaming; (d) integration of climate issues; and (e) better integration of CGIAR research into benefits on the ground. Indeed, as the report recognizes, many of these issues have been addressed in the past two years and are fundamental components of the World Bank Group Agriculture Action Plan 2010–2012. Management also welcomes recognition of the critical role of analytical work and staffing capacity in the delivery of the portfolio.

II. Management Comments

The IEG report supports the Bank Group position (and the central conclusion of the *World Development Report 2008: Agriculture for Development[2]*) that agricultural growth remains central to poverty reduction and it recognizes the Bank Group's recent scaled-up support to the sector. Management notes the following:

- **IDA supported projects in Sub-Saharan Africa have significantly improved over the past 10 years.** Agriculture and rural development projects with satisfactory outcomes increased from 48 percent in fiscal 2000–02 to 62 percent in fiscal 2003–05 and to 73 percent in fiscal 2006–08. However, a 73 percent satisfactory rate is still too low. The Regions and the anchor will continue to focus on factors that contributed to improved performance, including: identifying and scaling up good practice projects, improving quality monitoring and proac-

tivity, expanding cross-regional learning, and increasing policy dialogue where the policy environment is weak.

- **IFC is extending its reach to small-scale farmers and small and medium enterprises** with direct investments, and indirectly through investments in larger companies. IFC's business model in the Regions is evolving to be more active in IDA countries, and particularly in Sub-Saharan Africa. For instance, IFC now has an agribusiness anchor in Sub-Saharan Africa with a dedicated team, and has more than doubled its investments in African agribusiness in the past three fiscal years, reaching a record $270 million in 2010.

- **Bank-IFC collaboration on agriculture has increased since the 1998–2008 IEG review period.** Recent examples of joint work include: (i) the World Bank Group Agriculture Action Plan 2010–2012, (ii) inclusion of a public and private sector window in the recently launched Global Agriculture and Food Security Program (GAFSP),[3] (iii) the Responsible Agro-Investment (RAI) initiative and toolkit,[4] and (iv) preparation of a new Bank Group framework for engaging in oil palm.[5]

- **There has been significant reform of the CGIAR since the end of 2008.** A major mechanism to improve the effectiveness and relevance of the CGIAR's science is the establishment of a relatively small number of high-impact "mega-programs"[6] to replace the many, often fragmented, research programs of the past.

- **The integration of gender equality into agriculture** and rural development projects was already higher than in other sectors and has further improved since the period covered by the IEG report. However, management fully agrees that more needs to be done.

Finding the right balance between analytical and project work, and between technical and generalist staff is a challenge. The report raises concerns, which management shares, that (a) the number of analytical products has declined as the amount of lending has more than doubled; and (b) the share of agriculture subsector technical "specialists" has declined relative to broader agriculture sector "generalists" across the Bank. As the number of agriculture sector staff has remained relatively constant while lending has increased, there is less time available for analytical work. Moreover, the increase in decentralizing staff to country offices has increased a perceived demand for generalists to engage on multiple sector topics. These trends have increased since the end of the IEG review period, and will remain challenges unless overall staff numbers increase and/or changes are made in terms of how staff are recruited and managed. This balance between generalists and technical staff in a decentralized organization is being addressed by the actions under way as set out in the Board paper "New World, New World Bank Group: (II) the Internal Reform Agenda; March 22, 2010."[7] To mitigate these challenges in the shorter term, the Anchor and Regional ARD units will (a) conduct a Bank-wide ARD strategic staffing exercise to determine more precisely staffing gaps, especially in the context of current 3-5-7 senior staff rotation exercise; and (b) consider targeted cluster recruitment, based on lessons learned from the current Social Development pilot cluster recruitment exercise.

III. IEG Recommendations

Management welcomes and agrees with the IEG recommendations. These recommendations fit well with what the World Bank Group is currently doing and are consistent with the World Bank Group Agriculture Action Plan 2010–2012.

Management Action Record	
IEG Recommendations	Management Response
I. Synergies and complementarities. In the areas that drive productivity, such as irrigation and drainage, agricultural research and extension, access to credit, access to land, transport infrastructure, and the policy environment, complementarities and synergies are key drivers of effectiveness. To take better advantage of these complementarities:	
1. Step up *IFC's engagement in Sub-Saharan Africa* including supporting public-private partnerships and adapting the integrated trader-processor model for more effective use with small-to-midsize indigenous companies in the agriculture-based economies.	**Ongoing/Agree** IFC's business model in the Region is evolving to be more active in IDA countries and IFC is extending its reach to small-scale farmers and small and medium enterprises through: (i) direct investments in larger companies with a significant development reach to farmers and SMEs; (ii) indirect financing of medium-size companies and cooperatives through financial intermediaries; and (iii) indirect financing of smaller size agribusiness farms and enterprises through risk-sharing facilities with financial intermediaries. IFC now has an agribusiness anchor in Africa with a dedicated team of 9 full-time and 4 part-time staff, which is double that of the previous year, and IFC has more than doubled its investments in African agribusiness[8] in the past three fiscal years, reaching a record $270 million in fiscal 2010.
2. Set up a *knowledge network* linking agriculture and agribusiness supply-chain specialists across the World Bank Group to strengthen communication and collaboration among sector departments within the Bank and IFC, as well as across the World Bank Group.	**Ongoing/Agree** Management will broaden the existing informal World Bank Group thematic group on food safety to include agribusiness supply-chain specialists in the Bank and IFC. Bank-IFC collaboration on agriculture has increased since the 1998–2008 IEG review period. Recent examples of joint work include: (i) preparation of the World Bank Group Agriculture Action Plan 2010–2012; (ii) inclusion of both a public and private sector window in the recently launched Global Agriculture and Food Security Program (GAFSP); (iii) the Responsible Agro-Investment (RAI) initiative, including the recently launched RAI Toolkit, and;

IEG Recommendations	Management Response
	(iv) preparation of a new Bank Group framework for engaging in oil palm.
	In addition, there is increasing Bank-IFC in-country coordination. Examples include:
	(i) a review of smallholder participation in the Liberian rubber sector;
	(ii) possible interventions in the cocoa sector in Côte d'Ivoire;
	(iii) commercial agricultural development in Ghana;
	(iv) a first loss agribusiness finance facility in Cambodia; and
	(v) an agribusiness logistics study in the Philippines.
3. **Work with partners to ensure that CGIAR research and other *global and regional efforts* are translated into benefits on the ground, and facilitate partnerships among countries to encourage south-south knowledge exchange.**	**Ongoing/Agree** Since the end of 2008 (i.e., after the IEG evaluation period), there has been a significant reform of the CGIAR. A major mechanism to improve the effectiveness and relevance of the CGIAR's science and facilitate partnerships is the establishment, currently under way, of a relatively small number of high-impact "mega-programs," to replace the many, often fragmented, research programs of the past. Criteria which will guide approval of the mega programs include quantity and quality of partnerships included in design and implementation. Institutionally, the major reform is to separate the CGIAR "doers" from the "funders," including the recent creation of the Consortium of CGIAR Centers (i.e., the "doers"), and the CGIAR Fund Council (i.e., the "funders"), supported by a Fund Office, which, like the previous CGIAR Secretariat, will be hosted by the Bank.
II. Knowledge and capacity building. Experience points to the importance of capacity and how analytical work can highlight issues and raise awareness—particularly when capacity is weak:	
1. **Ensure sufficient quantity and quality of *Bank AAA and IFC advisory services in agriculture-based economies,* link them closely to lending, and use them to build counterpart commitment and to address constraints along the production chain.**	**Agree** Management agrees with this recommendation and notes that the number of Bank analytical products declined from a peak of 183 in 2000 to 131 by 2008, which was a period when lending more than doubled. As the number of agricultural sector staff has remained relatively constant, more time spent on project preparation and supervision to meet rising demand and improve portfolio quality has reduced the resources available for analytical work. This trend has actually worsened since the end of the IEG review period and requires further attention. The issue will be addressed in part through the staff review highlighted in response to Item II.3.
2. **Establish mechanisms to confirm ex ante if *project M&E frameworks* are adequate—with clear, relevant, and realistic objectives, thorough cost-benefit analysis, appropriate indicators, and adequate baseline data.**	**Ongoing/Agree** Management agrees that this is clearly an area where it is possible to do better, while noting that considerable progress has been made. Bank management has introduced core implementation status and result (ISR) indicators which serve to both standardize and improve indicator quality. Core ISR indicators for agricultural research and extension, irrigation and drainage, and land administration have also been prepared

IEG Recommendations	Management Response
	and will soon be introduced. Furthermore, baseline data are now required to be included in the first ISR and, finally, economic analysis courses are being offered regularly. As for IFC, the tracking of financial, economic and environmental outcomes has progressively been built into the appraisal of new investments and monitoring of the portfolio since IFC deployed its Development Outcome Tracking System (DOTS)[9]. For new investments, coverage of IFC's standardized agribusiness indicators is at 100 percent. Monitoring and evaluation of development impacts is an area of priority for IFC, and indicators will continue to be reviewed and improved continuously for their relevance. In particular, agribusiness indicators will be adjusted as part of IFC's forthcoming implementation of its Corporate Development Goals.
3. Review the *human resource base and skill gaps* (also in light of the increased lending), and develop and implement a strategic plan to enhance the technical and policy skills of Bank and IFC staff working in the agriculture sector, particularly in agriculture-based economies.	**Agree** Management shares the concerns about the proportion of Bank "subsector technical specialists" relative to "broader agricultural sector generalists" within the Bank's agriculture and rural development sector family. One factor driving this shift has been the increase in decentralizing staff to country offices where the need for "generalists" is often considered higher (to engage on multiple sector topics with government and other in-country development partners). The trend toward decentralization has increased since the end of the IEG review period, and will remain a challenge unless overall staff numbers increase and/or changes are made in terms of how staff are recruited and managed. This balance between generalists and technical staff in a decentralized organization is being addressed by the Board paper "New World, New World Bank Group: (II) The Internal Reform Agenda; March 22, 2010." To mitigate these challenges in the shorter term, the Regions and the anchor will: (a) conduct a Bank-wide ARD strategic staffing exercise to determine more precisely staffing gaps, especially in the context of current 3-5-7 senior staff rotation exercise, and; (b) consider targeted cluster recruitment, based on lessons learned from the current Social Development pilot cluster recruitment exercise.
III. Efficiency and sustainability. The impact of increased resource flows into agriculture will depend on the efficiency of resource use and the financial, social, and environmental sustainability of investments:	
1. Increase World Bank Group support to *medium-term expenditure planning* to help ensure the adequacy of funding for operations and maintenance, and work with clients	**Ongoing/Agree** Management agrees with the need for medium-term expenditure planning and sustainable financing. In order to assist governments

IEG Recommendations	Management Response
to ensure *sustainable financing*—including cost recovery where appropriate—for irrigation, transport, and research and extension services.	do so, the Bank is currently finalizing an agriculture public expenditure toolkit[10] to help better guide medium-term expenditure planning.
2. **Take stock of experience in water management and crop technologies in *rainfed areas* to inform future World Bank Group support.**	**Ongoing/Agree** Management fully supports this recommendation. For example, the Bank has recently undertaken analytical work on "Improving Water Management in Rainfed Agriculture,"[11] and carried out a portfolio review of rainfed agriculture projects. This ongoing stock taking has focused on gathering lessons learned from past experience to better inform future lending on rainfed agriculture. In addition, several analytical studies examining the impact of climate change on agriculture, including rainfed agriculture, are being undertaken by the Regions.
3. **Ensure that *gender concerns* are adequately mainstreamed and monitored in World Bank and IFC agriculture operations.**	**Ongoing/Agree** Although the integration of gender equality into agriculture and rural development projects was already higher than in other sectors, and has improved since the period covered by the IEG report, management fully agrees that more needs to be done. The percentage of rural projects with "gender responsive design" (as defined by the PREM Gender Department) in the Africa Region, which already met the 50 percent target in fiscal 2008, increased even further—from 59 percent in 2008 to 65 percent in 2009. In April 2010 the ARD Sector Board set a target of 75 percent for gender responsive design in agriculture and rural development projects in all Regions by fiscal 2014. After the period covered by the IEG review, the Bank compiled a good practice sourcebook with FAO and IFAD, the "Gender in Agriculture Sourcebook,"[12] and completed a study on access to extension services in India, Ghana, and Ethiopia[13] (World Bank & IFPRI 2010). These efforts complement the Gender Action Plan, which specifically provides operational support to agriculture. Going forward it is envisioned that these actions will significantly improve mainstreaming of gender into agriculture operations. Gender is mainstreamed across sectors and industries through explicit requirements in IFC's Sustainability Policy and Performance Standards (PS).[14] The social assessment process required in PS1 provides guidance on disaggregating stakeholder groups by key social identities, including gender, and ensuring that any potential adverse impacts are addressed. Throughout the PS, there is explicit reference to addressing risks, ensuring opportunities, and providing appropriate consultation for women. As examples, PS2 addresses non-discrimination; PS4 addresses gender-disaggregated aspects of health and vulnerability; PS5 addresses women's tenure and livelihoods in cases of resettlement; and PS7 & and PS8 both include specific attention to women's views in decision-making processes.

IEG Recommendations	Management Response
	As part of its PS review and update, IFC proposes to strengthen client's requirements not to employ trafficked persons as part of a revised version of the Performance Standards (version 1).
	IFC has been tracking the implications of its investments on employment by gender through its DOTS system. It agrees with IEG that more can be done to mainstream and monitor gender concerns in agribusiness. This will be done as part of the next revision of the sector's standardized indicators.
4. Expand the application of *IFC Performance Standards* to material biodiversity and other environmental and social aspects along the supply chain for primary suppliers (and for secondary suppliers to the extent the client has leverage), and enhance IFC support to the development and application of internationally accepted commodity certification systems.	Management agrees that IFC policies did not contain a requirement to examine supply chains in the early years of the review period; this was only addressed in the IFC Performance Standards (PS) which became effective April 30, 2006. PS 1 requires that the impacts associated with supply chains be assessed in two cases: (1) where the resource utilized by the project is ecologically sensitive (e.g., wood products) or (2) in the case where low labor cost is a factor in the competitiveness of the item supplied (e.g., textile and some agribusiness activities); then child and forced labor should be examined for supply chains. IFC's approach to supply chains has been to focus client actions on the most immediate and serious risks in their supply chains—such as child labor, forced labor, and potential clearing of critical habitats.
	As part of its PS review and update, IFC proposes to: (i) strengthen its supply chain assessment methodology as part of project appraisal; (ii) make changes to the PS by adding significant occupational health and safety issues as a new risk factor to be considered in the supply chain assessment; and, (iii) to continue supporting certification schemes, through investments and advisory services, including engagement in a number of global commodity roundtables. The ongoing review and update of IFC's Sustainability Policy and Performance Standards will address climate change, supply chains, and biodiversity issues among others.
	IFC is generally supportive of international certification schemes and has an active engagement in a number of global commodity roundtables. In addition, IFC has been actively working with its clients (especially producers and traders) to increase the traceability and certification of their products in their respective supply chains. Efforts in the coffee, cocoa, and cotton sectors, among others, are under way to develop corporate policies that emphasize purchasing of sustainable products, and compliance with national environmental legislation and IFC's PS requirements.

Chairperson's Comments: Committee on Development Effectiveness (CODE)

On September 22, 2010, the Committee on Development Effectiveness (CODE) considered the report *Growth and Productivity in Agriculture and Agribusiness: Evaluative Lessons from the World Bank Group Experience,* prepared by the Independent Evaluation Group (IEG), and the *Draft Management Response.*

Summary

The Committee welcomed the informative IEG report, underlining the critical importance of the agriculture sector for food security, poverty reduction, and development. In this context, the renewed World Bank Group attention to the agriculture sector was welcomed, and members underlined the critical need to maintain focus on this sector. They also sought to better understand why support to this sector had contracted in the past, not only by the World Bank Group but also by other donors. In disseminating the report's findings, IEG was encouraged to reflect the renewed Bank Group focus on the sector.

Management's response to the IEG report was appreciated. The Committee noted the convergence of views between management and IEG, and management's ongoing efforts that address many of the issues highlighted by the IEG. A range of issues was discussed, including Bank Group support to the Africa Region and the need to also provide support to other Regions, link and balance of focus between food security and agricultural productivity, provision of analytical and advisory services, IFC support in the sector, coordination and synergy between the Bank and IFC, and human and budgetary resources.

Recommendations and Next Steps

The Committee requested a Board discussion on the overall World Bank Group strategy in the agriculture sector, for which the IEG evaluation report may serve as background information. Suggestions were made to deepen the Management Response to the IEG report, including to better reflect the positive measures taken to strengthen Bank Group support for the agriculture sector and key lessons learned.

Main Issues Discussed

General Comments on the IEG Findings. Further to the informative IEG report, some members sought more elaboration on coordination of Bank and IFC support with other agencies (such as the U.N.) and differentiation of policies for low- and middle-income countries. A note of caution was expressed about the reference to low country commitment for agriculture in the Africa Region; a mention was made of the country commitment to agriculture declared through, among others, the 2003 Maputo Declaration, and that one issue is the constraints in availability of IDA resources and competing demands in use of resources. Bank management added that notwithstanding country commitment, client capacity remains a challenge. There was a suggestion to further elaborate on a range of factors contributing to the lower productivity in Sub-Saharan Africa. IEG said that it would work with Bank management to address differences in data used in connection with the assessment of project outcomes in the Africa Region. While agreeing with the IEG recommendations, some members felt they could have been more specific. In this respect, IEG noted the challenges of making more specific recommendations given the diversity of Regions and country circumstances.

Trend in World Bank Group Support. The Committee commented on the renewed Bank Group attention to the agriculture sector following the 2008 *World Development Report*, the global food crisis, and the articulation of the World Bank Group Agriculture Action Plan and the importance of maintaining this focus. Participants reflected on a confluence of factors, including the availability of food and greater priority given to other areas by many countries, which led to a decline in agriculture support by the Bank Group and by other development agencies. Noting that the IEG report covers the period between 1998 and 2008, when Bank Group support for agriculture declined and then started to recover, several speakers urged IEG to clearly communicate the context of renewed Bank Group attention to agriculture during its dissemination efforts.

Focus of World Bank Group Support. While acknowledging the need to support agricultural growth and productivity in Sub-Saharan Africa, some speakers noted that other regions, such as Central America, also continue to face food security issues, which should be addressed by the Bank. The Committee discussed the link and balance of focus between food security and agricultural productivity and issues of reliance on global market and domestic production to meet local food demand, which were recognized as complex issues driven by country context and choice. In addition, a member observed the need to consider the role of agriculture for development in countries emerging from conflict. Comments were made on the importance of a comprehensive approach; cross-sectoral work to address agricultural productivity issues, including with infrastructure; strengthening monitoring and evaluation; and further mainstreaming of gender.

A few members encouraged more attention by the Bank to rainfed areas, and a member noted the value added of Bank Group support in the palm oil sector. Regarding IFC investments, some members supported greater engagement in Sub-Saharan Africa, including to promote public-private partnerships in the sector. The importance of deepening coordination between Bank and the IFC was noted.

Knowledge Work and Capacity-Building Support. Noting the contribution of analytical and advisory work and its linkage with lending, speakers raised concerns about the IEG findings on the declining level of analytical work, and also stressed the importance of ensuring quality. Emphasizing the Bank Group's role as a knowledge institution, some members encouraged concrete actions to strengthen the Bank and IFC's advisory work in this sector. Members echoed IEG in encouraging the greater use of CGIAR research work and expressed interest in Bank Group collaboration with the CGIAR, beyond its reform. A few members highlighted the importance of supporting south-south cooperation for knowledge transfer, and working with local institutions to leverage knowledge. In addition, there was interest in further analytical work on impact of overseas agriculture investment on growth and productivity in developing countries.

Human and Budgetary Resources. Expressing concerns about the decline in agriculture-related technical skills relative to agricultural generalists, members and speakers raised questions about reasons for this decline, including whether the decentralization of the World Bank Group is a factor, and concrete actions, including timeline, to address this issue. Bank management noted that it is working on staffing strategy and briefly commented on the challenges of addressing staffing issues. This includes the differentiated demand at the country level for agriculture generalists (including agricultural policy and economics experts) and for specialized agriculture-related technical experts for whom there may not be a full work program in a single country or Region. IFC remarked on its ongoing decentralization initiative, including of staff, which is expected to strengthen its country engagement, particularly in Sub-Saharan Africa. In view of the recent reorganization at IFC, IEG observed the need for IFC to ensure alignment between its new organizational structure and strategic priorities for the sector. Some speakers also raised concerns about the gap between demand for agricultural support and constraints in budgetary resources.

Carolina Renteria, Vice Chairperson

Statement of the External Advisory Panel

This External Advisory Panel statement for the IEG assessment of agriculture and agribusiness programs over the past decade (1998–2008) is the result of a careful reading by the panel of the draft IEG assessment in March 2010, a vigorous two-day workshop with the entire panel and the full IEG team during March 18–19, 2010, and a series of e-mail interactions among the panel members after reading the draft final report in June 2010.

This statement has been signed by all panel members. Several individual panel members also offered detailed comments on the final draft, which were submitted directly to the IEG team. Consequently, this statement focuses on several larger issues and themes raised by the IEG assessment and also identified through the involvement of most panel members with World Bank activities in agriculture and agribusiness over the past several decades.

The panel stresses three main questions:

(1) Has the World Bank Group adequately prioritized its investment portfolio across regions, countries, and activities for the largest impact?

(2) Does the World Bank Group have the necessary technical capacity to design and assess its interventions in agriculture and agribusiness?

(3) Does the World Bank Group have specific monitoring and evaluation (M&E) indicators that clearly reflect its strategic vision?

The first question involves the strategic vision of the World Bank Group, and how it uses its analytical and advisory activities (AAA) to inform that vision. The panel is concerned that a lack of coordination across key groups within the World Bank Group—for example, between the World Bank and the IFC, across regions, and across sectors that have significant impact on the performance of the agricultural sector, such as transportation and finance—has impaired the ability of the World Bank Group to deliver the maximum impact from its agricultural investments in terms of contributions to economic growth and poverty reduction. Improving coordination should be a high priority.

The second question is primarily about the number, training, experience, and quality of core technical staff with skills in agriculture and agribusiness, but it also raises the larger question of scale effects, that is, whether World Bank Group projects add up to measurable impact. The IEG assessment expresses concerns about the impact of reduced staff capacity on the ability of the World Bank Group to meet its sectoral objectives, and the panel shares these concerns.

The third question asks whether the World Bank Group has the necessary M&E tools, data, and methodologies in place to know whether it is successful or not in reaching its specific project goals and its broader strategic objectives.

The IEG assessment addresses these questions in its comprehensive, almost exhaustive, analysis of World Bank Group activities in agriculture and agribusiness during the decade from 1998 to 2008, a period of great change in the global food economy and in World Bank Group activities in the sector. The panel congratulates the IEG team for this thorough and detailed effort, and especially for being highly responsive to extensive concerns expressed at the workshop on March 18–19 by the panel with respect to a perceived disconnect between the data analysis and reported findings and recommendations. The narrative and the conclusions are now carefully attuned to the actual analysis. The panel finds the current document to be highly credible and persuasive.

Accordingly, this panel statement draws out from the IEG assessment further implications for the World Bank Group on how it manages its involvement in agriculture and agribusiness. The IEG assessment points to serious deficiencies in the ability of World Bank Group leadership to articulate a clear and consistent strategic vision of the role of agriculture in economic development and poverty reduction, weaknesses in the AAA that would link a strategic vision to country programs, and in the capacity of core technical staff to design and implement projects. A special concern raised in the IEG assessment is the adequacy of the M&E process to provide useful insights into what is working and what is not, and hence feed back into the design and implementation process. The panel feels it is important to support these findings and to emphasize the need to improve significantly in these areas.

We offer some additional observations to stimulate that process.

I. Strategic Vision and Analytical Capacity

The World Bank abandoned agriculture when it was politically correct and market friendly to do so, and has re-engaged with the sector for the same reasons. The significant decline in World Bank Group investments in agriculture from the mid-1980s to the mid-2000s reflects a serious failure of strategic leadership and vision by the World Bank Group. The *World Development Report 2008: Agriculture for Development* was the Bank's first effort in 25 years to establish intellectual leadership in the field, but it has had relatively little impact on day-to-day activities within the World Bank Group. A very small group of highly skilled and dedicated specialists within the agriculture team has managed to push up the volume of Bank lending quite significantly in the past two years (beyond the review frame of the IEG assessment), a real achievement given the realities of the project approval process in the Bank, but we know nothing about the ultimate contribution of these projects to agricultural development and poverty reduction.

II. Project Design and Implementation Capacity

The IEG assessment notes the declining numbers of core technical staff in agriculture and agribusiness and comments on the observations of several former country directors that getting good technical assistance was difficult. The relatively ineffective use of AAA, especially in the poorest countries, may be partly linked to this human resource issue. But the panel feels the problem may be deeper than just hiring policies and staff levels. More than almost any other field in which the World Bank Group is actively engaged, agriculture and agribusiness activities require specialized skills, often gained mostly through experience, that are difficult

to replace with newly minted graduates who have general development training. Thus the quality and effectiveness of the agriculture and agribusiness staff may well have declined much more than just the numbers would suggest. Only a long-term vision of personnel needs can rebuild this staff competence over a period of decades.

III. Monitoring and Evaluation

The panel found the poor state of M&E of agriculture and agribusiness projects that is documented in the IEG assessment to be very worrisome. This is clearly not just a case of poor data entry, missing files, and confusing or cross-cutting categories. The apparent correlation between poor M&E and poor outcomes for the projects involved almost certainly implies a systematic problem at the stage of design and implementation. Poor projects do not have good M&E protocols built in. The panel urges the World Bank Group, at the highest level, to undertake a thorough assessment of their whole approach to M&E.

In closing, the panel would like to thank the entire team of the IEG assessment for dealing with some harsh criticism early on and for bringing to fruition this highly detailed and critical assessment of the World Bank Group involvement in agriculture and agribusiness. If there had been any doubt before 2007 about the importance of this sector to the mission of the World Bank Group ("we dream of a world without poverty"), the message is now crystal clear: we cannot solve the problem of poverty without sustainable increases in agricultural productivity. The IEG assessment presents a sobering picture of how little the World Bank Group has done over the past decade or so in that task and the need to do more and do it better. The panel fully agrees with that assessment.

Michel Debatisse

P. K. Joshi

Ramatu Mahama

C. Peter Timmer

The Members of the External Advisory Panel

Michel L. Debatisse's fields of expertise include agricultural marketing, corporate strategy related to the agricultural marketing and processing industry; adjustment of institutions and policies in developing countries; financing of industrial projects; and food and agriculture policy, particularly in relation to agro-industrial and agricultural development. He is presently a consultant and lecturer on agriculture and food policies, market development, agro-industrial and trading strategies, and risk management. He worked at the World Bank as thematic team leader, principal agro-industry specialist, and advisor until he retired in 2000. He has also been a professor at the ESSEC Business School, at the University of Maryland, and at the University of Clermont-Ferrand.

"P.K." Joshi is currently the Director, National Academy of Agricultural Research Management at Hyderabad, India. Previously he was Director, National Centre for Agricultural Economics and Policy Research (NCAP) in India. Prior to this he was the South Asia Coordinator/Research Fellow at the International Food Policy Research Institute (IFPRI), Principal Scientist and Theme Leader (Technology Policy) at NCAP, and Senior Economist at the International Crops Research Institute for the Semi-Arid Tropics (ICRISAT), Hyderabad. P.K. has focused on agricultural policy in India, with particular concern for sustainable resource management and the role of science in fostering agricultural development.

Ramatu Mahama Al-Hassan is an agricultural economist. She teaches agricultural economics at the University of Ghana, Legon, where she is also head of the Department of Agricultural Economics and Agribusiness. Her research works have dealt with many aspects of agricultural development, from household food security to issues of smallholder access to high-value markets, agricultural service provision, and agricultural policy in general. She works with many international agencies, including centers of the CGIAR such as IITA and IFPRI and has evaluated several development programs. Ramatu's work has covered several countries of Sub-Saharan Africa.

C. Peter Timmer wrote the signal book *Food Policy Analysis* for the World Bank in the early 1980s (with a little help from his friends Falcon and Pearson). He put these skills into practical application as a policy advisor on food and development issues in East and Southeast Asia. Peter joined the Center for Global Development as a senior fellow in March 2004 and became a nonresident fellow in 2007. He has served as the Thomas D. Cabot Professor of Development Studies at Harvard University and as dean of the Graduate School of International Relations and Pacific Studies at the University of California, San Diego (UCSD). Peter's work focuses on four broad topics: the nature of "pro-poor growth" and its application in Indonesia and other countries in Asia; the supermarket revolution in developing countries and its impact on the poor (both producers and consumers); the structural transformation in historical perspective as a framework for understanding the political economy of agricultural policy, and the functioning of the world rice market.

Chapter 1

EVALUATION HIGHLIGHTS

- Agricultural growth and productivity are essential to reduce poverty.

- Though development assistance for agriculture declined following the Green Revolution, it has recently begun to increase.

- Productivity is lower in agriculture-based economies than in transforming or urbanized economies.

- This evaluation assesses World Bank Group lending and nonlending activities in agriculture and agribusiness from fiscal 1998 to 2008 and covers both the World Bank and IFC.

The Need to Boost Agricultural Productivity

One billion people around the world are still living with chronic poverty and undernourishment. The poor are concentrated in rural areas, and the donor community recognizes that the Millennium Development Goals (MDGs) will not be achieved without improvement in the growth and productivity of agriculture. The food crisis of 2007–08 pushed issues of agricultural growth and food production up toward the top of the development agenda.

While increases in food prices have been exacerbated in the near term by rising energy prices and the financial crisis, longer-run trends will continue to put upward pressures on food prices (table 1.1). During the first three months of 2008, international prices of major food commodities reached 30-year highs. More recently, although international food prices have declined, they remain high compared with 2005 levels, and in many countries domestic prices have not declined to the same extent as international prices. Population growth (as world population is expected to reach nearly 9 billion by 2050), shifts in demand toward animal protein as incomes rise worldwide, and increasing use of agricultural products for biofuels will fuel rising long-term demand.

Increasing the food supply will be critical if this burgeoning demand is to be met, yet growth in agricultural productivity has been slowed in recent years by land and water constraints, underinvestment in rural infrastructure and agricultural innovation, lack of access to inputs, and weather disruptions (ECG 2010; Fan and Rosegrant 2008). Support for agriculture declined gradually from the early 1990s to the mid-2000s, in part due to the success of

Photo courtesy of Curt Carnemark/World Bank.

TABLE 1.1	Factors in the Recent Global Food Price Crisis Relevant to Global Food Production	
Time horizon	Demand-side factors	Supply-side factors
Long run	Increasing population Rising incomes in developing countries leading to increased consumer purchasing power, increased demand for meat and dairy products, and increased indirect demand for grains	Limited availability of agricultural land and water for irrigation; insufficient investments in rural institutions and infrastructure, agricultural research, extension and water and soil management; poor policies in some developing countries; Organisation for Economic Co-operation and Development subsidies; climate change; inadequate systems to ensure food safety
Medium run	Biofuel demand	Rising energy prices and resulting increases in prices of fertilizers, pesticides, and transportation; subsidies for biofuel production
Short run, cyclical	Financial speculation that may exacerbate the price effects of food shortages	Adverse weather in major exporting countries, crop and animal diseases, exchange rate volatility, price controls and changes in export and import policies, speculative hoarding, untargeted subsidies
Recent	Financial crisis and resulting credit tightening and increased borrowing costs for food exports and imports (OECD 2009)	Food security concerns prompting major buyers in the world market (for example, countries in the Middle East and North Africa) to lease land for agricultural production in Sub-Saharan Africa Diversion of land from wheat and other crops to production of biofuel feedstock; increase in farmland prices (von Braun and Meinzen-Dick 2009); low global grain stocks; tighter credit availability for crop production because of the financial crisis (OECD 2009)

Source: Adapted from Elliott (2008).

the Green Revolution and the resulting impression that food shortages were a thing of the past. The *2008 World Development Report: Agriculture for Development* (World Bank 2007b) highlighted the importance of agriculture in reducing poverty and called for heightened investment in the sector.

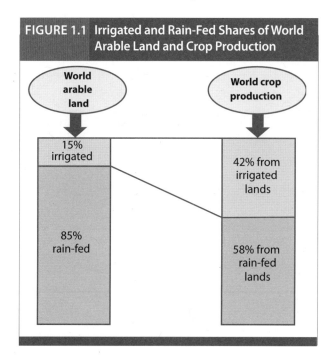

FIGURE 1.1 Irrigated and Rain-Fed Shares of World Arable Land and Crop Production

Crop production can be increased by expanding the area cultivated and by more intensive farming of existing arable land. The potential for area expansion is limited and largely confined to parts of Sub-Saharan Africa and Latin America (FAO 2009b), and the potential to increase output on the most productive agricultural lands has already largely been exploited (Fan and Hazell 1999; World Bank 2007b). The latest Food and Agriculture Organization (FAO) projections indicate that 80 percent of the increases in food production in the developing world will come from increases in yields and cropping intensity, and only 20 percent from expansion of arable land (FAO 2009e).

Most productivity growth will need to come in rain-fed areas, where most production occurs (figure 1.1). The rain-fed regions, home to most of the world's poor, were largely bypassed by the Green Revolution (World Bank 2006e). Though advances in technology could raise yields further in irrigated areas, much of the increase in crop production will need to come from drier, riskier production environments, which often have weak service from market infrastructure.

While there is potential to increase irrigation in Sub-Saharan Africa, where only 18 percent of the potentially irrigable land is under irrigation (Peacock, Ward, and Gambarelli 2007), the availability of water will be a growing constraint.

Water stresses are already mounting in many countries (IEG 2010f), and climate change is predicted to add to this problem. Meeting future food demand will require crop varieties and livestock that respond reasonably well in a range of production environments rather than flourishing only in a narrow set of climatic conditions (IFPRI 2009). Crop management techniques that help adapt varieties to local conditions and make them more resilient to biotic (such as insects and diseases) and abiotic (such as droughts) stresses will also be important in closing yield gaps between experiment stations and farmers' fields (FAO 2009e).

Rising energy prices could further constrain productivity growth through their impact on fertilizer prices. In the past two decades, expansion of fertilizer use has been high in many Asian countries but low in much of Sub-Saharan Africa, where infrastructure and institutional constraints have restricted its use (Heisey and Norton 2007). As a result, consumption of fertilizers in the more advanced economies is now seven times that of countries at lower levels of development (table 1.3). If fertilizers become more expensive with rising energy prices, increasing their use in Sub-Saharan Africa will be even more difficult.

Most productivity growth will need to come from rain-fed areas, where most production occurs.

Systems to ensure food safety and efficient transport will be critical to productivity growth, particularly as global trade in food products grows and markets become more integrated. Urbanization, globalization, and trade liberalization expand market opportunities, creating incentives for increased agricultural production, but these new markets demand quality products and timely delivery. Growth in animal husbandry enhances the risk of disease transmission within and across national borders (FAO 2006b). Unfortunately, the ability of smallholders to compete in these expanding markets can be limited by high transaction costs; insufficient access to credit, inputs, and extension; the need for training to meet food-safety and international sanitary standards; and procurement practices that favor larger transactions (World Bank 2007b).

Growth in global food trade will require attention to food safety and transport efficiency.

Recent developments suggest that it may be possible to harness private sector initiative more effectively to promote agricultural development. Growing demand for animal protein and biofuels provides increased opportunities for the private sector to invest profitably to grow grains for livestock feed and sugarcane and non-food crops (such as jatropha) for biofuels (UNCTAD 2009). Developing country governments are reviewing their policy frameworks and legislation to encourage foreign participation in their agricultural sectors. Progress over the past quarter-century in reducing anti-rural biases and international trade distortions in agricultural products (Anderson 2008) has also created a more supportive environment for private investments and for south-south cooperation.

Recent developments may have made it possible to harness private sector initiatives more effectively to promote agricultural development.

Cross-country analyses indicate that gross domestic product (GDP) growth originating in agriculture is at least twice as effective in reducing poverty as GDP growth originating outside the sector (World Bank 2007b; Barrett, Carter, and Timmer 2010). Improvements in agricultural productivity are critical for poverty reduction, as shown, for example, in the experiences of Brazil, China,

TABLE 1.2	Effect of a 1 Percent Increase in Crop Yields on Poverty Reduction		
Region	Percent of population in poverty	Number in poverty (millions)	Reduction in number of poor in relation to a 1 percent yield increase (%)
East Asia	15	278	0.48
South Asia	40	522	0.48
Sub-Saharan Africa	46	291	0.72
Latin America	16	78	0.10
Middle East and North Africa	7	21	—
Eastern Europe and Central Asia	5	24	—

Sources: World Bank 2005a, citing Thirtle, Lin, and Piesse 2003; Thirtle and Piesse 2007.

Note: Based on 2001 World Bank data.

TABLE 1.3 Countries in the Evaluation Portfolio as Classified in the 2008 WDR

	Agriculture-based	Transforming	Urbanized
Portfolio			
Countries in the World Bank evaluation portfolio[a]	Albania, Benin, Burkina Faso, Burundi, Cameroon, Chad, Côte d'Ivoire, Ethiopia, The Gambia, Georgia, Ghana, Guinea, Haiti, Kenya, Lao PDR, Madagascar, Malawi, Mali, Moldova, Mozambique, Nepal, Niger, Nigeria, Papua New Guinea, Paraguay, Rwanda, Tanzania, Togo, Uganda, Zambia N=30 (mostly in Sub-Saharan Africa)	Algeria, Angola, Bangladesh, Cambodia, China, Democratic Republic of Congo, Arab Republic of Egypt, Guatemala, Honduras, India, Indonesia, Islamic Republic of Iran, Kazakhstan, Kyrgyz Republic, Lesotho, Lithuania, Morocco, Pakistan, Panama, Romania, Senegal, Sri Lanka, Tajikistan, Tunisia, Vietnam, Republic of Yemen, Zimbabwe N=27 (mostly in South Asia, East Asia and Pacific, and Middle East and North Africa)	Argentina, Azerbaijan, Bolivia, Bosnia and Herzegovina, Brazil, Bulgaria, Colombia, Costa Rica, Dominican Republic, Ecuador, El Salvador, Jordan, Former Yugoslav Republic of Macedonia, Mauritania, Mexico, Mongolia, Peru, Philippines, Poland, Russian Federation, Serbia, Slovak Republic, Turkey, Ukraine N=24 (mostly in Latin America and Caribbean and Europe and Central Asia)
Countries in the IFC evaluation portfolio[b]	Côte d'Ivoire, Ghana, Kenya, Lao PDR, Moldova, Tanzania, Uganda, Zambia N=8 (mostly in Sub-Saharan Africa)	China, Arab Republic of Egypt, Guatemala, Honduras, India, Indonesia, Lithuania Vietnam, Republic of Yemen N= 9 (mostly in Asia, Latin America and Caribbean, and Middle East and North Africa)	Argentina, Azerbaijan, Belarus, Brazil, Bulgaria, Chile, Colombia, Dominican Republic, Ecuador, Mexico, Peru, Philippines, Russian Federation, Serbia and Montenegro, South Africa, Turkey, Ukraine, República Bolivariana de Venezuela N=18 (mostly in Latin America and Caribbean and Europe and Central Asia)

	Agriculture-based	Transforming	Urbanized
Agriculture			
Agriculture's contribution to growth, 1993–2005 (%)[c]	32	7	5
Share of agriculture in gross domestic product in 2008 (%)[d]	25	12	9
Agriculture value added in 2008 (2000 US$ billions)[d]	53	485	208
Agriculture value added per hectare of arable land in 2005 (2000 US$)[d]	316	1,047	565
Agriculture value added per worker in 2005 (2000 US$)[d]	599	1,398	3,357
Irrigated land in 2003 (% of cropland)[d]	9	24	14
Fertilizer consumption in 2005 (100 grams per hectare of arable land)[d]	208	1,523	1,553
Agricultural machinery, tractors per 100 square kilometers of arable land in 2005[d]	37	139	231
Public agricultural research and development expenditure per capita (1998–2005)[e]	1.8	3.4	5.0
Cereal yields in 2008 (kilograms per hectare)[d]	1,553	2,237	2,733
Transport (1998–2007) [d]			
Roads (% paved)	25	47	47
Roads (total network, '000 kilometers)	1,151	7,639	5,713

Sources: World Bank 2007b; World Bank Development Data Platform; evaluation calculations; CGIAR's Agricultural Science and Technology Indicators.

a. Twenty countries in the World Bank portfolio were not classified. Those countries account for 5 percent of total commitments to projects in the portfolio. Five regional projects in Sub-Saharan Africa (1 percent of total commitments in the portfolio) are also covered in this category. They could not be included with the agriculture-based economies because three of them had commitments that went to urbanized and transforming economies.

b. Seven countries in the IFC portfolio were in the not-classified category. Those economies accounted for 6.7 percent of total commitments in the portfolio, the regional projects for 5.8 percent.

c. World Bank 2007b, pp. 29–32, for country classification by the 2008 WDR into three country typologies and for associated indicators.

d. World Bank Development Data Platform (www.ddp.worldbank.org/) and evaluation calculations, numbers provided are for the latest year for which data are available; where data were not sufficient to provide accurate latest figure an average over the evaluation period is provided.

e. www.asti.cgiar.org/data; CGIAR's Agricultural Science and Technology Indicators and evaluation calculations. An average is provided because of insufficient data for the latest year for which data are available.

dress the first MDG of reducing extreme poverty and hunger (Hartmann 2004).

> GDP growth produced by agriculture is at least twice as effective at reducing poverty as growth in other sectors.

The goal of this Independent Evaluation Group (IEG) evaluation is to draw lessons from recent World Bank Group experience in the agriculture and agribusiness sectors to help inform future actions. The World Bank Group and other donors are rapidly scaling up support to this sector. Private foreign investment is also increasing. It is important to learn from both about the successes and the failures of past support.

and India (World Bank 2007b; de Janvry and Sadoulet 2010; Timmer 2007). Table 1.2 shows estimates of the effect of a 1 percent increase in crop yields on poverty reduction across regions. Indeed, some analysts view increasing food production as the most critical activity in Sub-Saharan Africa to ad-

Trends in Funding for Agriculture

Official development assistance (ODA) to agriculture declined after the success of the Green Revolution. It oscillated around $3.5–$4.5 billion per year between 1998 and 2004 (figure 1.2),

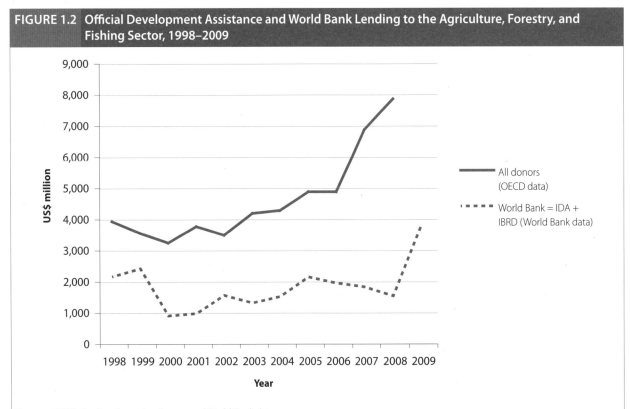

FIGURE 1.2 **Official Development Assistance and World Bank Lending to the Agriculture, Forestry, and Fishing Sector, 1998–2009**

Sources: OECD Creditor Reporting System and World Bank data.

Note: OECD and World Bank data are not entirely comparable. OECD data for ODA include IDA but not IBRD, and exclude countries that are members of the G-8 or the European Union, or that have a date of admission to the European Union. The reporting years also do not fully correspond, because the World Bank reports data by fiscal year while the OECD reports by calendar year. The OECD and World Bank data are presented to give an indication of World Bank lending in the context of overall ODA over time.

but the renewed focus on agricultural development has since led to increased support to the sector. ODA jumped to about 8 billion in 2008, and even further in 2009, with World Bank lending alone increasing from 1.5 billion in 2008 to 3.8 billion in 2009. The largest donors have been the World Bank, the European Union, Japan, and the United States; on a regional basis, the top donors have been the African Development Bank and the Asian Development Bank. China, India, and major foundations (such as the Bill and Melinda Gates Foundation) are increasingly important sources of funding for developing countries, particularly in Sub-Saharan Africa. The Republic of Korea, Mexico, Saudi Arabia, and Turkey have also begun to provide development assistance to agriculture (World Bank 2007c; Langenkamp 2008).

Development assistance to agriculture declined after the success of the Green Revolution.

The private sector arms of the multilateral development banks and bilateral agencies have also recently boosted their investments in this sector. In total, they invested about $12 billion in agribusiness in the private sector over 1998–2008. The largest investors are the International Finance Corporation (IFC), with a 48 percent market share; the European Bank for Reconstruction and Development (EBRD), with 31 percent; and the African Development Bank, with 7 percent.

The private sector flows to the sector have also increased.

Foreign direct investment (FDI) flows to agriculture in developing countries tripled, to $3 billion annually, between 1990 and 2007. These flows remain small compared with global flows, but in many low-income countries agriculture accounts for a relatively large share of total inflows. FDI in the entire agricultural value chain is much larger, with annual flows in the food and beverage sectors alone amounting to more than $6.5 billion. Developed-country transnational companies are dominant in the upstream (suppliers) and downstream (processors, retailers, traders) ends of the agribusiness value chain. In agricultural production, transnational companies from developing countries are as significant as those from developed countries.

Conceptual Framework

Farming is essentially a private sector activity (though in some countries there has also been cultivation of government-owned farms) in which farmers apply their labor and capital to land to produce crops, but they require a range of support services, inputs, and market access. The support services can be provided by the public sector, the private sector, a partnership between the two, or by nongovernmental or community-based organizations (NGOs and CBOs). Experience shows that farming inevitably requires some public support, because some services are never provided in sufficient quantity or quality by market institutions (Stiglitz 1998). Clear cases of such services are public goods whose consumption is not exclusive, such as agricultural research and development services that generate non-rival and often non-excludable knowledge (Barrett, Carter, and Timmer 2010). Other cases where some exclusivity might be arranged, such as roads (if tolls are feasible) and education (if fees can be collected), are also generally treated as public goods that governments need to provide (Fan 2008a,b).

The agriculture production chain is a highly complex system.

Figure 1.3 shows a simplified crop production chain and how various activities come together to enable agricultural production. A similar production chain can be constructed for animal husbandry. Variations in agro-ecological conditions across regions and countries influence the kinds of crops produced and their productivity, but the basic story remains the same: a number of factors—seeds, water, and agrichemicals (where available)—come together on a piece of land with human or animal labor or machines to allow crops to grow. The productivity of land and labor will be more or less dependent on soil quality and cultivation techniques, seed quality, extent of fertilizer and water application, and measures taken for disease and weed control. Just as soil fertility determines fertilizer need, disease and the availability of disease-resistant cultivars determine pesticide demand. Once a crop is produced and harvested, a range of agribusiness activities link farmers to consumers. Agribusiness activities are also important on the input side to provide seeds, agricultural chemicals, and pesticides as inputs for agricultural production. All the activities along the crop production chain are facilitated by the availability of credit, transport, marketing infrastructure, and a favorable legal and policy environment, including clear land rights.

The World Bank Group provides support to its clients to facilitate production and increase productivity along the crop production chain and to build relevant public and private sector capacity. Most World Bank interventions occur on the left-hand side of the production chain shown in figure 1.3, and most IFC direct interventions occur

FIGURE 1.3   Crop Production Chain and the World Bank Group

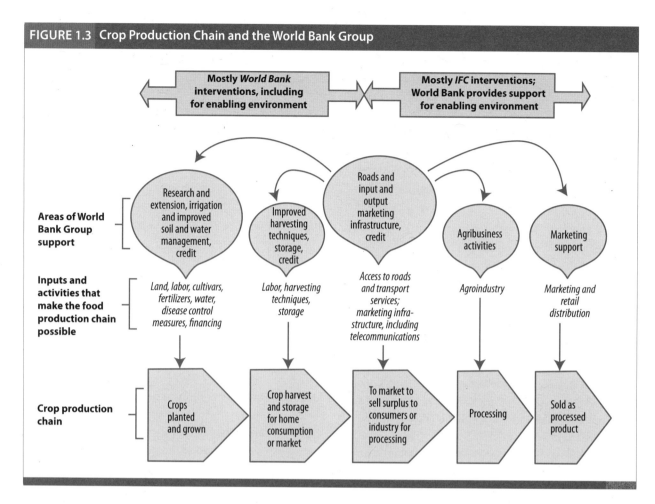

on the right-hand side. This evaluation assesses the World Bank Group's contributions along all of these dimensions in the past decade.

A production chain exists in all economy types, but productivity is lower in agriculture-based economies than in transforming and urbanized settings. The gap in labor productivity (agricultural value added per worker) between the agriculture-based economies and the transforming and urbanized ones is large—the figures were $599 for the agriculture-based, $1,398 for the transforming, and $3,357 for the urbanized settings in 2005 (in 2000 dollars, table 1.3; see appendix A for productivity trends). Productivity in agriculture-based economies is constrained by limited access to modern inputs, irrigation, communication, markets, transport, and credit (table 1.3).

> Productivity is lower in agriculture-based economies than in transforming or urbanized settings.

In agriculture-based economies, farmers are more likely to use seeds that they save from previous harvests or

purchase locally because the agribusiness sector is less developed and public sector production capacity is limited (see chapter 4). In these economies, farmers often self-process crops instead of selling to agroindustries that can exploit economies of scale. Inadequate incomes and limited access to credit further limit the ability of farmers to purchase available improved seeds and fertilizers that can help increase productivity. As economies develop and livestock and crop productivity increase, agribusiness activities grow in importance, typically rising from under 20 percent of GDP to more than 30 percent, before declining as economies become industrial (World Bank 2007b).

Evaluation Scope and Methodology

This evaluation assesses the World Bank Group's lending and nonlending activities in agriculture and agribusiness from fiscal 1998 to 2008, and covers both the World Bank and IFC. The evaluation of World Bank activities focuses on their contribution to agricultural growth and productivity, while the evaluation of IFC activities focuses on food and agribusiness (F&A) growth and development. The evaluation does not explore broader issues of rural or forest sector development. It also does not cover education and other social development activities that could, in the long run, support agricultural growth.

The evaluation addresses the following questions, with an eye toward gathering lessons to help inform future activities:

Strategy: What strategic approach has the World Bank Group taken toward agriculture and agribusiness, how has it evolved, and how has it influenced the choice of activities?

World Bank Group Engagement and Results: What have been the trends in World Bank Group lending and investments and in nonlending and advisory activities? What have been the results of these activities at both the project and country levels?

Drivers of Results: What sector-specific constraints has the World Bank Group faced, and how have they been addressed? To what extent do institutional factors, whether in client countries or in the World Bank Group, contribute to outcomes?

Evidence for the evaluation was gathered from a number of building blocks and triangulated to support evaluation findings. These are described briefly below (see detailed description in appendix A):

Portfolio Review. The full population of lending and investment activities from fiscal 1998 to 2008—including 633 Bank projects and 275 IFC investments—was identified and analyzed. In the Bank case, a random sample of 84 closed and ongoing projects was selected for further in-depth analysis. Projects in related subsectors were also reviewed, as was a sample of development policy loans (DPLs). The population of Bank and IFC nonlending and advisory services from fiscal 1998 to 2008 was identified, and a sample from the 1,110 pieces of Bank analytic and advisory activity (AAA) and all 211 IFC advisory services was analyzed.

Strategy Review. Relevant World Bank and IFC strategy documents were identified and the implementation of the strategies was reviewed as appropriate. For the Bank, these included Country Assistance Strategies, Poverty Reduction Strategies prepared by borrowers, and the Bank's rural strategies. For IFC, these included all relevant corporate, department, and country strategies.

Country Case Studies. For the Bank, 11 client countries were selected for detailed review: the 2 largest borrowers, India and China, and 9 others selected randomly. Together these countries accounted for more than one-third of the Bank's agricultural lending during the period. For IFC, seven countries were purposively selected based on the intensity of their operations: Argentina and Peru, which had large operations; India, which had midsize operations; and Egypt, Ghana, Nicaragua, and Nigeria, which had small to negligible operations.

Literature Review. Bank Group and external literature were reviewed to gather information about the complexities of the agriculture sector and the World Bank Group's role in various countries and regions. Included in the review were sector and subsector analyses, a recent IEG review of impact evaluations in agriculture (IEG 2010c), and research produced by academia, research centers, and donor organizations. Numerous previous IEG project, sector, country, and thematic evaluations were also reviewed for relevant information and data.

Stakeholder Interviews. Interviews were conducted with IFC and World Bank staff; clients (both current and past); donors' representatives (multilateral and bilateral); and representatives of the business community, government, and NGOs in the context of the desk and field work. In addition, 23 previous and current World Bank country directors covering 28 randomly selected countries were interviewed about the Bank's contribution to agricultural development and the institutional factors that affect that contribution.

Additional Analysis. A regression analysis was undertaken to examine the determinants of project performance, drawing on IEG ratings of overall outcome and sustainability of all closed projects in the World Bank evaluation portfolio (appendix D). In-depth impact evaluations were undertaken of a World Bank irrigation project and an IFC investment, both in Peru, and an impact evaluation of a land project in Malawi. The evaluation also drew on the Consultative Group on International Agriculture Research (CGIAR) Agricultural Science and Technology Indicators to measure agricultural technical capacity within countries and on World Bank Group Human Resources data as an indicator of staff skills.

The analysis draws on a country typology with three country classifications—agriculture-based, transforming, or urbanized—defined in the 2008 *World Development Report* (WDR) on agriculture. This evaluation adopts the WDR country classification based on the share of aggregate growth originating in agriculture and the extent of poverty (below $2.15 a day) in the rural sector, and the characteristics, challenges, and future outlooks for the sector are very different in the three country types.[1]

In the agriculture-based economies, which include most countries in Sub-Saharan Africa, agricultural development is essential to growth and poverty reduction, yet productivity lags substantially behind that of transforming and urbanized economies (appendix figure A.1). The transforming economies consist mainly of countries in South and East Asia and the Middle East and North Africa. These countries are less dependent on agriculture for overall growth than are the agriculture-based, but agriculture and rural development are needed to reduce poverty and narrow the urban-rural divide. In the urbanized economies, which include most countries in Latin America and Europe and Central Asia, poverty is no longer primarily rural, and agriculture contributes only modestly to growth.

Agriculture is a competitive sector and can contribute to poverty reduction by including the rural poor as producers and providing them with jobs in modern food markets. World Bank interventions during the evaluation period were distributed relatively evenly across the three categories of countries, whereas IFC interventions were concentrated in the urbanized category (with IFC investments in only eight agriculture-based economies).

Chapter 2

EVALUATION HIGHLIGHTS

- Agriculture and agribusiness accounted for about 8 percent of World Bank Group financing over the period.

- Although Sub-Saharan Africa had the largest share of projects and commitments, it had the lowest share dedicated to agricultural sector growth and productivity.

- Performance of World Bank agricultural lending was about the same as lending in other sectors. Europe and Central Asia performed better than average, and Sub-Saharan Africa notably worse.

- Less attention has been given to enhancing the impact and sustainability of analytic and advisory work at the country level, and there were fewer activities in agriculture-based economies compared with transforming economies.

- IFC investments were largely focused on Europe and Central Asia and Latin America.

- IFC's agribusiness investments and advisory services have increased since the sector was made a strategic priority, but the share of the agribusiness department has declined due to the rapid increase in the financial market departments.

- Development and investment outcomes of IFC investments in food and agriculture have improved; outcomes for advisory services have been mixed.

Photo courtesy of Ray Witlin/World Bank.

Strategy and Interventions

During the evaluation period, fiscal 1998–2008, the World Bank Group provided $23.7 billion in financing for agriculture and agribusiness activities in 108 countries. Seventy-six percent, $18.1 billion, of this support came from the World Bank and 24 percent, $5.6 billion, came from IFC. In addition to providing financing, both the World Bank and IFC have provided non-lending technical assistance and advisory services to their clients. The World Bank has also supported several global and regional programs and partnerships in the agriculture sector.

World Bank

The Bank's strategic approach to agricultural development has come full circle in the past 50 years, beginning with strong emphasis on agricultural development in the 1960s through the 1980s, moving away to focus on broader rural development in the 1990s and early 2000s, and returning to an agricultural focus since 2007 (box 2.1). The World Bank Group has recently formulated an Agriculture Action Plan that emphasizes support for agricultural productivity growth.

Lending Trends and Outcomes

World Bank lending to the agriculture sector was about 7 percent of total Bank lending over the evaluation period

---

BOX 2.1   THE THREE PHASES OF THE BANK'S STRATEGIC APPROACH TO AGRICULTURE

1968 to 1990—Agriculture sector development becomes a central focus

In October 1968, President Robert McNamara pledged to devote particular attention to agriculture. This led to the founding of the Consultative Group on International Agricultural Research (CGIAR) in 1971 and publication of the World Bank's first Agriculture Sector Study in 1972. The study discussed the role of agriculture in achieving the development goals of greater production and exports, increased employment, and better income distribution. The food crisis of the mid-1970s provided the impetus for continued focus on the sector into the 1980s. The 1982 *World Development Report* (WDR) focused on agriculture and emphasized the strong association between agricultural development and economic growth and poverty alleviation. It discussed some of the main policy, institutional, and technical issues involved in stimulating rapid agricultural development.

1990s and early 2000s— The shift to rural development

In the early 1990s, the Bank began to expand its work in human development, and then in environment and sustainable development. Meanwhile, the Green Revolution pushed food production to new heights, which contributed to complacency about the abundance provided by global food production. *Rural Development: From Vision to Action*, the 1997 strategy, shifted the Bank's focus to "the entire rural productive system." *Reaching the Rural Poor: A Renewed Strategy for Rural Development*, the 2003 strategy, supported an even broader rural agenda focused on creating an investment climate conducive to rural growth and empowering the poor to share in the benefits of that growth. Among its five strategic objectives, only one emphasized enhancing agricultural productivity and competitiveness. The rest focused on building an enabling environment for broad-based and sustainable rural growth, fostering nonfarm economic growth, improving social well-being, managing and mitigating risk and reducing vulnerability, and enhancing the sustainability of natural resource management.

Since 2007—The return to agriculture

With the recent WDR on agriculture, and the more recent food crisis, agricultural development is now back near the top of the development agenda. The Bank has prepared an *Agriculture Action Plan 2010–12* with five focal areas: raising agricultural productivity, linking farmers to markets and strengthening value addition, enhancing environmental services and sustainability, reducing risk and vulnerability, and facilitating agricultural entry and exit and rural nonfarm incomes. This has been accompanied by renewed attention to food security issues.

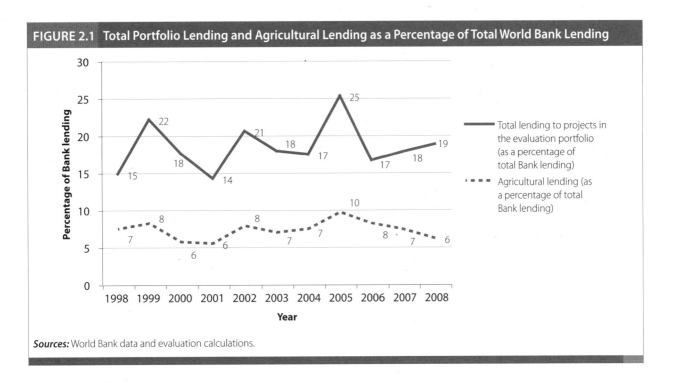

FIGURE 2.1 Total Portfolio Lending and Agricultural Lending as a Percentage of Total World Bank Lending

Sources: World Bank data and evaluation calculations.

(figure 2.1).[1] The evaluation portfolio consists of 633 projects with agricultural activities, in most cases combined with nonagricultural activities in the same project. Of the 633 projects, 506 were investment operations and 127 were development policy loans (DPLs). The total lending commitment of the portfolio was $45.2 billion, with about 40 percent of this—$18.1 billion—devoted to agriculture.[2]

> The agriculture sector accounted for 7 percent of World Bank lending over the evaluation period.

Agriculture lending was also part of projects with overall objectives that were not focused primarily on improving agricultural growth and productivity. Forty-six percent of the 633 projects in the evaluation portfolio were primarily focused on promoting agricultural growth and productivity and were largely composed of agriculture activities (figure 2.2).[3] The remaining 54 percent, many of them community-driven development (CDD) interventions, were largely nonagricultural projects, although they contain some agricultural activities (including forestry).

Agriculture lending has been distributed over several agriculture-related activities in investment and DPL operations, including irrigation and drainage (34 percent); general agriculture, fishing, and forestry (26 percent); agricultural research and extension (11 percent); crops (8 percent); forestry (7 percent); agricultural marketing and trade (6 percent); and animal production

and agroindustry (both 4 percent). Several of these subsectors, such as irrigation and drainage and research and extension, can be traced along the crop production chain shown in figure 1.3. Others, such as animal production, are part of a parallel production chain as noted in chapter

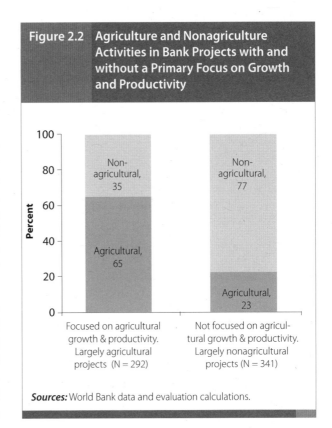

Figure 2.2 Agriculture and Nonagriculture Activities in Bank Projects with and without a Primary Focus on Growth and Productivity

Sources: World Bank data and evaluation calculations.

1 (also box 2.2). Rural finance and transport interventions that support agricultural development, as demonstrated by the crop production chain, are not considered part of the Bank's agricultural lending (appendix figure B.2a). The DPLs in the evaluation portfolio provide support for agricultural reforms (along with reforms in other sectors), including changes in the legal and policy framework.

The Sub-Saharan Africa Region accounted for the highest number of projects (193) and largest lending commitments in the evaluation portfolio ($11.5 billion) of any Region (figure 2.3), but had one of the lowest shares of that portfolio (32 percent) dedicated to agricultural growth and productivity (figure 2.4). Conversely, the Middle East and North Africa and Europe and Central Asia Regions, where urbanized or transforming countries predominate, each had lower aggregate lending commitments in the evaluation portfolio but, within those commitments, a greater focus on agricultural growth and productivity.

Although Sub-Saharan Africa had the most projects and largest commitments, it had the lowest share of the portfolio dedicated to agricultural growth and productivity projects.

Support for projects focused on agricultural growth and productivity declined from 1998 to 2003 in line with the Bank's shift toward rural development. The share of commitments for projects focused on agricultural growth and productivity declined from 71 percent of the portfolio in 1998 to a low of 25 percent in 2003. Since then it has picked up slightly (figure 2.5). Analysis by the number of projects shows a similar profile (see appendix figure B.3a). Analysis

---

BOX 2.2   LIVESTOCK SECTOR AND FISHERIES IN WORLD BANK PROJECTS

The livestock sector is the major supplier of animal protein, and demand for this protein has grown rapidly in recent years. Livestock is also an important source of livelihood for millions of rural poor (Steinfeld and others 2006). Cattle provide traction[a] for about 50 percent of the world's farmers. Farmers' livestock holdings provide organic fertilizer, convert waste into high-value food, and serve as insurance for people without access to financial markets. They also buffer farmers against shocks, drought, and natural disasters (Delgado and others 1999; IFAD 2004; World Bank 2007b). Some of the factors needed to increase animal productivity, whether on a commercial scale or for an individual farmer, are similar to those for increasing crop productivity—availability of good animal breeds, water, feeds, research and extension, veterinary care, medicines, access to markets, and support with processing of animal products.

Animal production activities are not fully captured in the Bank's agriculture lending, but are also part of several natural resource management and environment projects. Sixty-seven projects in the evaluation portfolio have some animal (livestock, birds, fisheries) production activities. Of these, 19 (28 percent) were avian flu projects, 11 (18 percent) were fisheries/aquaculture projects, and the rest dealt with other livestock. These had a total animal production commitment of $645.7 million, 65 percent of which went to transforming economies, 22 percent to the agriculture-based, and 9 percent to the urbanized. East Asia and the Pacific had the highest commitments (51 percent), followed by Sub-Saharan Africa (18 percent), South Asia (17 percent), Latin America and the Caribbean (7 percent), Europe and Central Asia (4 percent), and the Middle East and North Africa (3 percent).

The livestock projects have supported various activities, including rangeland management, pastoral development, animal research and extension (for breeding and nutrition, for example), and processing and marketing of livestock products. Fisheries projects have supported investments in advanced hatchery technology and marine aquaculture; improvement of inland open-water fisheries, including support for stock enhancement of floodplain fisheries, restoration of fisheries habitats, establishment of fish sanctuaries, and construction of fish passes; and expansion and quality improvement of storage, processing, and marketing facilities. The performance of the 10 closed projects was in line with the average performance of projects in the evaluation portfolio.

Sources: World Bank data and evaluation findings.
Note: A list of projects with animal components obtained from the Agriculture and Rural Development Department showed that 57 more projects in the evaluation portfolio had animal production components. When these are added, total animal commitments increase to $1,053 million. Fifty-nine percent of this amount went to transforming economies, 23 percent to the agriculture-based, and 11 percent to the urbanized economies. By Region, East Asia and the Pacific received 42 percent, Sub-Saharan Africa, 25 percent; South Asia, 16 percent; Latin America and the Caribbean, 8 percent; Europe and Central Asia, 5 percent; and the Middle East and North Africa, 4 percent.

a. Animal traction refers to the use of draft animals to provide the motive power for vehicles or machinery.

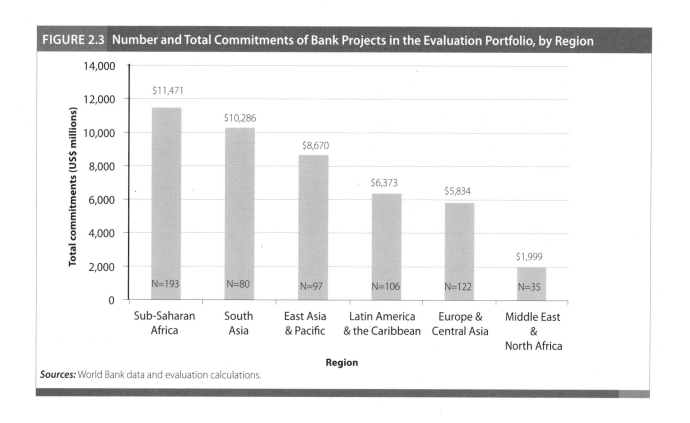

FIGURE 2.3 Number and Total Commitments of Bank Projects in the Evaluation Portfolio, by Region

Sources: World Bank data and evaluation calculations.

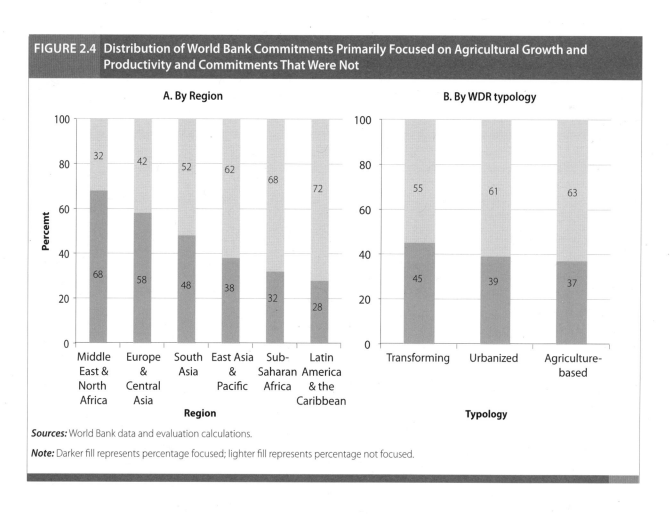

FIGURE 2.4 Distribution of World Bank Commitments Primarily Focused on Agricultural Growth and Productivity and Commitments That Were Not

A. By Region

B. By WDR typology

Sources: World Bank data and evaluation calculations.

Note: Darker fill represents percentage focused; lighter fill represents percentage not focused.

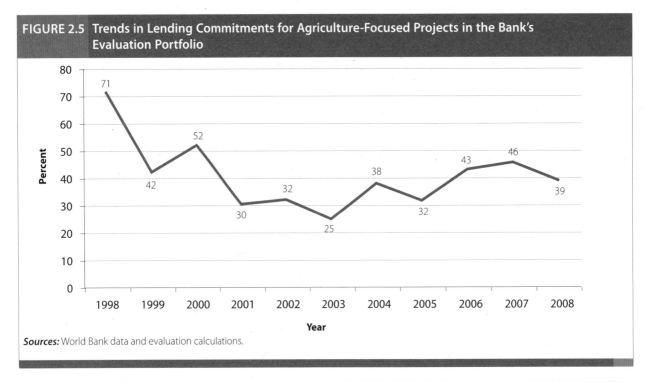

FIGURE 2.5 Trends in Lending Commitments for Agriculture-Focused Projects in the Bank's Evaluation Portfolio

Sources: World Bank data and evaluation calculations.

of the commitments by WDR typology indicates that focus on growth and productivity in agriculture declined most strongly in the agriculture-based economies until 2006. The slight upturn since then is largely attributable to the avian flu interventions in that year (figure 2.6).[4] Similarly, analysis by Regions shows that Sub-Saharan Africa followed the pattern of agriculture-based economies.

Support for agriculture-focused projects declined as the Bank shifted focus to rural development.

Investment operations were more likely to be focused on agricultural growth and productivity than DPLs. Fifty-one

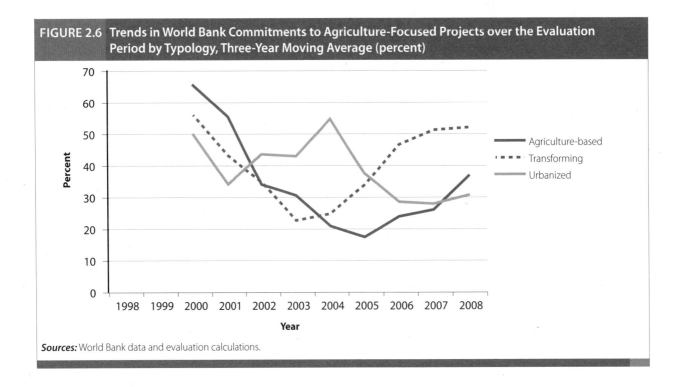

FIGURE 2.6 Trends in World Bank Commitments to Agriculture-Focused Projects over the Evaluation Period by Typology, Three-Year Moving Average (percent)

Agriculture-based
Transforming
Urbanized

Sources: World Bank data and evaluation calculations.

percent of the investment loans (49 percent by commitments) were focused on growth and productivity, versus 28 percent of the DPLs (27 percent by commitments). Over time, the total number of DPLs in the evaluation portfolio has increased, particularly in agriculture-based economies and in Sub-Saharan Africa (appendix figures B.3b, c).

Performance of projects in the evaluation portfolio, measured against their stated objectives, was comparable with those of all Bank projects over the decade. Seventy-seven percent of projects with agriculture activities had moderately satisfactory or better outcomes compared with 79 percent Bank-wide. Seventy-three percent of projects with agriculture activities had likely sustainability compared to 76 percent Bank-wide.

Outcome ratings for agriculture projects were comparable to those for nonagriculture projects, but their sustainability was lower.

Outcome ratings for the agriculture-focused projects in the evaluation portfolio were also the same as non-agriculture Bank projects over the decade, though their sustainability was lower (appendix figure B.4). Though only 67 percent of the agriculture-focused DPLs were rated satisfactory compared with 79 percent of the agriculture-focused investment operations, the difference is not significant. The achievements on the reforms related to the agriculture sector in these DPLs, which usually also included reforms in

sectors other than agriculture, were broadly in line with the overall outcome rating.

The outcome ratings of the agriculture-focused projects in the evaluation portfolio declined in the second part of the evaluation period, from 80 percent moderately satisfactory or better in fiscal 1998–2001 to 65 percent in fiscal 2002–08 (figure 2.7), while the performance of nonagriculture projects did not change. Performance of DPLs Bank-wide improved from 74 percent rated moderately satisfactory or better between fiscal 1998 and 2001 to 83 percent moderately satisfactory or better between fiscal 2002 and 2008, while performance of agriculture-focused DPLs declined from 82 percent moderately satisfactory or better to 57 percent between fiscal 2002 and 2008, driven to a large extent by the weaker performance of DPLs in Sub-Saharan Africa.

Problems in the performance of the agriculture portfolio appear to be concentrated primarily in Sub-Saharan Africa. The agriculture-focused projects performed better than the nonagriculture ones in Europe and Central Asia, but worse than the nonagriculture projects in Sub-Saharan Africa (figure 2.8.A). The performance of agriculture-focused investment operations and DPLs was similar, but below average in Sub-Saharan Africa. These results suggest that the Bank's agriculture activities face unique challenges in the poorer countries, which may help to explain the Bank's declining engagement until the recent uptick. Poor performance was certainly a factor in IFC moving away from agribusiness projects in the early part of the evaluation period. As shown

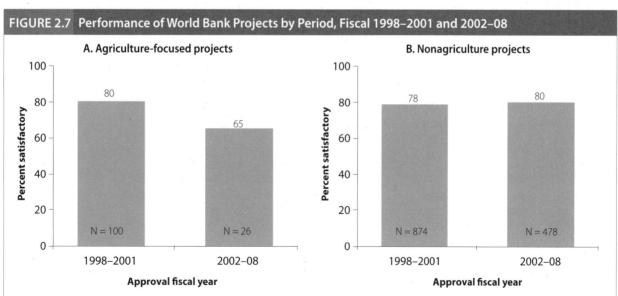

FIGURE 2.7 Performance of World Bank Projects by Period, Fiscal 1998–2001 and 2002–08

A. Agriculture-focused projects

B. Nonagriculture projects

Sources: World Bank data and evaluation calculations.

Note: Difference is statistically significant for the agriculture-focused projects. The agriculture-focused projects are those that included increasing agricultural growth and productivity among their objectives. The nonagriculture projects are all the others, including those outside the evaluation portfolio. All rating comparisons over the two periods (including those of DPLs discussed above) are based on data available as of May 5, 2010.

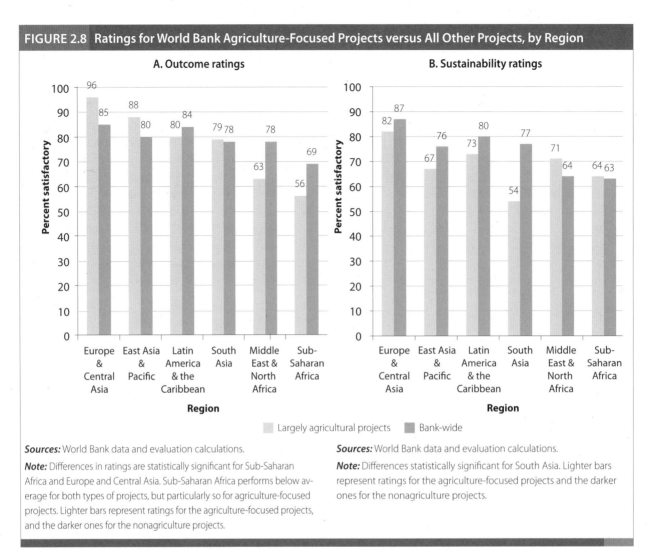

FIGURE 2.8 Ratings for World Bank Agriculture-Focused Projects versus All Other Projects, by Region

A. Outcome ratings

B. Sustainability ratings

Largely agricultural projects ■ Bank-wide

Sources: World Bank data and evaluation calculations.

Note: Differences in ratings are statistically significant for Sub-Saharan Africa and Europe and Central Asia. Sub-Saharan Africa performs below average for both types of projects, but particularly so for agriculture-focused projects. Lighter bars represent ratings for the agriculture-focused projects, and the darker ones for the nonagriculture projects.

Sources: World Bank data and evaluation calculations.

Note: Differences statistically significant for South Asia. Lighter bars represent ratings for the agriculture-focused projects and the darker ones for the nonagriculture projects.

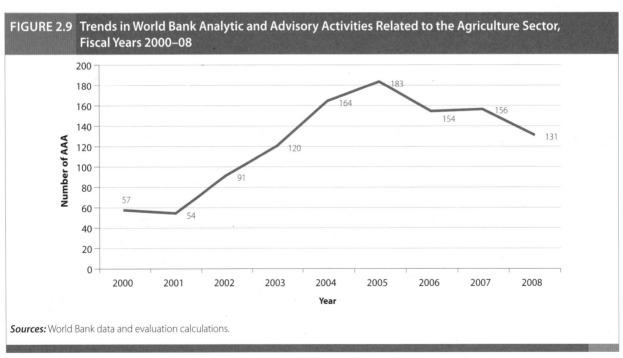

FIGURE 2.9 Trends in World Bank Analytic and Advisory Activities Related to the Agriculture Sector, Fiscal Years 2000–08

Sources: World Bank data and evaluation calculations.

in chapter 4, the poorest countries are often the ones with the weakest governance environment, and the Bank has used other approaches, such as CDD, to engage them. The low sustainability rating in figure 2.8.B (54 percent likely) for projects in South Asia can be explained by the weak performance of the large number of irrigation projects in the Region, as discussed in chapter 3.

> Performance problems in the portfolio appear to be concentrated primarily in Sub-Saharan Africa.

Analytic and Advisory Activities and Results

The recorded number of pieces of agriculture-related AAA increased until about 2005, when it began to taper off (figure 2.9).[5] This increase is in keeping with the emphasis on increased analytical work in the Bank's rural strategy (World Bank 2003d).

The quality of AAA is generally sound, and most AAA addresses issues of strategic relevance.[6] Assessment of a sample of agriculture sector–related AAA in 14 countries done for this evaluation found that the work is generally of sound technical quality and that the vast majority of products addressed issues that had been identified as sectoral development constraints in earlier work or in policy dialogue with

clients (see appendix B for the main findings from the IEG assessment of AAA). About three-quarters of assessed AAA pieces were delivered in time to help inform government policy decisions.

> Analytic work was generally of sound quality, relevant, and even influential.

Even AAA that focused on topics that had not yet been recognized as issues in the country was sometimes influential. Bank work on land policy and administration in Nicaragua, for example, was undertaken without much government interest. Once the work was completed, however, it aroused the interest of the ministers of agriculture and finance and contributed to land reform legislation. A separate evaluation of economic and sector work in all sectors (IEG 2008n) found a positive relationship between cost of economic and sector work (ESW) and its quality. That evaluation also found that the average cost of ESW tasks was higher in International Bank for Reconstruction and Development (IBRD) than in International Development Association (IDA) countries in all Regions and was lowest in Sub-Saharan Africa. Analysis undertaken for this evaluation corroborates this finding: The unit cost of AAA undertaken in IDA countries was $180,000, significantly below the average cost of AAA in IBRD and IBRD/IDA blend countries ($223,000 and $256,000, respectively).

Bank AAA has helped raise stakeholders' awareness; change policy, law, or regulation; and build coalitions for change. The AAA assessment, the evaluation's country studies and project assessments, and a review of Bank-supported land interventions support this finding. For example, the China country study found that Bank-supported AAA was influential among policy makers and academic communities and helped further rural reforms. The Bulgaria country study found that AAA was instrumental in the policy dialogue with the government, in helping the government prioritize reforms, and in generating public support for the reform process.[7]

A recent IEG review of seven farm restructuring projects in five Europe and Central Asia countries, undertaken as part of project assessments, also noted the important role of agricultural sector reviews in informing policy dialogue (IEG 2010a). Indeed, the Azerbaijan country study reported greater governmental interest in the Bank's nonlending contributions than in the lending ones. A review of the Bank's land interventions showed that the Bank's analytical work in this area, including the Policy Research Report, *Land Policies for Growth and Poverty Reduction* (World Bank 2003b), has contributed to the understanding of land rights issues both inside and outside the institution.

But insufficient attention has been given to enhancing the impact and sustainability of AAA at the country level. The AAA assessment also found that less than a quarter of the AAA reviewed led to sustained engagement on a particular topic in the country, suggesting that inadequate dissemination may be limiting the results achieved. Most reports were presented at a seminar and discussed with senior policy makers, but dissemination tended to stop there. In Malawi, for example, an IEG Country Assistance Evaluation (CAE) for the period 1996–2005 noted the need to strengthen consultations on analytical work with key stakeholders and promote its wider dissemination (IEG 2006c). IEG's assessment found that ESW followed by technical assistance scored higher results at the country level than freestanding ESW. Translation, particularly where English was not the official language, also led to better results.

> Less attention has been given to enhancing the impact and sustainability of AAA at the country level.

AAA results can be boosted through partnerships with domestic research organizations. One reason AAA seems to have had significant impact in China is the Bank's partnerships with domestic and international think tanks. The possibility of partnership with domestic research organizations has been lim-

ited in the agriculture-based economies by the weak technical capacity of their domestic institutions, as noted in chapter 4.

AAA has influenced the scope of lending and strategy formulation. The AAA assessment found that about two-thirds of sampled AAA served to inform Bank lending, and one-third was used to help formulate the Bank's country sector assistance strategy. The Peru country study found that AAA on sustainable fisheries (fiscal 2004) was critical to formulating the 2009 environmental DPL that is the Bank's main intervention for reforming management of the over-exploited marine fisheries in the country. The India country study found that existing policies, especially subsidies and regulations, were the major concerns of the Bank's agricultural policy dialogue during the review period. This dialogue was informed by a number of studies, among others, the "India Power Supply to Agriculture" (World Bank 2001), *India: Re-energizing the Agricultural Sector* (World Bank 2005e), "India: Taking Agriculture to the Market" (World Bank 2006c), and state-level agricultural sector reviews. The Georgia CAE (IEG 2008d) found that Bank studies contributed to the government's decision to end direct price interventions, liberalize trade, privatize land and distribution systems, and establish a financial intermediary system for agribusiness and large farmers through commercial banks.

The Bank has recently increased its attention to agriculture-related public expenditure with the intention of grounding the scale-up in sound budgetary planning and execution. This is an important step, particularly for Sub-Saharan Africa, given the high dependency on donor funding and the sustainability problems that have plagued many donor-funded projects in the Region.

> Projects whose preparation had drawn on Bank analytic work were more likely to have outcome ratings of satisfactory or better than those that did not.

The analysis of the sample portfolio found that projects whose documents stated that preparation had drawn upon Bank AAA were more likely to have outcome ratings of moderately satisfactory or better and sustainability ratings of likely than those with documents that did not mention the use of AAA (table 2.1). The Quality Assurance Group (QAG) quality-at-entry data for projects in the portfolio show similar findings for adequacy of country and sector knowledge, which is often developed through AAA to inform the design of lending products (table 2.1). IEG's earlier evaluation of ESW (IEG 2008n) also had similar findings. Only half (49 percent of the 84 project documents) of the sample port-

TABLE 2.1 Relationship between Analytic and Advisory Activities and Satisfactory Outcome Ratings in the World Bank

Portfolio	Outcome moderately satisfactory or higher (percent)	Sustainability likely (percent)
IEG sample portfolio		
AAA (ESW and technical assistance)		
Yes (N=26)	**92.3**	76.9
No (N=11)	**63.6**	71.4[a]
QAG		
Quality-at-entry rating on adequacy of country and sector knowledge		
Quality-at-entry rating high (N=47)	85.1	**78.9**[b]
Quality-at-entry rating low (N=6)	66.6	**50.0**

Sources: World Bank data and evaluation calculations. See also appendix table B.9.

Note: Bold numbers are statistically significantly different from each other.

a. N was equal to 7.

b. N was equal to 38.

folio mentioned that preparation had drawn on Bank or non-Bank sector work (appendix table B.8). IEG's ESW evaluation further found that Sub-Saharan Africa had the lowest share of investment loans preceded by relevant ESW that could have informed the loans.[8] While acknowledging the importance of AAA in informing Bank lending and policy dialogue, country studies report that there are no systematic procedures to ensure that this happens.

BOX 2.3   THE FOUR PHASES OF IFC'S STRATEGIC APPROACH TO AGRICULTURE

1998–2000

The strategies focused on geographic diversification, support for privatization, rehabilitation of cooperatives, and integration with the World Bank country and sector strategies. Some of the companies IFC invested in during the period later became local and regional agribusiness leaders (and south-south investors), but more were unsuccessful. The latter group strengthened the perception that food and agriculture carried high risks and contributed to a lower strategic emphasis on the sector.

2001–04

IFC corporate strategies did not mention food industries, agriculture, or agribusiness, and the sector was demarketed (that is, lost focus in IFC), except in the case of financial crisis or links to environmental issues (appendix box B.1). Meanwhile, the Agribusiness Department (CAG) strategies began to consider supply-chain linkages, a broader range of financial products, and country and subsector strategies.

2005–06

Agribusiness reappeared in the corporate strategies as an area where IFC would differentiate itself from investment banks by its emphasis on environmental and social issues (appendix box B.2). IFC would intervene in countries and sectors where there is a perception that economic development and sustainability concerns may diverge (through "demonstration impacts").

2007-present

Agribusiness became a corporate strategic priority in 2007 (appendix box B.3). It was rediscovered as a source of economic growth and a cornerstone of poverty reduction in frontier markets. Meanwhile, CAG strategies began to consider strengthening business development, growing commitments, focusing in Sub-Saharan Africa, and working with large trader-processors to reach the farm level. Agribusiness has additionally been presented as a strategic tool in response to the food crisis. The stated goal is to "Deliver development impact along the global agri-supply chain, through investments and advisory services with the private sector, to create opportunities and improve people's lives."

There were fewer agriculture AAA interventions in agriculture-based economies than in transforming economies (appendix figure B.5). Country studies in some of the poorer IDA countries, such as Nepal and Guinea, show that little AAA was done on the agriculture sector, limiting the possibility of positive impact on policy dialogue and lending. IEG country assistance reviews show that agriculture-focused AAA was not carried out in Ethiopia and Ghana for extended periods—Ethiopia during 1997–2005 (IEG 2008c) and Ghana during 2004–07 (IEG 2007e), even though the two countries had substantial agriculture lending from the Bank.

There were fewer analytic and advisory activities in agriculture-based economies than in transforming economies.

It is unclear how much the scale of IDA funding influences the extent to which AAA is done in some of the Bank's poorest client countries. However, the Guinea country study did find that the country's low Country Performance and Institutional Assessment (CPIA) rating led to a small IDA allocation, which in turn led to an administrative budget too small to support significant analytical work to build a knowledge base. That said, a significant proportion (22 percent) of the AAA that was initiated was ultimately dropped, which raises questions about the effectiveness with which limited resources are used. The likelihood of the AAA being dropped was higher in the agriculture-based economies (25 percent) than transforming and urbanized economies taken together (19 percent) (appendix table B.7).

IFC

IFC's strategic approach to the agribusiness sector has varied over time, much like the Bank's approach to the agriculture sector. Four phases can be identified (box 2.3) that have influenced the extent of IFC investments and advisory services in the sector.

IFC's strategies for agribusiness have set out a context of promoting economic growth and poverty reduction.

For agribusiness, the department and corporate strategies have set out a context of promoting economic growth and poverty reduction. Within this context, IFC seeks to: (i) increase supply through global agricommodity players; (ii) strengthen and integrate supply chains to link farmers to global agrisupply chains and to bring land into sustainable production through private equity investments; (iii) provide financing through working capital and trade-finance products, increase rural credit through investments and advisory services focused on wholesaling facilities (through financial intermediaries), and explore development risk management products; (iv) set standards and promote policy/regulatory dialogue for setting environmental and social standards, water efficiency and irrigation infrastructure through public-private partnerships, and land and trade policies reform; and (v) focus on Sub-Saharan Africa. The strategies also discuss the need to allocate more resources to agribusiness-related IFC units.

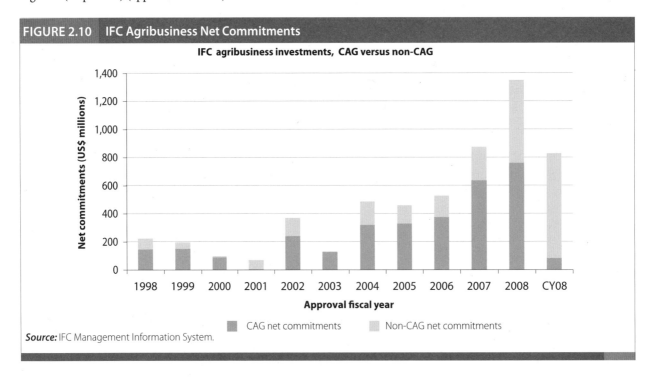

FIGURE 2.10   IFC Agribusiness Net Commitments

IFC agribusiness investments, CAG versus non-CAG

Net commitments (US$ millions) / Approval fiscal year

■ CAG net commitments   ■ Non-CAG net commitments

Source: IFC Management Information System.

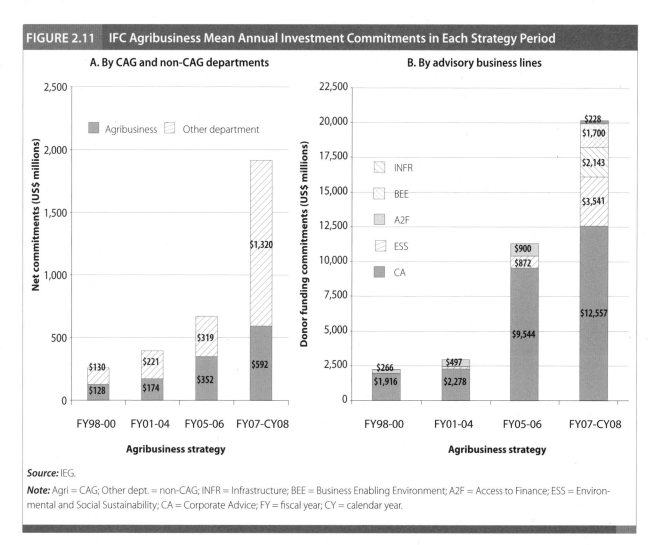

FIGURE 2.11   IFC Agribusiness Mean Annual Investment Commitments in Each Strategy Period

A. By CAG and non-CAG departments

B. By advisory business lines

Source: IEG.

Note: Agri = CAG; Other dept. = non-CAG; INFR = Infrastructure; BEE = Business Enabling Environment; A2F = Access to Finance; ESS = Environmental and Social Sustainability; CA = Corporate Advice; FY = fiscal year; CY = calendar year.

Investment Trends and Outcomes

IFC agribusiness investments have increased sharply since the sector became a corporate strategic priority in 2007 (figure 2.10). However, such an increase has not occurred in agriculture-based economies in general, and in Sub-Saharan Africa in particular. Over the evaluation period, IFC's commitments totaled $5.6 billion (275 projects). Fifty-four percent of total investments (44 percent of projects) were committed in fiscal 2007–calendar 2008, up from 18 percent (12 percent of projects) in fiscal 2005–06 (appendix table B.10). Before the evaluation period, agribusiness commitments had grown rapidly (fiscal 1991–97), but disappointing project outcomes brought an equally rapid decline.

IFC's agribusiness investments have increased sharply since 2007, when the sector became a strategic priority.

Over time, the share of commitments undertaken by the Agribusiness Department (CAG) has declined, large-ly because of the rapid growth of the global financial markets department (figure 2.11A). The fast growth in commitments was a consequence of agribusiness projects being developed independently of CAG, as will be discussed in chapter 4.[9] Overall, CAG accounted for 57 percent of agribusiness commitments over the evaluation period, but its share of commitments was only 37.5 percent in fiscal 2007–calendar 2008. The breakdown of agribusiness commitments by IFC departments is illustrated in figure 2.12 and appendix box B.4.

The share of commitments undertaken by the agribusiness department has declined because of the rapid growth of the global financial markets department.

Latin America and the Caribbean and Europe and Central Asia have been IFC's main Regional investment targets; Brazil and Argentina were its largest country operations. The Latin America and Caribbean Region has

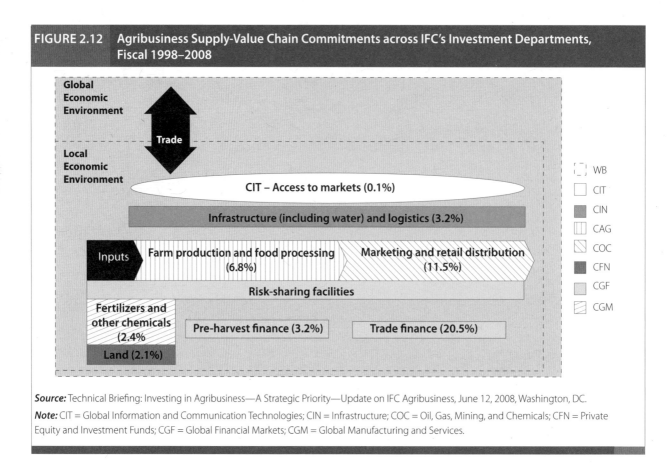

FIGURE 2.12   Agribusiness Supply-Value Chain Commitments across IFC's Investment Departments, Fiscal 1998–2008

Source: Technical Briefing: Investing in Agribusiness—A Strategic Priority—Update on IFC Agribusiness, June 12, 2008, Washington, DC.

Note: CIT = Global Information and Communication Technologies; CIN = Infrastructure; COC = Oil, Gas, Mining, and Chemicals; CFN = Private Equity and Investment Funds; CGF = Global Financial Markets; CGM = Global Manufacturing and Services.

received 46 percent of commitments, followed by Europe and Central Asia (24 percent), East Asia and the Pacific (8 percent), and Sub-Saharan Africa (6.7 percent). By number of projects, Latin America and the Caribbean again is first, with 35 percent, followed by Sub-Saharan Africa, with 24 percent, and Europe and Central Asia, with 19 percent. The Sub-Saharan Africa projects include 22 small investments in the Africa Enterprise Fund program.[10] Brazil received 15 percent of total agribusiness commitments (8.4 percent by number of projects), followed by Argentina with 12 percent (6 percent by number), and the Russian Federation with 8 percent (4 percent by number). Urbanized and transforming economies received 77 percent of agribusiness investments (67 percent by number).[11]

BOX 2.4   IFC'S SUPPORT FOR ANIMAL PRODUCTION AND PROCESSING

IFC has achieved generally satisfactory development outcomes in the slaughtering and poultry subsectors, lower investment outcomes in dairy production, and mostly poor development and investment outcomes in aquaculture and fishing.

The factors for success in slaughter, poultry, and dairy are good sponsors with market leadership, technical strengths to drive efficiencies, competitive feedstock, strict bio-security on farms and in the supply chain, and effective management of contract farming and sustainability of supply chains. A Ukrainian poultry processor is a good example of the unique role that IFC can play in the subsector in terms of economic growth, employment, and small and medium enterprise opportunities (appendix box B.6).

The poor outcomes were a consequence of investments in small-scale companies operating in almost monopolistic markets or under challenging business environments caused by government intervention or poor IFC screening and appraisal. The poor outcomes of the earlier aquaculture and fishing investments were due to market, sponsor, and technical weaknesses. For example, IFC supported a company to renovate and remove bottlenecks from a 7,000-ton per year export fish processing plant by Lake Victoria in Uganda. The company did not achieve the expected outcomes because of energy outages and reduced fish stocks in the lake; IFC also incurred a financial loss.

Source: IEG.

The top agribusiness subsectors are food and agriculture, finance, and distribution.

The top three agribusiness-related subsectors are food and agriculture (F&A), finance, and distribution. As further discussed in chapter 4, IFC's organizational structure and industry knowledge may have encouraged the subsector distribution. Its breakdown is as follows: food and agriculture (57 percent), mostly animal production and processing (box 2.4 and appendix box B.5), vegetable fats and oils, beverages, and sugar; finance (25.8 percent), mostly agribusiness-related trade guarantee transactions, with a few investments in private equity and banks; distribution (11.5 percent), with investments in agribusiness-related distribution and logistics companies; infrastructure (3.3 percent), mainly warehouses, port terminals, and electronic trading platforms focused on agribusiness; and agrichemicals (2.4 percent), with investments in fertilizer plants.

IFC has diversified the range of financial instruments used in the sector—from loans to guarantees and quasi-equities, reflecting the increasing trends in international agribusiness trade and deeper IFC commitment to its agribusiness clients. IFC investment products included loans (61 percent), guarantees (23 percent), equity (10 percent), and quasi-loans (5 percent). The loan proportion significantly decreased (from 92 percent to 49 percent) between fiscal 1998–2000 and fiscal 2007–calendar 2008.[12] Meanwhile, the share of guarantees materially increased (from ~0 percent to 40 percent) over the same period. Quasi-loans and quasi-equity investments have recently multiplied: 51 percent of total commitments were committed in

fiscal 2007–calendar 2008; this had been a recommendation of an IEG evaluation. IFC mobilized a total of $1.06 billion from B-loan[13] investors through its agribusiness projects. Consequently, other financial institutions have invested 19 cents per IFC dollar invested in agribusiness projects, which is lower than the 34 cents per IFC dollar in IFC projects worldwide.

The development outcome (DO) and investment outcome (IO) ratings of the food and agriculture investments have significantly improved. IFC seems to have found a way to successfully support the trader-processor model after the poor performance at the beginning of the review period. This achievement is related to the layering of risk factors, which will be discussed in chapter 4. From fiscal 1998 to calendar 2008, 77.6 percent of the invested volume (65 percent by projects) achieved outcomes that met or

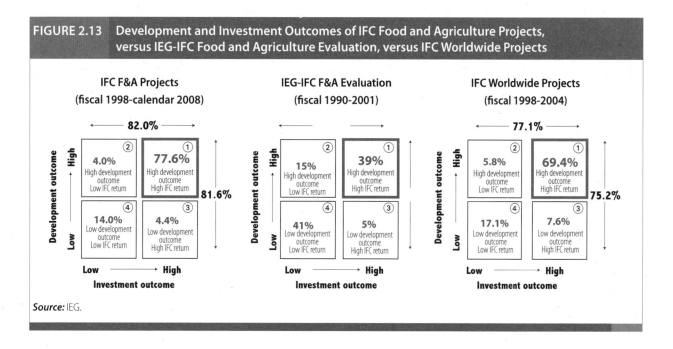

FIGURE 2.13 Development and Investment Outcomes of IFC Food and Agriculture Projects, versus IEG-IFC Food and Agriculture Evaluation, versus IFC Worldwide Projects

Source: IEG.

exceeded specified business, economic, environmental, and social performance criteria and made positive contributions to private sector development beyond the project. This compares with only 39 percent of the invested volume achieving higher ratings in fiscal 1990–2001, as found by earlier IEG evaluation work. The F&A projects have also done better in DO/IO than the worldwide IFC projects[14] evaluated by IEG over the same period (figure 2.13).

Development outcome and investment outcome ratings of food and agriculture investments have improved significantly.

The F&A projects in South Asia and Europe and Central Asia have achieved the highest DO/IO, and those in Sub-Saharan Africa the lowest (see appendix figure B.6). The former is because of a relatively higher proportion of projects in the brewery and soft drink subsectors using the processor model. The latter is associated with several country-level factors that have negatively affected IFC's performance in Sub-Saharan Africa: difficult business environments, paucity of indigenous entrepreneurs, small size of the potential investments, and lack of access to markets. These issues are discussed more fully in chapter 4. By WDR typology, the transforming economies achieved better outcomes than the urbanized and agriculture-based economies. The outcomes of the urbanized economies were negatively affected by the poor-performing investments of fiscal 1998–2001 (appendix table B.11).

The most frequent project objective[15] was to provide long-term financing. Objectives related to environmental and social aspects and to links to farmers lagged. First, long-term financing was a stated objective in 96 percent and was attained in 84 percent of the projects throughout the strategy periods. Second, improvement of environmental and social capacity was a stated objective in 95 percent of the projects and was attained in 65 percent. Ignoring the yet-to-be-evaluated fiscal 2007–calendar 2008 interventions, its realization rate[16] seems to have increased over time. Third, linking investments to farmers and small and medium enterprises (SMEs) was a stated objective in 84 percent of the projects and was attained in 64 percent (for details on the other objectives see appendix figure B.7).

Provision of long-term financing was the most frequently pursued project objective.

Advisory Services Trends and Outcomes

IFC's agribusiness advisory service expenditures have also recently increased (figure 2.14). However, Sub-Saharan Africa accounted for only 10 percent of expenditures. Overall, IFC's advisory service expenditures totaled $91 million in 211 projects. In fiscal 2007–calendar 2008, IFC spent more than 55 percent (or 43 percent by number of projects) of the total agribusiness advisory expenditures for the evaluation period, up from 25 percent (or 17 percent by number of projects) in fiscal 2005–06 (see figure 2.11B and appendix table B.12).[17]

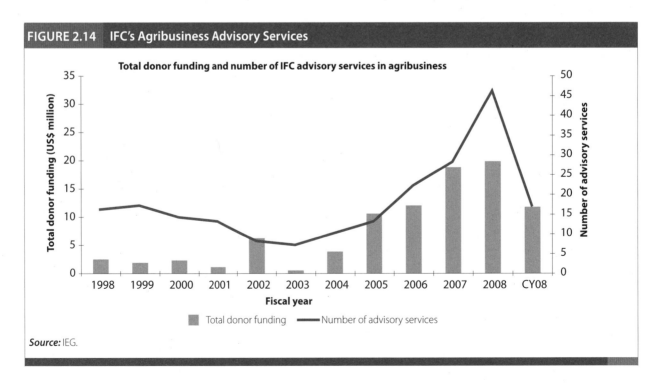

FIGURE 2.14   IFC's Agribusiness Advisory Services

Total donor funding and number of IFC advisory services in agribusiness

Source: IEG.

Advisory services expenditures in agribusiness have also increased, in particular for the Corporate Advice and Sustainability business lines.

The Corporate Advice and Sustainability advisory-business lines[18] **have contributed the most to the sector, the Business Enabling Environment and the Infrastructure lines the least** (appendix box B.7). Corporate Advice has supported areas such as corporate governance, linkages to farmers, feasibility studies, export programs, sector reviews, land reform, livelihood programs, farming, and processing. Sustainability has addressed issues related to biodiversity, carbon finance, cleaner technologies, gender entrepreneurship markets, social responsibility, sustainable energy, and traceability along the supply chains and food safety in areas such as bamboo, animal production and processing, sugar, other food, and biofuels. Over time, however, the share of Corporate Advice decreased and that of Sustainability rose. Corporate Advice ($65 million in 149 projects) accounted for 62 percent of expenditures in fiscal 2007–calendar 2008, down from 86 percent in fiscal 1998–2000. Meanwhile, Sustainability ($11 million in 40 projects) grew from 1 percent to 18 percent of expenditures over the same period. Since investment climate constraints are detrimental to the development of agriculture and agribusiness, IFC can add value by helping countries reduce the cost and burden of regulatory and administrative barriers in supply chains (for example, export policies, trade logistics, and constraints to the adoption of sustainability and quality standards). The implications of the lower share of expenditures of the Business Enabling Environment[19] and Infrastructure business lines are also discussed in the business environment section of chapter 3.[20]

Projects in the Sustainability business line performed better than those in Corporate Advice.

The Sustainability projects performed better those in Corporate Advice. The Sustainability projects generally responded to clients' demands and focused on activities such as water efficiency, cleaner energy, and integrated pest management. They have achieved a development effectiveness success rate of 81 percent and role and contribution of 57 percent; the Corporate Advice projects have achieved 73 percent and 51 percent, respectively. The Access to Finance, Business Enabling Environment, and Infrastructure business lines had very small numbers of projects and could not be compared in a meaningful manner.

Photo courtesy of Anatoly Rakhimbayev/World Bank.

IFC has largely focused its advisory work on Europe and Central Asia; Ukraine and the Russian Federation were its largest country operations. The advisory work in Europe and Central Asia mainly focused in helping clients and outgrowers to access knowledge, financing, and markets following the collapse of the Soviet Union. Europe and Central Asia has received 39 percent of dollars spent (or 32 percent of the projects); East Asia and the Pacific, 16 percent (or 20 percent of the projects); and Latin America and the Caribbean, 14 percent (or 15 percent of the projects). Ukraine received 17 percent of expenditures, followed by Russia (8.9 percent), and Indonesia and India (7 percent each). Urbanized and transforming economies received 78 percent of expenditures.[21]

Agribusiness advisory expenditures were equally split between the production of reports and on-site consulting work, with little subsector overlap with the investment subsectors. The reports focused on subsector and feasibility studies, business plans, and linkage assessments. The balance was spent for on-site consulting on subsectors such as bamboo-wood-forestry and finance, among others (see appendix box B.8). The bamboo-wood-forestry subsector, with 11 percent of expenditures ($9.7 million in 22 assignments), has mostly sought to strengthen the supply chain, assist SMEs, and emphasize sustainability. The finance sector, with 9 percent of expenditures ($8 million in 11 projects), has focused on agricultural insurance development; agricultural industrial financing; post-harvest, grassroots entrepreneurs; and farm financing. The small overlap between the subsectors focused by the investment and by the advisory services operations partly explains the low percentage of investment projects linked to advisory projects, as discussed below.

Overall outcomes for agribusiness advisory services are mixed.

The overall outcomes of the agribusiness-related advisory services projects are mixed; IFC was more successful in delivering positive development impacts than in playing an additional role. This can be attributed partly to the disconnect between advisory and investment projects—an issue also discussed in chapters 3 and 4.[22] Seventy-six percent of these projects[23] achieved a satisfactory development effectiveness rating, which is better than that of IFC's advisory services projects overall (67 percent). However, in only 52 percent of the agribusiness advisory projects has IFC provided a special contribution or additional role (that is, attained a satisfactory role and contribution rating), compared with 85 percent achieved by IFC in its projects worldwide.[24]

Throughout the evaluation period, the development effectiveness rating decreased and the role and contribution rating increased. These trends can be explained by the normal lag between intervention and achievement of long-term results, by the efforts of IFC to focus its advisory work as discussed in chapter 4, and by IFC's ongoing advances in training and quality control in advisory project reporting and monitoring. On the one hand, the development effectiveness success rate decreased from 85 percent in fiscal 2005–06 to 69 percent in fiscal 2007–calendar 2008.[25] On the other hand, the role and contribution success rate has risen throughout the strategy periods, even though it has remained low overall (see appendix figure B.8).

Agriculture-based economies have outperformed the other types on the role and contribution rating.

Agriculture-based economies have outperformed the other two types of economies on the role and contribution rating (74 percent, see appendix table B.13), but urbanized economies have outperformed the others on the development effectiveness rating (85 percent). This suggests that there is room for agribusiness advisory services projects to play a special role in difficult business environments, and for delivering positive impacts once the enabling environment allows the private sector to grow (see appendix figure B.9). Europe and Central Asia achieved the best development effectiveness success rate, followed by Latin America and the Caribbean and East Asia and the Pacific.[26]

Summary and Implications

The World Bank and IFC strategic approaches to the agriculture and agribusiness sector evolved over the evaluation period. During the early part of the period, the Bank's strategic focus was on the broader issues of rural development. Recent world events have helped to restore agricultural development as a strategic priority for the Bank. In 2007, for the first time, agribusiness became a corporate priority for IFC; more recently, there has been a specific focus on Sub-Saharan Africa.

The broader rural strategic focus was accompanied by reduced Bank attention to agricultural growth and productivity in the early 2000s, particularly in low-income countries, though this may be reversing now. Much Bank agriculture lending during the evaluation period—particularly in Sub-Saharan Africa—was incorporated in projects whose principal objectives were not focused on agriculture. While project outcomes of the evaluation portfolio (which includes all projects with agriculture activities) were broadly comparable to outcomes in other sectors, those for the subset of projects focused primarily on agriculture were lower. Furthermore, these agriculture-focused projects performed the worst in Sub-Saharan Africa—worse than other Sub-Saharan Africa projects—while in Europe and Central Asia and East Asia, the agriculture-focused projects performed better than other projects.

IFC's agribusiness investments and advisory services have increased significantly and performed well in recent years, except in Sub-Saharan Africa. In dollars invested, Latin America and the Caribbean has been the dominant Region, followed by Europe and Central Asia and East Asia and the Pacific. Investments remain low in Sub-Saharan Africa and in agriculture-based economies. IFC's investments generally did well over most of the evaluation period, though performance has lagged in Sub-Saharan Africa. The outcome of the advisory services projects is mixed, but it provides evidence that IFC can play a larger role in agriculture-based economies.

These results suggest that it is particularly difficult for the World Bank Group to achieve satisfactory results in agricultural projects in poor countries and that extra care will need to be taken, given the importance of boosting agricultural productivity in agriculture-based economies and the recent increases in World Bank Group engagement in the sector. One factor that seems to boost results is good analytic work and IFC advisory services prior to lending, and country programs may need to be more focused and selective than in the past to be able to fund AAA adequately and use it more efficiently given tight administrative budgets.

Chapter 3

EVALUATION HIGHLIGHTS

- The Bank Group's support for irrigation and drainage infrastructure has improved farmer access to water, but sustainability has been challenging.

- World Bank performance has been lower for extension than for research, and cost recovery has been a problem.

- The Bank's rural finance approach to credit access appears to be beneficial, but sustainability is problematic; IFC's main value added in credit has been the provision of long-term finance to its clients.

- The evidence of the impacts of land administration projects on agricultural productivity is sparse, but projects promoting access to land can increase agricultural production by bringing underutilized land under cultivation.

- The Bank Group's transport interventions have generally been successful, but results have varied by Region and have been lowest in Sub-Saharan Africa.

- In their work on the enabling environment and access to input and output markets, the Bank and IFC need to coordinate much more closely.

- All six areas covered in this chapter must function together effectively for success and growth in agriculture.

World Bank Group Activities and Results

This chapter examines the Bank Group's contribution along the crop production chain shown in figure 1.3 in six areas: irrigation and drainage; research and extension; access to credit; access to land and formalization of land rights; transport and marketing infrastructure; and policies, markets, and agribusiness.

As shown in chapter 2, three of these areas—irrigation and drainage, research and extension, and markets and agribusiness—are formally regarded as part of agricultural lending in the Bank. Roads and market infrastructure, support for land issues, and rural credit are classified separately. The critical importance of the latter three in promoting agricultural development is recognized in the recent Agriculture Action Plan (World Bank 2009e), which refers to them as "other agriculture-related investments." For IFC, these six areas are covered under five investment sectors—agribusiness, infrastructure, financial markets, manufacturing, and chemicals.

These six broad areas were selected because of their importance to sustainable improvement in agricultural productivity. Cross-country studies by the International Food Policy Research Institute (IFPRI) have found that investment in both *research and extension* and *road infrastructure* have some of the largest returns for agricultural growth and poverty reduction (Fan 2008b). *Irrigation* investments have also made significant contributions to increasing crop production (Fan and Hazell 1999; Fan, Hazell, and Thorat 1999; Fan, Zhang, and Zhang 2002), and *water management* is important for increasing food production in an environment of increasingly stressed water resources (IEG 2006e). Improving *access to credit* is critical for meeting a range of farmer and agribusiness needs and for the success of development programs (World Bank 2004a; Conning and Udry 2007). Secure *rights to land* can encourage farmers to invest in irrigation and drainage, soil conservation measures, and other natural resource management practices to improve the productivity of their land (World Bank 2003b). *Efficient markets* allow farmers and agribusinesses to capitalize on market opportunities and benefit from increased farm productivity (World Bank 2004a). Figure 3.1 shows IEG's estimate of World Bank and IFC commitments in the six areas.[1]

Irrigation and Drainage

The Bank provided $6.2 billion (34 percent of total agricultural lending) for irrigation and drainage in 173 proj- ects over the evaluation period. Forty-five percent ($2.8 billion) went to South Asia, mostly India, followed by 20 percent to East Asia, mostly China and Indonesia. Seven percent went to Sub-Saharan Africa, which has the least amount of land under irrigation. There is considerable scope for expansion of irrigation in Sub-Saharan Africa, though resource constraints (including limited IDA allocations)—in some cases low prioritization (Peacock, Ward, and Gambarelli 2007), and in other cases lack of consensus on regional water sharing arrangements, such as those over the Nile basin—have constrained investments in this sector.

The $6.2 billion the Bank has lent for irrigation and drainage over the period has addressed three interconnected issues.

The Bank's irrigation and drainage portfolio tackles three interconnected issues: improving access to water, enhancing recovery of operation and maintenance costs, and improving water-use efficiency. The majority of projects in the portfolio focus on surface irrigation, and about 20 percent (37 projects) address groundwater-related activities. Over time, the frequency of activities that support

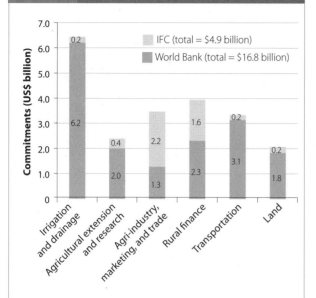

FIGURE 3.1 World Bank and IFC Contributions by Investment Area, Fiscal 1998–2008

IFC (total = $4.9 billion)
World Bank (total = $16.8 billion)

Sources: World Bank Group data and evaluation calculations.

Note: IFC figures are total net commitments to projects that address the area among other, broader objectives. World Bank commitments labeled "rural finance" and "transportation" refer to the agriculture portfolio of 633 projects that also include rural finance or transportation activities. World Bank land commitments are for stand-alone land projects.

groundwater extraction has declined, while those addressing groundwater recharge, conservation, or its more efficient use have remained unchanged.

> IFC support for irrigation and drainage was often embedded in broader packages of support.

Unlike the World Bank, IFC tended to include its support for irrigation in broader packages of support to its clients. IFC invested $241 million (4.3 percent of total commitments) and spent $2.6 million for advisory services (2.8 percent of total expenditures) for clients that have used part of these funds for new or improved irrigation systems. These clients have generally sought to address their own plantations' needs (as did a sugar producer in Peru), but in exceptional cases clients have also sought to address the needs of their outgrowers (as did an irrigation equipment and vegetable processing company in India), or both own-plantation and outgrower needs (as did a rice producer in Uganda). Latin America and the Caribbean has dominated, with 70 percent of commitments, followed by Europe and Central

Asia (12 percent). Only 2 projects out of 20 were located in agriculture-based economies (Kenya and Zambia).

Though it was not a strategic priority over most of the review period, in the past three years IFC has also focused on bringing rain-fed land into sustainable production. IFC has invested in private equity funds—that seek to introduce improved inputs and practices in rain-fed areas. The business model of one fund is to identify farm operators working under rain-fed conditions and provide them with capital to create platform companies that can be scaled up, such as in Latin America, Eastern Europe, and Africa.

About 80 percent of the Bank's irrigation projects increased farmers' access to water by meeting their targets for physical infrastructure development (figure 3.2). Sixty projects with irrigation and drainage objectives have closed and been evaluated by IEG, and 26 of these were categorized as largely irrigation projects and reported results related to irrigation outcomes.[2] Projects supported construction or rehabilitation of canals or drainage systems, provision of equipment for small–scale on-farm irrigation, construction of water cisterns, drilling of boreholes, and construction of tubewells for groundwater extraction.[3] Commonly reported outcomes included increased water availability and improved water flow in canals, timeliness and reliability of water supply, and water quality. The Azerbaijan Irrigation and Drainage Rehabilitation Project (fiscal 2000), for example, led to a more reliable and timely supply of water for irrigation and drainage activities. It also reduced waterlogging and salinity on approximately 36,500 hectares.

> Bank irrigation projects have improved farmer access to water.

Cost recovery has been challenging, however, which has made it difficult to fund operation and maintenance of the physical infrastructure and promote water saving. Fifteen of the 26 closed projects attempted to achieve some level of cost recovery through pricing and improvements in collection rates.[4] The increases in cost recovery that have been achieved have generally been insufficient to cover operation and maintenance requirements, contributing to the low sustainability performance of the subsector noted earlier.[5] Political and institutional factors typically impede cost recovery, including the difficulties associated with imposition and enforcement of pricing policies, lack of capacity or motivation of collection agencies to enforce water charges, and a vicious cycle of low operations and maintenance expenditure leading to poor performance and increasing reluctance of farmers to pay (FAO 2004; IEG 2006e; World Bank 2005d, f, 2007i). Moreover, depending on pricing and cost

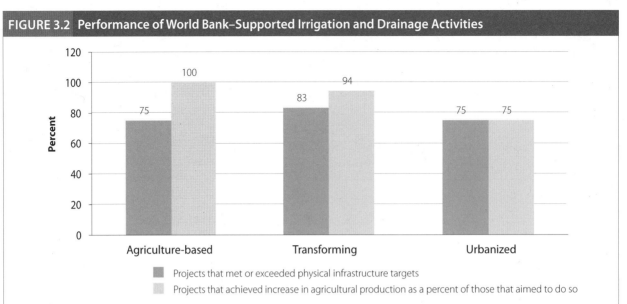

Projects that met or exceeded physical infrastructure targets

Projects that achieved increase in agricultural production as a percent of those that aimed to do so

Note: These data are based on performance of 26 closed investment projects with a focus on irrigation and drainage. There were few closed projects in agriculture-based and urbanized economies.

recovery to reduce water consumption is complicated by the inelastic nature of demand for water (IEG 2010f, World Bank 2005d).

But cost recovery has been a challenge, which has made it difficult to fund operation and maintenance of infrastructure.

Other approaches have also been promoted to help reduce water consumption, including crop diversification and the use of more efficient irrigation technologies (World Bank 2005d). While Bank-supported projects such as the Morocco Water Resources Management Project (fiscal 1998) have promoted drip irrigation and other water-saving technologies, measurement of water savings is often poor. For water-saving approaches to work, farmers must have incentives to diversify crops or invest in improved technologies, as were provided in the China Irrigated Agriculture Intensification Loan II (fiscal 1998) and the China Water Conservation Project (fiscal 2000). A lesson emerging from the first project is the importance of giving equal attention to both agricultural innovation and irrigation improvement to ensure that water-saving goals are met (see also box 3.13).

Bank projects have also provided support to reform public agencies in charge of irrigation management to make them more responsive to farmers' demands. This issue has been one of the most politically challenging to address,

particularly in South Asia and, to some extent, in Europe and Central Asia. The Pakistan National Drainage Project (fiscal 1998), for example, made some initial progress toward institutional reform, but vested interests ultimately impeded these reforms. The India country study noted that difficulties in reform are tied to the complex political economy, and a champion within government is needed. It concluded that when the political will for reform is weak, undertaking analytical work on the issue might be the appropriate strategy for the Bank, and perhaps the best and most effective contribution Bank projects can make is to provide a platform that reform-minded government officials can use to stimulate change from within.

Bank projects have promoted water users associations (WUAs) as institutional models to promote farmer participation in improving water management, maintenance of irrigation systems, and fee collection. Bank projects have focused to varying degrees on the establishment of WUAs, building the capacity of their members, putting in place an appropriate legal environment for their operation, and transferring operation and maintenance responsibility to them.

This model has had varied success. According to the recent IEG evaluation of the World Bank's water-related activities (IEG 2010f), WUAs were established as planned less than half the time, but three-quarters of those that were established were reported to be working effectively at project closure. WUAs that did not provide sufficient training for members were often ineffective, leading to uncertainty and conflicts regarding the rights and obligations of the WUAs. This usually resulted in a low level of willingness to pay for service.

Sustainability has been a concern for various reasons: weak administrative and financial capacities of WUAs, lack of basic office equipment and vehicles, and inadequate recognition that user participation changes, but does not eliminate, the role of government agencies in irrigation (IEG 2010f, 2006e). Recent Bank sector work, while noting some achievements, also acknowledges that efficiency has risen from participatory irrigation management "only marginally, and there are many schemes where O&M is beyond farmers' capacity" (World Bank 2007g). Box 3.1 highlights three lessons that could improve these results.

Bank projects have promoted water users associations in an attempt to improve water management and maintenance of irrigation systems.

Irrigation projects also report positive agricultural outcomes, particularly when supported by complementary activities. Ninety-two percent of the 26 closed Bank projects reported increases in agricultural production. Half of the projects included complementary activities, and most noted that these activities—such as credit, market access, and research and extension—are important for increasing agricultural outcomes. A recent IEG project assessment of a water project in Morocco (fiscal 1998) noted how inadequate extension advice limited the uptake of new irrigation technology. An earlier IEG study, *Water Management in Agriculture* (IEG 2006e), also noted the scope for increasing complementarity between irrigation investments and credit, extension, and marketing services. An IEG impact evaluation of an irrigation project in Peru also reported positive complementarities between modern on-farm irrigation technology and infrastructure (box 3.2), and similar findings were reported by an IEG review of impact evaluations in agriculture (IEG 2010c).

Irrigation had positive agricultural outcomes, particularly when supported by complementary activities.

There is limited evidence on the Bank's contribution to water-use efficiency. Of the 26 closed investment projects in the irrigation portfolio, about half specifically aimed to increase water-use efficiency, and 7 measured changes in water productivity or spillage and reported results at completion. However, only three of these seven reported actual reduc-

tions in water consumption. One of these, the China Water Conservation I Project (fiscal 2001), successfully piloted an evapotranspiration-based approach to water management using remote sensing technology. Some DPLs reviewed for this evaluation addressed water-use efficiency through support for related policy and legal reforms, but project completion reports did not provide information on changes in water use.

There is limited evidence on the Bank's contribution to water-use efficiency.

Water management in rain-fed agriculture has been neglected (World Bank 2006e). In part because they were largely bypassed by the Green Revolution, rain-fed areas continue to have much lower productivity than irrigated lands (figure 1.1). However, in a world of increasing water scarcity, addressing the yield challenge may require the wider use of management practices that will improve efficiency of water use, such as conservation agriculture (that also plays a wider resource-conservation role) and water harvesting techniques (FAO 2009e). The literature notes the greater marginal impact on agricultural production and poverty alleviation of an additional unit of investment in rain-fed areas compared to irrigated areas (Fan 2008b; Fan and Hazell 1999; Fan, Zhang, and Zhang 2002).

The Bank does not track projects that are promoting rain-fed agriculture separately, thus missing an opportunity to deal strategically with the subject. The activities related to better harvesting and efficient use of rainwater are scattered among irrigation and environment interventions supported by different Bank sector units whose work is often not coordinated, as will be discussed in chapter 4. A recent portfolio review of water management in agriculture carried out by the water anchor (World Bank 2010b) estimated that about 5 percent of total commitments to the sector over fiscal 1999–2008 were for agricultural water management in rain-fed agriculture. In recent years, the Bank has also supported countries with drought warning systems and weather insurance schemes to reduce the risks of farmers in rain-fed agricultural systems.

IFC investments have also contributed to improving client irrigation systems. The investments have generally achieved satisfactory DO/IO ratings, except for the projects in Sub-Saharan Africa and for the very early projects in Latin America and the Caribbean (discussed in chapter 2). An investment in a fruit producer in Guatemala shows how a typical IFC investment can help a client address constraints in their access to water, while also contributing to economic growth and employment opportunities for farmers (box 3.3).

IFC investments and advisory services have also helped improve irrigation systems.

Public-private partnerships in irrigation were the focus of two advisory service projects, neither linked to an IFC investment. The Moroccan and Indian (in Maharashtra state, the project was partly funded by the World Bank) projects both sought to advise the government on how to implement public-private partnerships focused on irrigation. The Moroccan project was successful because it mobilized private sector funds in a traditional public sector area and created employment opportunities for about 2,000 people. However, the Indian project has been delayed by political and security challenges and by objections from NGOs.

IEG carried out an impact evaluation of an irrigation project in Peru (the Irrigation Subsector Program, fiscal 1997–2004) to inform this evaluation. The project had a total commitment of $85 million in support of two on-farm components to directly benefit farmers and an off-farm component to benefit WUA members. The on-farm components provided a one-time subsidy for private farmers to acquire modern irrigation technology and financed extension officers to train farmers to use new irrigation technologies and farming practices. The off-farm component supported irrigation and drainage infrastructure and building of managerial and operational capacities in 40 WUAs. Using a mixed-methods approach, the evaluation sought to discover whether the project improved the agricultural performance of beneficiaries and their economic welfare; the multi-component design of the project improved agricultural productivity and economic well-being; and there were spillover effects of on-farm investments of benefit to households in surrounding areas that did not receive direct project support.

The impacts of the project were largely positive:

- Support for improved irrigation infrastructure and management of WUAs led to increases in demand for farm labor of 27 percent and in the wage income of farmers of 47 percent.

- The on-farm modern irrigation technology increased the proportion of agricultural output that was sold in the market (versus consumed) by 12 percent compared with the output of control farmers, increased the probability of growing permanent crops by 15 percent, and bolstered production and productivity when off-farm irrigation infrastructure was also improved.

- Extension and training were also positive. The demonstration and lessons on irrigation techniques and farming offered by the program increased productivity in treatment localities by over 20 percent. Extension increased the proportion of agricultural production sold in the market by a similar amount (12 percent) compared to farmers in control localities. In specific crop production, farmer training increased production of export crops such as rice, cotton, maize, onions, and grapes. Some of these are nontraditional crops that experienced a boom in the agricultural sales market in Peru and abroad.

- Both poor and nonpoor farmers increased their proportion of cultivated land and farming of permanent crops by approximately 14 percent relative to poor farmers in control localities.

- There were mixed results on effectiveness of multicomponent design: There were positive complementarities between on-farm, modern irrigation technology and infrastructure projects when they were implemented in the same locality. These results partially agree with the qualitative insight that modern irrigation technology, when implemented alone, was unable to achieve such positive results. However, quantitative results on impacts of on-farm extension and infrastructure rehabilitation do not seem to be complementary. The evidence shows that productivity and the total value of production were negatively affected in localities with both components.

The quantitative analysis shows that there was a spillover effect of on-farm irrigation technology on farming outcomes, particularly a shift toward export and industrial crops and increases in the proportion of the production sold in the market from the total harvest produced. There is qualitative evidence that beneficiaries were more likely to hire manual laborers to work on their plots, suggesting that some of the spillover effects were through labor and the promotion of new work opportunities in the local market.

Source: IEG 2009f.

Research and Extension

New technology was essential to the Green Revolution, and further technological advances will be needed if world food production is to substantially increase in an environment of scarce natural resources. For technology to contribute to agricultural productivity growth (for crops and livestock), it must be generated, and then reach farmers and be adopted by them. The process is not a simple one-way path—it is essential that farmers' needs and local conditions feed back from the field to the researchers. Historically, publicly supported research and extension systems have been important in agricultural technology generation and transfer, and this will continue to be true. The private sector may have sufficient incentives to invest in innovation in some product areas (generally where the benefits of innovation can be partially appropriated by the companies creating them), but not in others. For example, for self-pollinating crops, farmers can reuse seeds from year to year, which would make it difficult for private developers to enforce patents and recover their costs (Elliot and Hoffman 2010).

Technology advances will be needed to double world food production by 2050.

In areas where incentives for private sector engagement are weak, governments rely on direct funding of research and development activities to subsidize the development of technologies with large social returns (Elliot and Hoffman 2010). Public and private research are complementary; the availability of a strong public education and research system can help provide not only a pool of scientists and technicians to staff private research firms but also basic inputs for private research, such as elite breeding lines for crops that the private sector can use as parent material for developing high-yielding varieties (Pray and others 1991; Pray, Fuglie, and Johnson 2007).

World Bank agricultural research interventions have focused mainly on helping increase in-country capacity, whether through building government institutions (for example, the Senegal Agricultural Services and Producer Organizations Project, fiscal 1999); providing training for researchers and funding for postgraduate education programs for young scientists; rehabilitating laboratories, offices, and other facilities; or supporting partnerships with research institutions, universities, and farmers' organizations in institutional models such as the Competitive Grant Scheme (CGS).[6]

The Bank's research interventions have focused mainly on helping build in-country capacity.

The Bank has also supported global and regional research through its financing for the CGIAR, which began in 1971 and has helped produce a range of yield-enhancing and yield-stabilizing technologies. The institutions in CGIAR not only conduct research on crop breeding

---

BOX 3.3 IFC DEVELOPMENT OF A NEW PLANTATION AND IRRIGATION SYSTEM BY A FRUIT PRODUCER

A fruit producer invited IFC participation in a $20 million investment to develop 1,412 hectares of banana plantation, including an irrigation system for two leased farms on the southern coast of Guatemala. IFC supported the client with a $7 million loan disbursed in 2000. The development was completed in 2002, and the loan was fully repaid in April 2007.

The development required an irrigation system to ensure the operation of the plantation during the dry season. The client built a system that draws water from adjacent rivers and eight on-site boreholes. A sprinkler irrigation system was also installed at both farms to improve irrigation efficiency.

The investment produced impacts at the client, economy, and common people's levels. At the client level, the development provided a hedge against natural disasters through spatial diversification from the Pacific coast. At the economy level, the investment brought previously poorly managed land into production, increasing both yields and quality. At the people's level, the farm sites were leased from nonresident owners, and the employees of the former lessees were reemployed by the client.

Source: Portfolio review.

and genetic improvement, disease control, natural resource management, and policy research, but also help build capacity in the agricultural research systems of developing countries. The Bank has provided $50 million per year to help fund the core activities of CGIAR during the evaluation period. CGIAR studies show that the level of adoption of modern varieties has been high in Latin America and Asia but has lagged in Sub-Saharan Africa (Evenson 2003; Evenson and Gollin 2003; Renkow and Byerlee forthcoming). Weak in-country capacity, as will be discussed in chapter 4, has contributed to lagging performance in Africa.

The Bank has put more resources into extension and advisory services than into research.

More World Bank resources have gone to extension and advisory services than to agricultural research. Of the approximately $2 billion in World Bank support for research and extension and advisory services (about 11 percent of agricultural lending) provided through 160 projects over the evaluation period, about 40 percent ($72 million a year) was for research and about 60 percent ($109 million a year) was for extension and advisory services.[7] In this subsector, 32 percent of the interventions were in Sub-Saharan Africa and 30 percent in South Asia, followed by 14 percent in Latin America and the Caribbean, 13 percent in East Asia and the Pacific, 8 percent in Europe and Central Asia, and 3 percent in the Middle East and North Africa.

During the evaluation period the Bank moved away from supporting the publicly funded agricultural extension training and visit system, and toward demand-driven approaches to extension. The nature of these approaches is still evolving. Training and visit was largely abandoned in Bank-supported operations by 2000. Subsequently, the Bank placed more emphasis on strengthening the ability of farmers and their organizations to demand better research, extension, and advisory services and to hold providers accountable. At the same time, new strategies aimed to involve the private and the nonprofit sectors in service provision. Moreover, the Bank identified new strategies to foster linkages between agricultural research, extension, and education (box 3.4), which often involved efforts to decentralize government functions in general.

The newer demand-driven extension approaches have a wider scope than the technology transfer role of the training and visit system. Farmers are advised or educated through various extension methods on specific practices or technologies to solve an identified problem or produc-

tion constraint.[8] One approach, the farmer field school, championed by the FAO, largely constitutes an adult learning process. Various limitations to this approach have been identified, including elite capture, shown by a recent study in Indonesia, and high cost, causing sustainability problems in the post-project era (Anderson 2007; Feder, Murgai, and Quizon 2003). Other approaches supported by the Bank and their evolution over time are discussed in box 3.4.

Newer demand-driven approaches to extension have wider scope than the training and visit system.

The ratings of World Bank activities supporting agricultural research were on a par with the broader agricultural portfolio, but those of extension activities were lower, with wide variation among Regions. Of the 160 research and extension and advisory service projects in the portfolio, 48 were closed and had been evaluated by IEG. It was possible to rate the performance of research activities in 30 of them and extension activities in 39. Seventy-three percent of the research and 67 percent of the extension activities were rated satisfactory on achievement of outcomes, compared with 77 percent for all agriculture projects.

Achievement of outcomes for activities supporting research was similar to that in the rest of the agriculture portfolio, but extension activities performed below average.

Agriculture-based economies performed significantly worse than the urbanized ones on extension, and significantly worse than the transforming economies on research (figures 3.3 and 3.4). Nearly 100 percent of the extension activities and about 83 percent of the research activities in Europe and Central Asia were rated satisfactory—the best performance among the Regions. About 40 percent of the research and 45 percent of extension activities in Sub-Saharan Africa were unsatisfactory.[9] Among the reasons for unsatisfactory performance were overly ambitious design with limited capacity to implement and lack of availability of complementary inputs such as seeds and fertilizers.

Several improved management practices and institutional models could be attributed to Bank interventions, though there is limited evidence that Bank-supported projects have resulted in adoption of improved technologies. The country studies found that adoption of management practices and institutional models, such as CGSs, often occurred because of their use and promotion through Bank-financed projects.

BOX 3.4 ENGAGING PRODUCERS IN THE AGRICULTURAL KNOWLEDGE SYSTEM

Agricultural Knowledge and Information Systems (AKIS)

In 2000 the Bank and FAO articulated an approach to agricultural services in which the farmer was seen as a responsible entrepreneur, managing complex agricultural and off-farm activities to maximize well-being within many constraints. To achieve this goal, the farmer interacts with input suppliers, extension agents, traders, NGOs, community members, and others to acquire information and knowledge for his or her farming operation. The underlying realization is that improving rural productivity, social equity, and competitiveness requires effective and efficient agricultural knowledge and information systems.

The AKIS concept focuses mainly on linking farmers with public and private institutions in extension, research, and education. Examples of Bank projects that have supported this approach include Uganda's National Agricultural Advisory Services Project (fiscal 2002), designed to complement the earlier Bank-supported Agricultural Research and Training Projects (fiscal 1992, 1999) that helped to restore functionality in both the National Agricultural Research Organization and the Makerere University faculties engaged in human capital enhancement for the Ugandan AKIS, and the Romania Agricultural Knowledge and Information Systems Project (fiscal 2005).

Evaluations of the National Agricultural Advisory Services Project show that the administrative arrangements introduced over the years have led to capture of project resources by relatively well-off farmers (Feder and others 2010). More recent changes introduced by the government under its Prosperity for All program are reported to have aggravated the tendency for capture, because this program component focuses not on groups but on individual, selected model farmers, who receive substantial amounts of subsidies. The committee to select the model farmers explicitly includes a representative of the ruling party (Birner and Resnick forthcoming).

Agricultural Innovation Systems (AIS)

The AKIS concept is evolving toward the more comprehensive AIS idea, which integrates farmers (often in producer organizations), researchers, extension workers, various private sector actors (including traders, input dealers, and supermarket procurement officers), and civil society organizations active in rural areas to harness knowledge and information from various sources for better farming, processing, and marketing to improve livelihoods and agribusiness development. Examples of projects using this approach include the Peru Agricultural Research and Extension Project (fiscal 2005) and the India National Agricultural Innovation Project (fiscal 2005), although it is too early to draw on evaluative experience with most such projects. But the evidence concerning the extension model being pursued in conjunction with the project in India and its predecessor is positive. The Agricultural Technology Management Agency (ATMA) model (Singh, Swanson, and Singh 2006) of participatory decentralized extension was implemented originally as a pilot program in the earlier World Bank–supported National Agricultural Technology Project in India. It has since been expanded to a national program of the Indian government. The program operates at a district level (there are some 600 districts in the 28 states of India). Each district has a semiautonomous agency (referred to as ATMA) that deals with extension matters. The agency can receive both public and private funds, as well as charge fees to clients. Each ATMA is directed and overseen by a governing board that includes representatives of all farmer classes in the district, as well as other stakeholders (private sector, rural banks, NGOs, and official agencies dealing with agricultural development).

Sources: FAO and World Bank 2000; Feder and Savastano 2006; Friis-Hansen, Aben, and Kidoid 2004; Parkinson 2008; Singh, Swanson, and Singh 2006; Swanson 2008; Tripp, Wijeratne, and Piyadasa 2005; van den Berg and Jiggins 2007.

There is limited information reported in Bank documents to link technology adoption levels and Bank interventions. A review of all 48 project completion reports for research and extension projects found that only 23 percent discussed adoption of technologies, and only 15 percent reported some level of adoption, partly a reflection of inadequate monitoring and evaluation (M&E). Twenty-one percent of the research and extension projects also provided support for agricultural inputs such as seeds and fertilizers. However, even for these activities, information on adoption rates is scant.

> There is little evidence that Bank projects have resulted in the adoption of improved technologies.

The extent of reporting on increases in agricultural productivity is even more limited. A recent IEG assessment of CGS projects in four countries (Brazil, Colombia, Nicaragua, and Peru) found that, with the exception of Peru, there is no evidence to show whether the various small subprojects led to

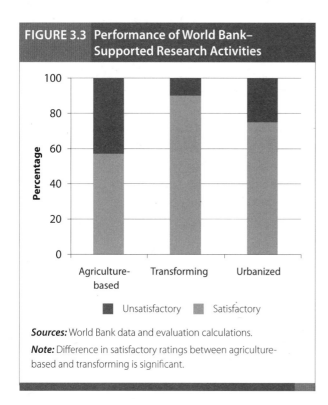

FIGURE 3.3 Performance of World Bank–
Supported Research Activities

Sources: World Bank data and evaluation calculations.

Note: Difference in satisfactory ratings between agriculture-based and transforming is significant.

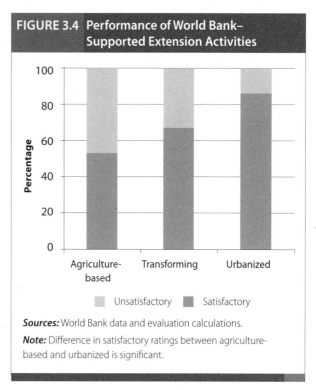

FIGURE 3.4 Performance of World Bank–
Supported Extension Activities

Sources: World Bank data and evaluation calculations.

Note: Difference in satisfactory ratings between agriculture-based and urbanized is significant.

successful new technologies and, if they did, whether these were taken up by farmers. In these projects there is also limited information on the share of CGS-funded subprojects that led to improved technologies at the research level, not to mention the farm level (IEG 2009i).

World Bank interventions have had limited success in ensuring adequate support for research and extension activities after the Bank project closes. This is particularly evident in Sub-Saharan Africa, where the sustainability of 57 percent of projects is at risk because of the limited availability of government funding after project completion, an issue discussed in chapter 4. An IEG assessment of the Tanzania Agricultural Research Project II (fiscal 1998) stated that "the evidence suggests that, yet again, research activities build up and develop linkages with clients during the peak funding period of a project only to sink back down to a power-conserving, almost hibernation mode once the project closes" (IEG 2007i). Inadequate budgetary commitments also created problems in retaining trained personnel and scientific skills supported by Bank projects. In the Chad Agricultural Services and Producer Organization Project (fiscal 2004), for example, the tight funding situation led to the loss of many experienced project staff.

> Interventions have had limited success in ensuring adequate support for research and extension activities after Bank project closure.

Cost recovery for extension services was promoted in about a quarter of the projects, but with limited success. The demand-driven extension approaches in Africa, as tried in projects such as the Uganda National Agricultural Advisory Services Project (fiscal 2001), have faced sustainability challenges because poor farmers have had limited capacity to pay. Most (80 percent) of the costs of these activities are being supported through donor programs (Feder and others 2010; Swanson and Rajalahti 2010). In the Kyrgyz Agricultural Support Services Project (fiscal 1998), which laid the foundation for a pay-for-services extension model, there is a concern that government intervention in commodity markets may risk lowering the returns to farmers and decrease their ability to pay for agricultural services. An IEG assessment of the Armenia Agricultural Reform Support Project (IEG 2009a) also highlighted the significant risks to sustainability of advisory services created by, among other reasons, the reluctance of the rural clientele to pay for them. The assessment notes that this has prompted the government to consider whether to adjust the self-financing ratios mandated for the agricultural support centers and whether extension services should be offered free of charge and funded from the budget. Swanson and Rajalahti (2010) concluded that public funding of extension services will be needed to deal with the difficulty of cost recovery from poor farmers and smallholders who "are generally unwilling and unable to pay for advisory services that deal with public knowledge and information."

Research results from CGIAR institutions need to be mainstreamed consistently in country-level Bank projects. A previous IEG study noted the weak link between CGIAR centers and national programs (IEG 2004b), and a review of project documents carried out for this evaluation found that the weakness has persisted. A study commissioned by the CGIAR Secretariat (Anderson 2008) also found that research results are not always recognized or mainstreamed as they should be in World Bank operations, despite their considerable potential for increasing agricultural productivity and improving food security in vulnerable countries, especially in Sub-Saharan Africa. Recent technology projects appear to emphasize strengthening this link, as in the Bangladesh National Agricultural Technology Project (fiscal 2008). Strengthening the synergies will require concerted efforts by both the World Bank and the CGIAR system, as is being attempted in the three contemporary, multidonor, Bank-coordinated regional agricultural research projects in Sub-Saharan Africa.

IFC's support for agricultural research has been limited.

In contrast with the Bank, IFC's support for agricultural research has been limited. IFC's role was catalytic in the one private equity fund in which it invested in this area. That fund, in turn, invested in agribusiness technology companies in Brazil and Argentina. The fund's investee companies are seed producers and manufacturers of advanced agricultural equipment and export-oriented hog processors. This is a promising line of engagement for IFC, as small and medium agribusiness technology companies are in need of the type of financing and convening power that IFC can provide at early stages of their lives.

IFC supports extension indirectly by investing in agribusiness trader-processors who in turn assist farmers, as well as in private equity funds that finance agribusiness-technology companies. In the trader-processor model, the cost of the extension service is generally embedded in the price paid to farmers for their product. IFC committed $396 million in F&A (or 7 percent of total commitments) and spent an additional $7.8 million in advisory services (or 8.6 percent of total expenditures) in clients that used part of these funds to provide extension services to farmers. Clients have sought to address their own needs (as did a shrimp farmer in Venezuela, or an egg producer in China), and sometimes both their own and their outgrowers' technical needs (as did a wine producer in China). The Latin America and the Caribbean Region has dominated this activity, with 54 percent of commitments, followed by Europe and Central Asia (21 per-

cent). Only 2 projects out of 20 were located in agriculture-based economies (Côte d'Ivoire and Zambia).

IFC supports extension indirectly by investing in agribusiness trader-processors.

IFC has made greater use of advisory services in extension than in the other five areas (credit, irrigation, transport, land, and marketing). The portfolio review found that 49 percent of investment commitments were linked to advisory projects, and that 27.5 percent of advisory expenditures were linked to investment projects. This is higher than the average for IFC (see chapter 4). Only three advisory service projects focused on agriculture-based economies. The one located in Sub-Saharan Africa was an exceptional success. It was designed to facilitate the development of a chain of small, third-party wholesaling units by a bottling company affiliated with a multi-national beverage company, and to provide them with access to finance through a working capital facility of a commercial bank.

When IFC has combined an agribusiness investment and an extension advisory service project, the intervention has achieved superior outcomes. This has happened when IFC has facilitated the building of partnerships between technical partners, client companies, and off-takers, and supported them with investment and advisory service projects. For example, IFC investment and advisory service projects that focused on a coffee-trader's operations in Central America have provided farmers with the opportunity to improve output quality, productivity, reliability, and ultimately income (see appendix box C.1).

When IFC has combined an agribusiness investment and an extension advisory service project, the intervention has achieved superior outcomes.

Conversely, where IFC has not followed up advisory service support with investments, results have been inferior because of the lack of an anchor investment client who can financially and technically support the advisory service and make the advisory service sustainable by providing market access to the farmers. For example, IFC delivered the Seaweed Farming Advisory Project in Indonesia, in an area where seaweed is a major source of income for tens of thousands of small-scale farmers. The program provided a spectrum of services, including training in planting, harvesting, and post-harvest handling. Two separate evaluations were conducted, in 2005 and 2006. Both evaluations found little evidence of success with respect to the project's objectives of improving farmers' knowledge, practices, and income.

Access to Credit

Access to credit, whether for short-term working capital or productive capital investments, plays an important role in facilitating and promoting agricultural production. Rural credit is complicated by the seasonal nature of much agricultural production, weather- and price-related risks, and the dispersed nature of farming (World Bank 2004a, 2005f). Access to credit was found to be a constraint to farming in every country study conducted for this evaluation.

Previous IEG evaluations found that World Bank support to rural credit has been weak, in part because of the weak performance of line-of-credit operations (IEG 1996, 2006b). In the mid-1990s, the World Bank shifted from directed agricultural credit to a broader rural finance approach,[10] prompted by a wider focus on rural poverty (see box 2.1) and evidence that well-managed financial intermediaries could reach rural areas and remain sustainable.[11] The approach since that shift has emphasized reforms to better enable financial institutions to operate in rural areas by strengthening their capacity and helping them to develop appropriate lending instruments and risk-management mechanisms.

The broader rural finance approach taken by the Bank makes it difficult to ascertain how much support has been provided specifically for agricultural credit. Thirteen percent of the 633 projects in the evaluation portfolio—81 projects with a total commitment of $2.32 billion, or an average of $211 million each year—included some aspect of agricultural credit and financial services. Forty-two percent of this commitment went to East Asia and the Pacific, 19 percent to Latin America and the Caribbean and to Sub-Saharan Africa, 12 percent to South Asia, 6 percent to Europe and Central Asia, and 2 percent to the Middle East and North Africa. Forty of the projects have closed and been evaluated by IEG, of which 78 percent were rated moderately satisfactory or better on outcome. The Europe and Central Asia Region has the best outcome performance (nearly 100 percent satisfactory), and Sub-Saharan Africa the worst (about 60 percent satisfactory). Given the administrative tracking arrangements in place in the Bank, it is difficult to tell precisely how much support has been provided for agricultural credit, and it is thus rarely possible to isolate the performance of the Bank in that area.

> It is difficult to ascertain how much support the Bank has provided to agricultural credit.

The findings from IEG project assessments and a desk review of 25 Bank-supported projects with relatively

Photo courtesy of Flore de Préneuf/World Bank.

large rural finance components show lagged application of the broader rural finance strategy and weak linkage with agriculture. The desk review found projects with features of both a line-of-credit and a rural finance approach—among them the Philippines Third Rural Finance (fiscal 1999) and First Moldova First Rural Investment and Services (RISP I, fiscal 2002) Projects—and others focused on the rural finance approach—the second Moldova RISP (fiscal 2006) and Mexico Savings and Rural Finance Project (2002). In the 25 projects reviewed, the needs of the agricultural sector were generally taken into account indirectly, and often unintentionally.

> The Bank's rural finance approach appears to be benefiting the agriculture sector.

That said, the Bank's approach to rural finance appears to be benefiting the agriculture sector. Although data are limited, it is likely that these projects benefited agriculture because it is the main rural activity in most developing countries.

Four recent IEG project assessments support this conclusion. The Romania Rural Finance Project (fiscal 2001) assessment found that although agricultural productivity and growth were not specified as development objectives, lending to agriculture increased almost threefold during the project period. The Moldova RISP I assessment found that the agriculture sector absorbed most of the lending and advisory assistance offered. The assessment of the Philippines Third Rural Finance Project found that even though an increase in agricultural productivity was not a stated objective, fisheries, aquaculture, grain milling, and poultry benefited substantially. An assessment of the Rural Finance Project in Vietnam had similar findings.

However, sustainability remains a challenge. In the Moldova case, for example, NGOs worked well as loan originators and delivered properly documented loan applications to banks and the Rural Finance Corporation. But without project financing, the NGOs needed to charge for their services, and up to the time of the assessment, intermediaries had refused to pay. To survive, NGOs may have to limit services to larger, established clients, which will make it difficult for poorer farmers to access their services. In the Philippines case, the sustainability of the Peoples Credit and Finance Corporation, the project's conduit for on-lending to participating microfinance institutions, remains in question in the absence of privatization. In Vietnam, the persistence of intermittent interest rate ceilings and subsidized lending jeopardizes sustainability. Finally, in Romania, the project's institution-building achievements have been put at risk by the global economic crisis.

Sustainability remains a challenge.

Microfinance lending appears to have benefited the agriculture sector. Of the 40 closed Bank projects, 10 had identifiable microcredit activities, and 90 percent of them were rated moderately satisfactory or higher. These operations, generally grounded in a CDD approach, have a wide range of objectives—reducing vulnerability and securing sustainable livelihoods for targeted populations (such as Afghanistan Emergency National Solidarity, fiscal 2004), enhancing social and economic empowerment of the rural poor (such as Bihar Rural Livelihood Projects, fiscal 2007), or simply increasing access to income-generation projects or infrastructure for certain groups (such as the Nepal Poverty Alleviation Fund, fiscal 2004). In these interventions, microcredit activities are not agriculture-focused but have a broader rural dimension. The agriculture sector has benefited when beneficiaries have used resources for rehabilitation of rural roads, irrigation channels, purchase of livestock, and similar activities.

It is difficult, however, to predict the extent to which demand-driven rural CDD projects with microcredit components can address agriculture sector credit constraints. IEG assessments of closed projects have found that broader poverty alleviation goals in microfinance interventions have sometimes caused project designers to neglect longer-term financial services needs. For example, IEG's assessment of the Indonesia Kecamantan Development Project (KDP, fiscal 1998) rated the outcome of the project's microcredit component unsatisfactory. The assessment noted that the joint group liability for repayment often did not work because there was no expectation of continuity, groups were hastily formed, and there were no institutional links to sustain the mechanism. The Implementation Completion Report (ICR) review of the follow-on KDP II (fiscal 2001) noted that the low repayment rates for microcredit suggest that the sustainability of the project's microcredit approach is unlikely. The completion report of the Colombia Productive Partnership Support Project (fiscal 2002) similarly found that it was not always possible to get producers' organizations to reimburse grants into the revolving fund. A recent Agriculture and Rural Development Department (ARD) discussion paper (World Bank 2007d) raises similar concerns and suggests that savings-led community organizations may have better prospects.

It will be important to increase the synergy and coordination between financial sector interventions and the Bank's agriculture lending. The country studies and ARD Rural Finance Reviews demonstrated that financial sector interventions may affect the availability of agricultural credit, and agricultural and community support interventions may affect the quality of the participating financial institution's loan portfolio. However, the weak coordination between sector units, discussed further in chapter 4, has been an issue. Some projects give a great deal of attention to coordination, others none at all. For example, the Moldova Rural Investment and Services Project put significant emphasis on business and agricultural support services. However, in the India Strengthening Rural Cooperative Project (fiscal 2007), which aimed to reform and revitalize the country's rural credit cooperative banks, the agriculture focus was largely limited to agricultural insurance systems. In the Vietnam Rural Finance Project there was no significant attention to the capacity of agricultural support services or analysis in the project documents of the extent to which they may constrain the quality of portfolio or project outcomes. At the strategic level, the Bank's Vietnam agricultural strategy document paid little attention to the role of rural finance, notwithstanding a significant ongoing rural finance lending program.

It will be important to increase the synergy and coordination between financial sector interventions and the Bank's agriculture lending.

Addressing weather and price risks that contribute to credit constraints in the agriculture sector also requires synergies between agriculture, the financial sector, and disaster- and risk-management lending. These risks are unpredictable and difficult to manage. In recent years the World Bank has supported countries with drought warning systems and weather insurance schemes to reduce farmers' risks in rain-fed areas. For example, in Malawi the Bank is supporting a government pilot of an index-based drought-risk-management mechanism to manage weather-related risks associated with maize production.[12] The Bank has also supported initiatives for cotton farmers in Mexico to hedge their price risks, and coffee producers in Tanzania to reduce their price risks, by using international derivative markets (World Bank 2005i). More recently, Bank Group projects in Kazakhstan and Mongolia have supported crop and livestock insurance. The World Bank Group is also helping countries access financial markets to cope with disasters. Effective coordination across different parts of the World Bank Group is critical in addressing agricultural risks and financing needs.

As with extension, IFC has traditionally supported farmers' access to credit through investments in trader-processors, which have generally achieved satisfactory DO/IO ratings. It has committed $360 million in F&A investments (representing 6.4 percent of total commitments) and spent an additional $7.2 million in advisory services (7.9 percent of total expenditures) in client countries that have used part of these funds to address farmers' financing needs. Latin America and the Caribbean has dominated this activity with 60 percent of overall commitments in F&A, followed by East Asia and the Pacific (16 percent) and Europe and Central Asia (11 percent). Three of 17 projects were located in Sub-Saharan Africa. As one example of success, the investment helped a trader-processor provide its outgrowers in Sub-Saharan Africa and Asia with working capital through a warehouse receipt program. However, an investment in India was rated unsatisfactory because the business model failed when the commercial banks withdrew credit support to farmers, and the farmers were provided no buy-back assurance.

IFC has traditionally supported farmers' access to credit through investments in trader-processors.

The advisory projects were generally stand-alone projects designed to develop capacity in small-scale financial institutions and entrepreneurs linked to agriculture and agribusiness activities. However, the South Tajikistan Cotton Lending Program is an example of an integrated (advisory plus investment) pilot initiative in support of a farmer-owned company that provides financing, inputs, and marketing services to cotton farmers in the Sugd region. The investment in a soy-producing and farming project in the Amazon, though affected by serious concerns about its environmental impact, also showed how an IFC trader-processor client can address farmers' access to credit issues (box 4.2).

IFC has recently diversified its agribusiness operations into guarantees, private equity, wholesaling, and risk management.

More recently, IFC has diversified its agribusiness operations from financing the trader-processor model to financing banks and funds (that is, guarantees, private equity, wholesaling, and risk management). IFC has provided trade finance guarantees for $1.15 billion and committed $117 million in private equity funds (representing, in the aggregate, 22.6 percent of total commitments). Through the Global Trade Finance Program, IFC has guaranteed financial institutions in developing countries that support agribusiness trade operations[13] (for south-south and south-north trade). These guarantees have covered mainly issuing banks in Latin America and the Caribbean (52 percent), the Middle East and North Africa (19 percent), and Sub-Saharan Africa (12 percent). IFC private equity fund commitments have either encouraged the diversification of existing funds into agriculture and agribusiness or facilitated the implementation of new agribusiness funds through financial support and convening power.

IFC had put the plan to boost agribusiness financing through wholesaling facilities on hold because of the recent financial crisis, but it has recently made a couple of investments. The wholesaling business model seeks to support financial intermediaries with investments (loans, risk-sharing mechanisms) and advisory services (underwriting capacity, product development skills, crop insurance technology) to reach farmers and agribusiness SMEs.[14] IFC is also using advisory funding to explore instruments for more efficient intermediation of financing and risk management. These efforts include financial products, such as warehouse receipts, weather index insurance, and the Global Index Insurance Facility.

In terms of access to credit, the main value added (additionality) of IFC's support to agribusiness clients has been the provision of long-term financing. The portfolio review and country-level reviews also revealed that IFC's presence has provided a kind of guarantee and created market comfort when support has been for new clients. For example, IFC supported the a food retailer in Peru when it decided to diversify from food retailing into sugar production and distribution, creating a new company.

The main form of IFC additionality in access to credit has been the provision of long-term financing.

IFC's ability to provide countercyclical finance to its agribusiness clients has been another reason clients chose to stay with IFC. IFC has been an important countercyclical financier in countries such as Argentina, where clients have reported that IFC has provided financing when it was not available to local commodities firms (for example, a soybean trader and food processor. However, during the recent financial crisis, IFC has been shifting its focus from innovative efforts to repeat business with existing clients.

IFC's financial support has focused on large local and regional trader-processors, and through them to their outgrowers, but the medium-size local agribusiness enterprises have been missed. IFC financing has been useful in addressing the clients' capital expenditures and working capital gaps, including the financing gaps of their outgrowers. The financial contribution has been complemented by advice from IFC industry specialists when the project fell within their area of expertise. However, medium-size local agribusiness enterprises have been too small for IFC direct financing, and too large for indirect financing through trader-processors.

Trade finance and private equity operations could partially bridge the financing gap for the missed medium-size local agribusiness enterprises.

IFC trade finance and private equity operations could help partially bridge the financing gap for the missed medium-size local agribusiness enterprises. Both kinds of operations target small and medium-size agribusiness enterprises, though the Global Trade Finance Program is focused narrowly on niche trade operations and does not meet the working capital needs of medium-size enterprises. The agribusiness private equity operations narrowly address the equity needs of agribusiness companies, and it is a very small and recent area of engagement for IFC. IFC's investment in a Latin American corporation is an example.[15] The wholesaling operations of the company could potentially play an important role, but it is still too early to assess their outcomes.

The only significant IFC intervention in risk management is an investment in a soybean trader-processor ($100 million) in Argentina. Through a reciprocal guarantee corporation and structured financial products, it facilitates credit access for its network of 6,000 farmers. The guarantees have allowed the outgrowers to obtain financing from local commercial banks for up to two years at competitive interest rates. The advisory-supported efforts to develop risk management mechanisms have so far not produced significant outcomes.

IFC has not focused its microfinance operations in agriculture and agribusiness. An IEG evaluation found only one example: IFC has successfully provided a microfinance intermediary with additional equity injections and a long-term loan to expand into small agribusiness lending with term loans (IEG-IFC 2007).

Access to Land and Formalization of Land Rights

Access to land and formalization of rights to that land enable crop cultivation. The scope of this limited[16] review is confined to rural land issues, although rural and urban land issues cannot be completely separated. Not only are rural and urban land often covered by the same legal rules, but there are economic and social links as well, because population growth and urbanization have contributed to declining availability of agricultural lands in many countries.

A critical issue, with both efficiency and equity implications, is the distribution of land rights. Farmers' access to land is determined primarily by land distribution and tenure patterns, which vary across countries and regions depending on the historical, social, and political context; level of economic development; and rate of population growth.[17] In some countries where inequality in land distribution has been high, governments have supported land reforms to reduce this inequality and to include the poor in the growth process. State-led land redistribution policies were high on the political agenda of some governments in Asia and Latin America following World War II. Land reforms became less popular in the 1970s, though sporadic reform efforts continued—for example, in Ethiopia (in 1975), Zimbabwe (1980), and the Philippines (1988), a result of shifts in the domestic balance of power between landowners and landless workers and peasants (ODI 1995). More recently, the Bank has supported market-led approaches that seek to match willing buyers and sellers.

A second critical issue is the formalization of land rights. Formalizing rights to land may enhance security, which can encourage farmers to invest in improved production technologies, while giving them the option of using land for

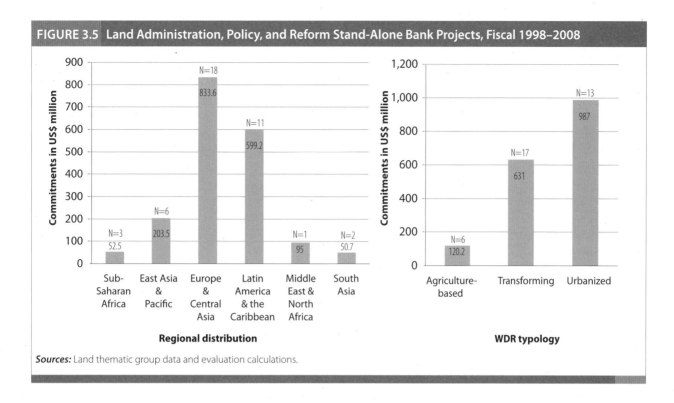

FIGURE 3.5 Land Administration, Policy, and Reform Stand-Alone Bank Projects, Fiscal 1998–2008

Regional distribution

WDR typology

Sources: Land thematic group data and evaluation calculations.

commercial transactions (including as collateral).Individual titling is a recognized way to formalize rights, particularly in the developed world. In many societies in Africa and elsewhere, access to land is governed by customary law and practices, and security of tenure may not require complete ownership as under individual titling (Wily 2006). In these scenarios, formalization of land rights is complex and can contribute to land grabs by the elite. In some other countries, such as Ethiopia and Vietnam, land ownership is vested in the state and farmers are granted use rights (World Bank 2008f, g).

During the evaluation period, the World Bank provided support both for increasing land access for the poor and for formalization of land-use rights. Between fiscal 1998 and 2008, the World Bank approved 168 land projects, with IBRD/IDA commitments totaling $13.05 billion. Forty-one of these were stand-alone land projects with total commitments of $1.84 billion (figure 3.5).[18] Twelve of those projects have closed and were rated. Overall, they performed as well as projects in the evaluation portfolio.

During the evaluated period, the Bank provided support for increasing land access for the poor and for formalization of land rights.

The World Bank Group has supported three kinds of land reform interventions to address issues of land access. One supports the acquisition of land through land funds in

a willing seller–willing buyer model, as demonstrated in the Malawi Community-Based Land Development Project (fiscal 2004), the Brazil Land-Based Poverty Alleviation Project (fiscal 2001), and the Honduras Access to Land Pilot (fiscal 2001)—the last leveraging private sector financing for land acquisition (box 3.5). Another kind supports implementation of farm restructuring programs in the transition economies of Europe and Central Asia, as in the Azerbaijan Farm Privatization (fiscal 1997) and Tajikistan Farm Privatization (fiscal 1999) Projects. A third type, while it does not directly provide access to land, supports agriculture and related support services to beneficiaries of state-supported land distribution programs, such as in the Philippines First and Second Agrarian Reform Communities Projects (fiscal 1997 and 2003).

Projects promoting access to land can increase agricultural production by bringing underutilized land under cultivation.

Projects promoting access to land can increase agricultural production by bringing underutilized land under cultivation. One reason many of these projects have achieved positive agricultural outcomes is that they have also supported on-farm investments. However, IEG project assessments, country studies, and a recent impact evaluation in Malawi found that productivity effects have

BOX 3.5   HONDURAS' ACCESS TO LAND PILOT: AN INNOVATIVE BUSINESS MODEL

In the Honduras Access to Land Pilot Project (PACTA), private sector lending institutions provided funds to landless or land-poor farmers to purchase land, and the project provided public financing for complementary investments and technical assistance to improve the productivity of the newly acquired properties. One of the main successes of PACTA is the good quality of the loan portfolio for land purchase, which has an average default rate of less than 5 percent. Many households paid off their debts ahead of schedule. Beneficiary incomes are reported to have increased through improved land productivity and output in project sites.

PACTA's approach is unique: other land fund programs have worked through public development banks rather than the private sector. Historically, commercial banks have not been interested in financing land purchases, even when the market value of the land used as collateral has been up to twice as high as the value of the requested loan. Studies have shown that banks are primarily concerned with beneficiaries' capacity to repay loans. An important feature of the PACTA model was the establishment of a loan guarantee fund, which helped encourage private sector participation. Beneficiaries were provided with a grant subsidy to fund technical assistance and productive investments, but rather than providing the full subsidy in the first year, a portion of the grant money was held in reserve until a number of loan payments had been made. Over time, participating lenders gained more confidence in the program and gradually improved their credit terms. They also increased their commitment to the program. By project close, only about 55 percent of the total loan portfolio was backed by the loan guarantee fund, and a payout was made only once during the lifetime of the project.

Another distinguishing feature was PACTA's emphasis on the whole productive enterprise rather than just on land acquisition. No transactions in land occurred without a realistic, detailed plan for how to develop the land. A lesson learned from this experience is that focusing exclusively on a single asset, such as land (or training, technology, credit, or technical assistance), does not by itself establish the conditions needed to create a sustainable family-based or cooperative enterprise. The success experienced by the vast majority of PACTA enterprises centered on an integrated business model that includes: enterprise development services, private financing for land, investment capital, market access, and a systematic learning process based on participatory M&E.

At the close of the pilot phase, the government indicated its intention to expand operations on a national level through a subsequent phase of the program. The government committed $865,000 annually for three years to continue PACTA-related activities beyond the closing date of the pilot project. According to the project's completion report, the government's allocation was insufficient to scale up, but it would enable the program to maintain operations while the new IDA-financed Rural Competitiveness Project was being prepared. That project became effective on May 27, 2010.

Sources: World Bank 2008i, 2005g; PACTA ICR; project files; Honduras country study.

---

varied. In the Malawi project, for example, increased access to land improved agricultural production but not productivity (box 3.6). An IEG assessment of the Guatemala Land Fund Project found that the technical assistance and subproject financing provided resulted in modest increases in agricultural productivity, though weak M&E made it difficult to say by how much. In contrast, increases in land productivity and outputs brought about by the Honduras Access to Land Pilot Project led to a doubling of farmer income. It is an example of an innovative approach that not only addresses access to land but also provides rural credit and technical support services.

The major emphasis (85 percent of stand-alone projects) of the Bank's lending support has been for land administration. This has involved support for clarification of rights, including mapping, legal regulatory reform, formalizing rights to land through titling, and development of institu- tional capacity to deliver land administration services for titling and recording transactions. Thailand was one of the first countries to receive World Bank support for land titling, through three projects over an 18-year period (1984–2002). Since then, there have been a number of similar projects—the Lao People's Democratic Republic First and Second Land Titling Projects (fiscal 1996 and 2003) in East Asia and the Pacific, El Salvador Land Administration (fiscal 1996) and Guatemala Land Administration (fiscal 1999) in Latin America and the Caribbean, Ghana Land Administration (fiscal 2004) in Sub-Saharan Africa, Ukraine Rural Land Titling (fiscal 2003) in Europe and Central Asia, and the Sri Lanka Land Titling and Related Services Project (fiscal 2001) in South Asia. Some Bank projects, such as the Ghana Land Administration Project (fiscal 2004), are also attempting to deal with formalization of rights under systems of customary tenure, though these projects are fewer in number.

The Malawi Community-Based Rural Land Development Project (CBLDP) provided poor families with a conditional cash and land transfer to relocate to larger plots of farmland. In addition, the program administered a farm development grant, assisted in the procurement of water infrastructure, provided extension services, and made sure that beneficiaries obtained group titles to their new land.

The project succeeded in increasing access to land. The amount of cultivable land increased for beneficiaries (by 1.01 acres), and they were 65 percent more likely than nonbeneficiaries to gain formal title to their land.

It also led to positive impacts on most production outcomes. Beneficiaries increased their maize cultivation by over 100 kilograms more than the control group, although maize yields were not affected. They also increased tobacco production by 53 kilograms and added to their livestock holdings.

Productivity of households did not significantly increase.

Impacts on agricultural outcomes were lower for beneficiaries that moved out of their district of origin.

Source: IEG 2009g.

The Bank's emphasis has been on formalizing rights to land through land administration programs.

It is difficult to link land administration projects directly to agricultural outcomes for two reasons:

- **Projects often focus exclusively on land administration and/or titling and rarely track the productivity of land registered under the project.** Most of the projects focus exclusively on modernizing the system for registering property rights, demarcation of land, improving information systems, and building capacity for land administration agencies. Typical indicators are number of parcels registered, reduction in time and cost to register a property, number of property transactions, and sometimes assessments of land value. The Slovenia Real Estate Registration Modernization Project (fiscal 1999), for example, focused on improving the efficiency and effectiveness of real estate administration systems, and the recent IEG assessment noted lack of attention to productivity. The Thailand and Lao PDR programs were also concerned with titling and related regulatory activities. In contrast, in some more recent projects in Europe and Central Asia, such as in Azerbaijan, support services are being provided through projects that parallel the land titling work, and agricultural productivity outcomes are becoming more visible.[19]

Land administration projects are not easily linked to agricultural outcomes.

- **Several Bank-supported land administration projects deal with these issues mainly in the urban context.**

Among these are the Peru Urban Property Rights Project (fiscal 1999) and the recently assessed Kyrgyz Land and Real Estate Registration Project (fiscal 2000). The projects started out as urban interventions; only during implementation did they begin giving attention to registration of rural lands. However, the project M&E and data systems were not updated to take into account the rural context, limiting the possibility of reporting on these results. Similarly, the Ghana Land Administration Project dealt with titling in the peri-urban areas of Accra.

IFC support was provided more through advisory services than through investment projects. Thirteen percent of total expenditures ($11 million) went to advisory service projects to advise governments on policy, procedure, and institutional land reform (for example, the Land Market for Investment Projects in Mozambique, Namibia, and South Africa) and supporting client and nonclient trader-processors and their outgrower farmers with ownership, titling, and privatization issues. For example, an advisory service project in South Africa is seeking to help farmers to access ownership of 30 commercial farms (in partnership with a nonclient orange trader-processor). The Europe and Central Asia Region received 77 percent of this support, most of which went to agriculture-based economies in that Region.

IFC provided proportionally more support for access to land through advisory work than through investments.

Four percent of total IFC commitments ($239 million) went to investment projects seeking to follow through on the privatization of agribusiness assets in Europe and Central Asia, Sub-Saharan Africa, and Asia. These investments in-

Photo courtesy of Julio Pantoja/World Bank.

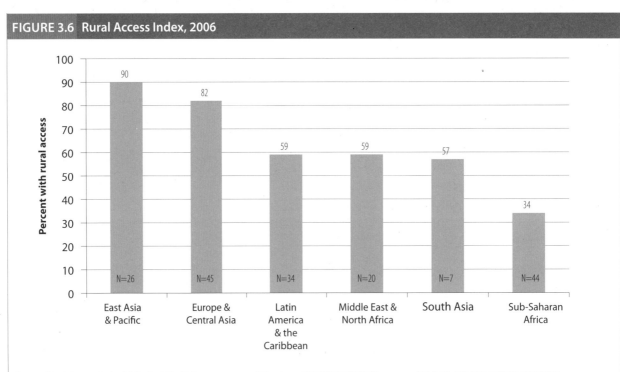

FIGURE 3.6 Rural Access Index, 2006

Source: Rural Access Index Web site http://siteresources.worldbank.org/EXTTRANSPORT/Resources/337115–1214499672078/5154009–1214508441379/rai-chart-values-by-region-20070308-2.pdf.

Note: N =Number of countries.

tended to help IFC clients acquire land and other government-owned agribusiness assets. In western Ukraine, for example, IFC invested in a multifaceted trader-processor involved in various agricultural markets: seeds, crop protection, fertilizers, machinery, spare parts, commodity trading, transportation, and farming. This investment supports the government's decree "On Accelerating Reform of the Agricultural Sector of the Economy" by making the breakup of Ukraine's collective farms economically feasible. Under a one-stop shop concept, the company distributes a full range of agricultural inputs and services to more than 6,500 farms, which account for 4 million of the approximately 34 million hectares of arable land available in Ukraine. These investments have achieved generally satisfactory DO/IO ratings. The Latin America and the Caribbean Region has dominated this activity with 43 percent of investment commitments, followed by Europe and Central Asia (20 percent); only 2 projects out of 20 were located in agriculture-based economies (in Côte d'Ivoire and Lao PDR).

> Satisfactory results have been achieved when IFC has combined advisory services for access with follow-up investments in trader-processors.

IFC has achieved satisfactory results when it has combined access to assets advisory service projects with follow-up investments in trader-processors. Examples of this type of support are the combination of two advisory service projects and a follow-up investment in a company in In-

dia. The aim of these projects was to reduce poverty among laborers at 24 tea plantations in Assam and West Bengal by implementing a sustainable employee-owned plantation model and providing technical and business training. The ownership scheme was rapidly oversubscribed: applications were received from 58 percent of the company's daily workers, 83 percent of the monthly rated workers, 97 percent of the nonmanagement staff, and 100 percent of the management staff. One of the advisory service projects also employed an additional 3,000 youths, after over a decade of creating no new employment opportunities (see also box 3.11).

Transport and Marketing Infrastructure

The inadequacy of roads and marketing infrastructure has hindered the development of agricultural activities in many developing countries. While access to markets is also affected by international trade and tax policies (Anderson 2009), this section focuses on physical and communication infrastructure. Primary roads, railways, warehouses, ports, and airports are important for movement of goods over long distances and for access to import and export markets. Rural and secondary roads are critical for linking farms and villages to local markets. Electronic communication networks provide farmers with up-to-date market and price information. An ongoing IEG evaluation of information and communications technology will examine World Bank Group support for information and communication technology regulation and infrastructure.

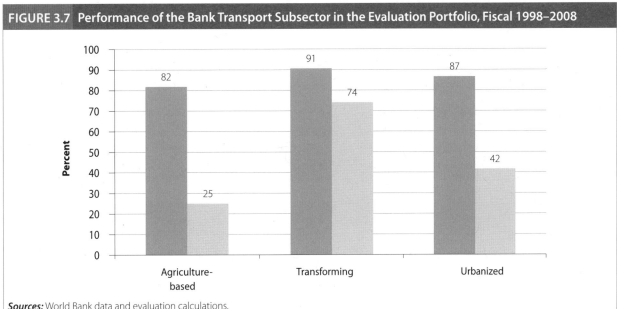

FIGURE 3.7 Performance of the Bank Transport Subsector in the Evaluation Portfolio, Fiscal 1998–2008

Sources: World Bank data and evaluation calculations.

Note: Darker bars represent percentage that achieved the physical transport intervention, the lighter bars represent those that reported achievement in agricultural production resulting from the transport component as a percentage of projects that intended to do so.

World Bank Group Activities and Results | 51

Inadequate transport infrastructure and services in rural areas can lead to high marketing costs that undermine local marketing and export of food staples (World Bank 2007b). The literature underscores the positive impact of improved road access on agricultural growth and productivity (Fan and Chan-Kang 2009; Fan, Zhang, and Zhang 2002; Felloni and others 2001). Access to roads[20] is much lower in Sub-Saharan Africa than in any other Region (figure 3.6), highlighting the difficulties farmers face in reaching markets. This problem is compounded by the large concentration of landlocked countries in Sub-Saharan Africa that face an additional cost of accessing international markets to export their crops (World Bank 2009k). Transport costs can be as high as 60 percent of total marketing costs in some Sub-Saharan Africa countries (World Bank 2007b).

The need to expand rural transport infrastructure has been emphasized by the strategies of both the rural and transport sectors of the World Bank. The World Bank provided extensive support for roads but only limited attention to railways and other transport infrastructure during the evaluation period.[21] IEG's transport evaluation showed that about 15 percent of road projects were for rural roads. In this evaluation's portfolio, 149 projects (24 percent) had transport components—mainly rural roads—with the share declining over the years of the evaluation period from 35 to 20 percent.[22] Two-thirds of these projects indicated that the transport component would contribute to improvements in agricultural production or productivity. A total of about $3 billion was committed to the transport components in the evaluation portfolio; 46 percent went to South Asia, 21 percent to East Asia, 15 percent to Sub-Saharan Africa, and 13 percent to Latin America and the Caribbean. The smallest shares went to the Middle East and North Africa (3 percent) and Europe and Central Asia (2 percent).

> The need to expand rural transport infrastructure has been emphasized by the sector strategies of both the rural and transport sectors of the Bank.

The Bank has also provided support for storage (including cold storage at seaports and airports), market infrastructure to reduce post-harvest losses, and infrastructure to reduce marketing costs such as construction of rural marketplaces, wholesale markets, and market information systems. Eighty-four of the 109 marketing projects in the portfolio reviewed featured such agricultural marketing infrastructure, mostly in Sub-Saharan Africa (35)

BOX 3.7   EXAMPLES OF BANK RURAL INFRASTRUCTURE PROJECTS THAT BENEFITED THE AGRICULTURAL SECTOR

The China Irrigated Agriculture Intensification Loan (fiscal 1998) had a component that aimed to expand the rural road network to promote the development of agricultural production and the rural economy in the project area. It supported the construction of 12,952 kilometers of gravel road and 27,250 kilometers of earth roads that contributed to substantial achievements in crop production—from a total of 16.3 million tons targeted at appraisal to 22.4 million tons. Average farm incomes also increased 40–65 percent. In three of the five provinces, the incomes of poorer households increased in percentage terms by more than the increases of the incomes of wealthier families.

The India Diversified Agricultural Support Project (fiscal 1998) aimed to increase agricultural productivity, in part through improving rural infrastructure. The project improved 2,728 kilometers of rural roads, connecting over 1,100 villages, and refurbished 114 rural (haat painths and cattle) markets. Impact assessments suggest that these improvements had a significant economic impact. There was an increase in crop productivity (over 10 percent), milk productivity (25 percent), and cropping intensity (from 169 percent at baseline to 203 percent at completion) in project areas. There was also significant diversification of area, out of cereals and into vegetables and other higher-value crops. The ICR noted that construction of roads contributed to these outcomes.

The Mali National Rural Transport Project (fiscal 2000) supported rehabilitation of 513 kilometers of feeder roads. The project also established a Road Authority that maintained about 10,000 kilometers of feeder roads over a 12-month period, serving 10 rural communities that were formerly inaccessible because of flooding in the rainy season and connecting several Malian towns with each other, as well as internationally with Mauritania. The project resulted in a 20–40 percent reduction in transport costs and facilitated better distribution of rice and other agricultural products, both domestically and to Mauritania. The ICR also reported that annual paddy production increased by 95,607 tons against a target of 26,000 tons after satisfactory development of the 9,330 hectares of new irrigated land. IEG's ICR review, however, cautioned that it is not clear if all of the increased production can be attributed to project activities.

Sources: World Bank documents and evaluation findings.

The new port has increased the efficiency of the transportation infrastructure of IFC's client by providing a low-cost operation for export of agricultural products from Argentina. Low-cost operations are key to competing in the international commodity markets in which the client participates and for paying competitive prices to farmers. IFC has played a catalytic role, because after this first experience of building and operating a port, the client has built similar ports in other emerging economies.

The project consisted of construction and operation of a grain port terminal at Timbues, on the lower Parana River, 340 kilometers north of Buenos Aires. Two hundred and one hectares of land with 1,800 meters of waterfront were acquired; a truck parking area and facilities for sampling, conditioning, and storage were constructed; and equipment was purchased. The Timbues port has a storage capacity of 120,000 tons and is designed to accommodate a throughput of about 2 million tons of grain per year, consisting mainly of export soybeans. The project cost was approximately $51 million. IFC has directly financed $18 million and syndicated an additional $28 million. Construction began at the end of February 2005, and the project was completed in November 2006.

Source: IEG portfolio review.

and Europe and Central Asia (18). The highly rated China Anning Valley Agricultural Development Project (fiscal 1999), Morocco Pilot Fisheries Development Project (fiscal 1999), Bangladesh Agricultural Services Innovation and Reform Project (fiscal 2000), Jordan Horticultural Exports Promotion and Technology Transfer Project (fiscal 2002), and Rwanda Agricultural and Rural Market Development Project (fiscal 2000) are noteworthy examples. Of 21 evaluated projects with such components, 20 were rated moderately satisfactory or higher.

Bank transport interventions have generally been successful, but results have varied by Region. Of 74 transport-related projects in the evaluation portfolio that had information on achievements, 86 percent were successful in constructing or rehabilitating infrastructure, with a somewhat lower success rate in agriculture-based economies (figure 3.7). Among the Regions, Sub-Saharan Africa had the lowest achievement rate, with 73 percent of interventions successfully implemented, compared with 86 percent in the Middle East and North Africa, 88 percent in East Asia and the Pacific, 90 percent in South Asia, and 100 percent in both Europe and Central Asia and Latin America and the Caribbean. The overall achievement rate of 86 percent is better than the performance of the agriculture portfolio Bank-wide (77 percent).

> Transport interventions have generally been successful, but results have varied by Region and sustainability is an issue.

However, IEG's transport evaluation found that projects with transport components not managed by the Transport Sector Board, such as those evaluated as a part of this study, often faced sustainability concerns. DPLs have also supported establishment of mechanisms for rehabilitation and maintenance of roads by encouraging increased budget allocations for road maintenance (in Cameroon, under the Structural Adjustment Credit III [fiscal 1998], for example). The evaluation also found that maintenance remained an issue, particularly in Sub-Saharan Africa (IEG 2007a).

Projects also often fail to show (in part due to weak M&E) that the transport improvements result in higher agricultural production. Of 58 closed projects, only half—and only 25 percent in Sub-Saharan Africa—showed that intended results in agricultural production were achieved. Box 3.7 provides some examples of rural infrastructure projects that have successfully benefited the agriculture sector.

IFC has helped its trader-processor clients finance specific marketing infrastructure and logistics gaps and has also supported companies seeking to develop trading platforms. To address these gaps, IFC invested $185 million in its trader-processor clients during the evaluation period (representing 3.3 percent of total commitments). For example, IFC investment in a company in Vietnam facilitated the construction and operation of a cold storage warehouse in support of seafood exports, which have been steadily increasing in recent years. Only 2 out of 15 projects were located in agriculture-based economies (Bolivia and Kenya). IFC also committed $20 million in two companies that provide trading platforms using the Internet and cell phones.

> IFC has helped its clients to bridge infrastructure and logistic gaps in their supply chains.

The Bank supported marketing reform in the cotton sector in six West African countries (Benin, Burkina Faso, Chad, Côte d'Ivoire, Mali, and Togo) during the evaluation period through analytic and advisory activities and various lending instruments, including Poverty Reduction Support Credits (PRSCs), investment loans, and economic recovery grants. The tightly controlled marketing systems have been plagued by inefficiencies and a lack of transparency and have created many opportunities for rent-seeking and mismanagement, effectively costing farmers by reducing the price paid at the farm level, although admittedly at less distorted levels than in other parts of the developing world.

The situation varied among countries, but Benin provides a good illustrative example of some of the challenges. The Benin Cotton Reform Project (fiscal 2002) was designed to increase efficiency by switching responsibility for operations related to cotton production from government-dominated parastatals to private entities—for ginning, to private operators; for provision of technical services, to contractors paid through producer groups; and for the provision of credit, to an organization reporting to and funded by producer, supplier, and processor groups. It was assumed that these groups would have a greater interest in achieving efficiencies and reducing costs as they assumed greater responsibility for covering relevant costs.

The outcome of the project was rated moderately unsatisfactory by IEG, which observed that "during implementation the Bank followed up continually on implementation issues and utilized leverage provided by budget support operations to press the issue of privatization, first in PRSC3 and again in PRSC5 in 2008, when it was finally achieved. The fact that despite this constant pressure, SONAPRA [an agricultural parastatal] was not privatized until after closing, and many other issues remained outstanding, suggests that, without the Bank efforts, even that limited institutional progress would not have been achieved."

Sources: Tschirley, Poulton, and Labaste 2009 and evaluation findings.

IFC has helped its agribusiness clients successfully bridge infrastructure (railway systems, trucks, barges, ports, warehouses) and logistics gaps that created bottlenecks along their supply-value chains. For example, IFC investment in a logistics services company in Peru has helped companies in the agricultural sector move, store, transport, and finance inputs and outputs (see chapter 4 "Coordination among IFC Departments" for more details). IFC investment in a client in Argentina supported the construction and operation of a dedicated soybean port in Timbues. It is an example of how IFC can support a soybean trader-processor client to address an infrastructure-related bottleneck (box 3.8). These physical and marketing infrastructure investments in trader-processors and logistics companies have generally achieved satisfactory DO/IO ratings.

IFC's strategic objective to step up infrastructure investments through public-private partnerships in Sub-Saharan Africa has not been achieved. Though the public physical and market infrastructure needs are immense in Sub-Saharan Africa, it is unclear to what extent there are opportunities for the private sector to complement the public sector in this area in the present difficult business environment.

> IFC's strategic objective to step up infrastructure investments through public-private partnerships in Sub-Saharan Africa has not been achieved.

Policies, Markets, and Agribusiness

Agribusiness, agro-industry, and market activities are integral to agricultural and rural development. They connect farmers to input and output markets and economic opportunities and enhance linkages between agricultural and nonagricultural economic activities— roles well described in the 2008 WDR (World Bank 2007b). As shown in figure 3.1, IFC committed $2.2 billion to marketing and agribusiness, and the World Bank committed $1.3 billion in 109 projects during the evaluation period. Thirty-four percent of World Bank resources went to Sub-Saharan Africa, 28 percent to Europe and Central Asia, 16 percent to East Asia and the Pacific, 14 percent to South Asia, 6 percent to Latin America and the Caribbean, and 2 percent to the Middle East and North Africa.

Business Environment and Policy Reform

The World Bank Group has long had an interest in improving the investment climate or, as it is sometimes expressed, enhancing the business enabling environment. This was epitomized in *World Development Report 2005: A Better Investment Climate for Everyone* (World Bank 2004b). The quality of a country's business environment is determined by the risks and transaction costs of investing in and operating a business, which in turn are determined by the legal and regulatory framework; barriers to entry and exit; and conditions in markets for labor, finance, information, infrastructure services, and other productive inputs. The World Bank endeavors to improve the business environment through its operations. IFC only invests in a country when minimum conditions for the private sector to operate are present, but even when the minimum conditions do not exist, IFC may seek to influence the investment climate through its advisory services to both the public and private sectors.

> The Bank has continued to support reform of agricultural policies in many of its interventions that deal with agro-enterprise development.

The World Bank has continued to support reform of agricultural policies in many interventions that deal with agro-enterprise development, such as in the cotton markets of West Africa (box 3.9), coffee markets in East Africa, and cereal markets in Eastern Europe. Support for policy reforms during the evaluation period was most common in agriculture-based countries (about two-thirds of countries compared with about half of other client countries). Support to public entities was also strongest in agriculture-based countries, while support to privatization and other private entities was more frequently seen in urbanized countries, where several governments (such as in Bulgaria, Turkey, and Ukraine) emphasized reform programs.

The experience with the Bulgaria First Agriculture Sector Adjustment Loan (fiscal 1999) confirmed a common lesson (IEG 2001a) that where there is a political consensus for reform, DPLs can effectively reinforce the reform agenda. There was similarly strong commitment from the government of Turkey for the Agricultural Reform Implementation Project (fiscal 2002). Country director interviews also confirm that the Bank has often found it difficult to engage with countries on policy issues when client countries did not share the Bank's view of the public sector's role in agriculture. The country directors pointed to a lack of staff who can effectively engage in a policy dialogue with Bank clients in the sector. Where the Bank has done this effectively, it has often used AAA as an entry point. Country director interviews suggest that this has happened more frequently in middle-income countries than in poor, agriculture-based economies.

BOX 3.10 THE POOR AND WOMEN HAVE BENEFITTED FROM IFC'S INVESTMENT IN A VEGETABLE PRODUCER

To measure the impact of the client on employment and economic welfare in its districts of influence, IEG used three methodological approaches: time-trend analysis, industry analysis, and counterfactual analysis. IEG was therefore able to isolate the client's impact from the general economic trends across poor and nonpoor population segments. The client was chosen as the subject of a quasi-experimental design evaluation for two main reasons: (1) it is a grower and exporter of fresh asparagus in Peru that self-produces all the asparagus that it processes, and (2) it represents a self-contained production and processing operation, which made it possible to clearly identify its economic and geographic areas of influence. The reasons behind the three encouraging the client impacts are as follows:

First, the indirect positive impacts on the poor probably result from:

- Increased agriculture-based economic activity in the area, which could have helped poorer farmers to buy inputs or sell products more efficiently

- Hiring of poorer farmers as seasonal workers

- Learning of more effective farming techniques and practices through exposure to Agrokasa's cutting-edge technology

- Hiring by the nonpoor employed by the client of the poor as peons to work their land rather than letting it sit idle.

Second, the positive direct impacts on nonpoor households are because male-headed nonpoor households have significantly increased their nonwage income, though there have been no significant impacts on formal employment and wage income.

Third, both poor and nonpoor households with a female member in the client industries have increased their net income and nonwage income significantly more than those in the control group (unlike households with only men in such industries). The main explanation for these positive effects for women could be spillovers from the client, such as labor opportunities for women in neighboring areas who may work as peons or seasonal workers for the firm. These opportunities may have existed locally or at a distance for men, but women would be less likely to be able to travel far for work. The lack of direct impacts through wage employment is corroborated by data provided by the firm, which show that only 18 percent of the client's employees were women (April 2008).

Source: IEG.

> Progress has been slow in countries where consensus on the need to limit the role of government in market functions has not developed.

Conversely, progress in Bank projects has been slow in countries where consensus has not developed on the need to limit the role of government in marketing functions—such as by eliminating or at least improving the efficiency of parastatals. Examples include the fiscal 2005 Tanzania Second Poverty Reduction Support Credit (PRSC) and the Malawi Fiscal Management and Accelerated Growth Project (fiscal 2004). The latter project emphasized reform of the parastatal Agricultural Development and Marketing Corporation, but that reform proved difficult.

Direct improvements in the enabling environment for agribusiness have not been a major focus of IFC's agribusiness interventions, though a few IFC agribusiness investments—primarily in Europe and Central Asia—have sought to indirectly influence the investment climate through demonstration effects. These investments represent only 2.3 percent (or $129 million) of total commitments over the review period. Examples include investments in a dairy producer in the Russian Federation (see appen-

dix box C.2) and a food processor and retailer in Croatia. Though the Business Enabling Environment and Infrastructure units have played a limited role in support for the sector, IFC has undertaken a few stand-alone sector, privatization, and investment climate studies not linked to any specific IFC investment.[23] A good example of advisory service combined with investment to address the business environment in Liberia is discussed in box 3.12.

> Direct improvements in the enabling environment for agribusiness have not been a major focus of IFC's interventions.

Input and Output Markets

The state control of agricultural marketing and food processing that prevailed in many parts of the developing world in the 1970s have undergone tremendous changes in the era of liberalization and globalization in the 1980s and 1990s (Swinnen and Maertens 2007). In transition countries, the liberalization of prices and trade and the privatization of state enterprises eliminated the state control and vertical coordination of commodity chains, and similar changes have reduced the role of state agencies in food and agricultural chains in many developing and emerging economies.

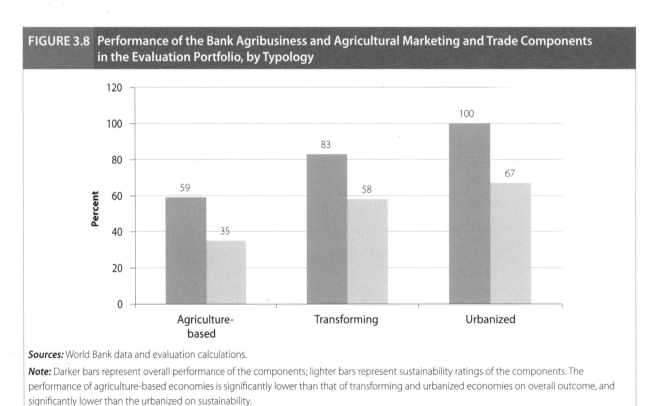

FIGURE 3.8 Performance of the Bank Agribusiness and Agricultural Marketing and Trade Components in the Evaluation Portfolio, by Typology

Sources: World Bank data and evaluation calculations.

Note: Darker bars represent overall performance of the components; lighter bars represent sustainability ratings of the components. The performance of agriculture-based economies is significantly lower than that of transforming and urbanized economies on overall outcome, and significantly lower than the urbanized on sustainability.

Most of the world has seen significant foreign and local investment in agribusiness and the food industry, including the rise of supermarkets (Reardon and Berdegué 2006). Increasingly, the aggregation of output for small-scale farmers is being done by large private purchasers such as food companies (trader-processors) and supermarkets. These firms want assurance that the goods meet stringent quality and safety standards, and these requirements make it difficult for smallholders acting individually to take advantage of these new marketing opportunities. Bank projects also recognize the importance of collective action and assist farmers in forming producer organizations and building links with exporters, as was done in the Senegal Agricultural Export Promotion Project (fiscal 1998).

World Bank Group activities seek to improve farmers' access to output and input markets.[24] Many Bank projects assist farmers with public infrastructure (as discussed above), and most of the Bank's agro-industry projects (nearly 10 percent of its agricultural lending) address weaknesses along supply chains, including marketing information, and compliance with food safety protocols.[25] IFC core F&A operations have traditionally supported trader-processors in accessing local and international markets and in providing their outgrowers with extension, financial, environmental, and social services and inputs for their production (the processor model).

> Bank Group activities seek to improve farmers' access to output and input markets.

Many Bank-supported agricultural projects have supported development of the seed industry. In agricultural research components, the Bank has supported plant breeding and crop improvement. Agricultural administration and agricultural extension components have supported multiplication, certification, and dissemination of seeds of improved cultivars. Agribusiness and marketing components have supported enhanced emergence and growth of input dealers and their networks. These activities span the public and private sectors and have important links to international entities, including the CGIAR on the public side and international agribusinesses (especially those with major crop biotechnology products) on the private side. Operations that support seed industry development are found in a range of country typologies: agriculture-based, such as the Rwanda Agricultural and Rural Market Development Project (fiscal 2000); transforming, such as the India Diversified Agricultural Support Project (fiscal 1998); and urbanized, such as the Philippines Diversified Farm Income and Market Development Project (fiscal 2004).

IFC has committed $1.7 billion in F&A investments (30 percent of total commitments) and spent an additional

---

BOX 3.11   IFC—A COMBINATION OF ADVISORY SERVICE AND INVESTMENT HELPED DEVELOP VEGETABLE SUPPLY CHAINS IN SOUTHERN UKRAINE

The transition to a market economy had left the vegetable sector in southern Ukraine in disarray. To rebuild the sector it was necessary to initiate policy dialogue with the government, to promote regulatory reform, and to build the entrepreneurial capacity of the farmers. IFC advisory work contributed to regulation improvements and supported farmers to:

- Raise productivity and quality
- Improve managerial and business skills
- Deal with legal issues related to land and property rights.

IFC investment helped the client vegetable processor to become a reliable off-taker partner to the farmers helped by the Southern Ukraine Vegetable Supply-Chain Development Advisory Service Project. Conversely, the advisory service project improved the vegetable supply chain of Sandora, a major juice processor in Ukraine. The client's supply-chain chokepoints were caused by the lack of reliable supply and the poor quality of tomatoes and carrots produced by local farmers. Thus, through its support to the processor and farmers, IFC has helped the development of the fruit and vegetable sector in southern Ukraine, the promotion of the production of value-added agribusiness products, local entrepreneurship, technology transfers, and the training of local people.

IFC invested in the client twice, in 2004 ($20 million) and in 2006 ($20 million). Through these investments, IFC directly helped the client carry out its expansion plans by providing the appropriate maturity match between assets and liabilities. In July 2007, the client was sold to an international beverage company, and it fully repaid its IFC loans in March 2008.

Sources: Portfolio review, IEG-IFC 2008b.

$22 million in advisory services (24 percent of total expenditures) for clients that have typically used part of these funds to address agribusiness and marketing issues (that is, concerns of small-scale farmers and suppliers). These clients have sought to address their own marketing and agribusiness needs (as did a noodle producer in Indonesia) and their outgrowers' needs (as did an apple juice producer in China). Latin America and the Caribbean has dominated these activities with 62 percent of commitments, followed by Europe and Central Asia (16 percent) and East Asia and the Pacific (13 percent). Nine of the 94 projects were located in agriculture-based economies (Côte d'Ivoire, Kenya, Lao PDR, Tanzania, Uganda, and Zambia).

The advisory service projects were generally stand-alone projects designed to develop capacity in different subsectors; to improve clients technology, quality, and environmental practices; and to link small-scale farmers to trader-processors (either IFC client or not). For example, the Olive Oil Supply Chain Development Project in West Bank and Gaza helps producers improve their practices and links them to an existing IFC client in Egypt. IFC has also invested $362 million (6.4 percent of total commitments) in clients that provide agribusiness services.

> The Bank's activities in input and output markets have performed about the same as the rest of the agricultural portfolio, but sustainability is weak.

With regard to outcomes, the marketing and agribusiness activities performed on a par with the Bank agricultural portfolio, though the sustainability record is weak. Of the 109 Bank projects in the evaluation portfolio, 37 were closed and have been evaluated by IEG. Seventy-eight percent of the activities were judged moderately satisfactory or higher, which is similar to the overall outcome rating of 77 percent for agricultural projects, as noted in chapter 2. However, only 54 percent of the activities in the marketing portfolio were judged likely on sustainability. By WDR typology, agriculture-based economies had the weakest performance (figure 3.8).

IFC has refined its approach to investments in trader-processors, and DO/IO ratings have improved substantially during the evaluation period, except in Sub-Saharan Africa. Some successful clients have become local and regional players and south-south investors, benefiting farmers, employees, and suppliers with increased income and opportunities, and positively affecting the economy through greater productivity and growth.

> The poor, the nonpoor, and women have benefitted from the IFC investment in a vegetable processor.

IEG carried out an impact assessment of an IFC-supported asparagus producer in Peru to get an indication of the impact of the trader-processor model on poverty, because such assessments are not done systematically by IFC. IEG found that IFC played a catalytic role by providing the client with long-term financing when it was not otherwise available. The impact evaluation also found that the client had three encouraging impacts on the surrounding communities (box 3.10 and appendix figure C.5):

- The poor appear to have benefitted indirectly, because their nonwage income improved compared with that of the control group.

- The investment appears to have brought about positive direct impacts on nonpoor households.

- Both poor and nonpoor households with a female member in one of the client's industries have increased their net income and nonwage income significantly more than the control group.

IFC has also refined its approach to agribusiness advisory service projects. More recently, there has been an effort to integrate the strategy of advisory-service business lines with the agribusiness investment operations and to focus on a few areas of engagement (see chapter 4 for more on coordination among IFC departments). The combined successful outcomes of an investment in a vegetable processor and the Southern Ukraine Vegetable Supply-Chain Development Advisory Project illustrate how IFC could increase its development impact (box 3.11). Similar case studies are a banana producer in Ecuador (appendix box C.3) and a sugar producer in India (appendix box C.4). Additionally, a large fertilizer company in Algeria is the first IFC project with an advisory service and a follow-up investment project designed to improve farmers' fertilizer practices. However, at the beginning of the evaluation period, advisory service projects lacked strategic focus and were mainly supply-driven. Many subsector reports were produced without any follow-up advisory service or investment projects. For example, unsuccessful projects were carried out in frog ranching (Peru), honey production (Kenya), and tomato production (Tajikistan; this failed because of the lack of a viable trader-processor anchor).[26]

> IFC has also refined its approach to agribusiness advisory service projects.

After nearly two decades of conflict, Liberia's economy, institutions, and human capacity had been devastated when the civil war ended in 2003. Following the election of a democratic government, Liberia is moving from the transitional post-conflict recovery phase to laying the foundations for long-term development. The government focus is on catalyzing economic growth by getting major transport corridors functioning to open up trade and commerce, revitalizing agriculture, getting energy infrastructure up and running, and generating employment. Liberia's government goal over the next three years is to firmly establish a stable and secure environment and to be on an "irreversible" path toward rapid, inclusive, and sustainable growth and development. Within the context of this improved business environment, the engagement of the private sector is critical to financing Liberia's recovery.

In a rare example of collaboration across the World Bank Group, support is being provided to develop Liberia's tree crop sector. IFC is providing technical assistance through sector studies and following up with investments. Foreign Investment Advisory Services (FIAS) and Private Enterprise Partnership for Africa (PEP Africa, funded by IFC and other donors) are providing input to the development of a model concession contract in the form of policy papers analyzing the issues that typically form part of a concession agreement. The World Bank, meanwhile, is supporting the policy capacity of the Ministry of Agriculture (the authority for agricultural concessions) under the Agriculture and Infrastructure Development Project and is leading the policy dialogue and the integration of these issues into the poverty reduction strategy. The joint PEP Africa–FIAS projects include:

- **Private Sector Development Growth in Post-Conflict Program: Phase 2 ($4.6 million)**

    Drawing on a 2006 mini-diagnostic, in consultation with the Ministries of Commerce and Finance, and the National Investment Commission, the program focuses on business registry, investment promotion, models for tree crop concession and outgrower engagement (in collaboration with the World Bank), and the business regulatory framework.

- **Liberia Trade Logistics Project ($0.85 million)**

    This project seeks to reduce time and cost for import and export transactions and to achieve efficiencies in trade logistics through targeted reforms.

- **Private Sector Development Growth Support through Special Economic Zones (active, $0.7 million)**

    The project seeks to assist the government in the creation of special economic zones where companies invest, create jobs, and produce goods within an improved business environment.

IFC has also contributed with an investment in a rubber producer ($10 million), demonstrating that it is possible for the private sector to invest in agribusiness in this post-conflict country. A World Bank economist based in Accra participated in the due diligence for this investment. The client is competing for exports with producers from West Africa and Southeast Asia, the latter being by far the world's largest producing region. Therefore, the client helped by IFC sustains a higher level of operational efficiency and improved plantation yields through new plantings and improved varieties. Additionally, the client has upgraded its outgrower program, including the provision of planting materials and fertilizers to outgrowers, delivering extension services, and extending financial advances.

Sources: IEG review of the portfolio, Poverty Reduction and Economic Management, and the draft 2010 CAS.

IFC can play a larger role in linking farmers and agribusiness SMEs, not only with its trader-processor clients but also with its food-retailer clients. The important role of retailers is recognized in a recent ECG paper (ECG 2010). IFC is exploring a business model in Eastern Europe that seeks to achieve integration of farming and food retailing.[27] The three types of clients (traders, processors, and retailers) can help each other by reducing barriers and costs to exchange and encouraging greater market integration between rural and urban areas. However, the outgrower farmer model is prone to contract ruptures and disputes between farmers and trader-processors in the absence of efficient dispute resolution mechanisms (Leles and Zylbersztajn 2007). IFC can help mitigate these by acting as a neutral broker.[28]

IFC can play a larger role in linking farmers and agribusiness SMEs with trader-processor and food-retailer clients.

Although not representative of generalized practice, the rubber sector in Liberia provides an example of how good results can be achieved in a complex sector such as agribusiness by coordination among the World Bank and the investment and advisory departments of IFC. The Bank and IFC have helped the public sector with knowledge instruments in their respective areas of expertise, and IFC investment operations have introduced demonstration effects both as role models for existing companies and in seeking to prompt new companies to enter the market (box 3.12).

Agribusiness projects in Sub-Saharan Africa will always demand more time and resources from the World Bank Group than traditional investments in urbanized and transforming economies. The constraints to doing agribusiness in Sub-Saharan Africa, discussed in chapter 4, contribute to longer lead times and higher transaction costs for the Bank Group. These constraints tax IFC more in Sub-Saharan Africa than in other Regions in terms of the number of investment officers per dollar of commitments.[29]

Summary and Implications Going Forward

The findings in this chapter offer lessons to consider as assistance is scaled up in the future.

In irrigation and drainage, the World Bank Group's support for physical infrastructure can help provide farmers with access to irrigation water and thereby raise agricultural productivity. But physical infrastructure is unlikely to be sustainable without reliable funding for operations and maintenance. The Bank Group needs to devote more attention and resources to helping governments design and implement politically and institutionally feasible mechanisms for cost recovery from beneficiaries, to facilitate a larger role for the private sector by enabling the environment for public-private partnerships to succeed, and to monitor results in this area more diligently. Greater attention to water-use efficiency and its monitoring is also needed, as emphasized in the recent IEG evaluation on water-related activities. The Bank needs to track its water management activities separately in rain-fed areas to allow the institution to take stock of what works in addressing the related water management issues.

With regard to agricultural research and extension, the public and the private sectors have important and complementary roles. The Bank Group needs to stay engaged in these areas at the country and global levels (the latter through support to CGIAR) and to facilitate the mainstreaming of research results from CGIAR institutions in Bank projects at the country and regional levels. The Bank Group can also

---

BOX 3.13   THE IMPORTANCE OF SYNERGIES AND PARTNERSHIPS: CHINA IRRIGATED AGRICULTURE INTENSIFICATION

This project was rated highly satisfactory on outcome. It aimed to increase agricultural production and farmers' incomes and to establish mechanisms for sustainable use, development, and management of water and land resources in irrigated areas in the Huang-Huai-Hai Plain, the most important region in China for agricultural production.

Project components included irrigation, soil improvement, increased forest cover on farmlands, rural roads and electricity development, improved agricultural technology (including training to farmers in integrated pest management), provision of agricultural inputs, and water resource management (including development of water user associations).

The project achieved high production and added value by using combined agriculture-irrigation approaches, placing as much attention on agricultural innovation and improvement as it did on rehabilitation of the irrigation networks. It did not treat the agriculture element as an add-on to what is still considered an irrigation project. The project also capitalized on synergies across projects. The project design built on lessons from a successful earlier project. It used an existing governmental comprehensive agricultural development program that had relevant sectoral staff at all levels of project management: central, provincial, and municipal.

Strong borrower commitment at the central and decentralized levels and strong Bank supervision efforts were also major contributors to success of the project. Task management from Beijing was proactive in response to government communications and needs, including the flexibility to make adjustments to project arrangements. Teamwork with government was good.

At the end of the project, almost all components exceeded their targets and objectives were achieved. The average net per capita income of project-area farmers increased substantially (in Anhui, by 60 percent; in Hebei, by 92 percent; in Henan, by 61 percent; and in Jiangsu, by 103 percent compared with pre-project levels).

Sources: IEG review and project documents.

help governments create the conditions for nascent agribusiness technology companies to thrive, both on their own and in partnership with public research institutions. Extension services should engage farmers while helping to link them with input suppliers and markets, and the World Bank Group is working with partners in the public and private sectors to design new approaches along these lines. Cost recovery is as difficult an issue in extension as it is in irrigation, and further work is needed to ensure sustainability. In addition, the Bank needs to build adequate M&E into projects, because there is limited evidence about creation and adoption of improved technologies as a result of Bank interventions.

Access to credit will continue to be a major constraint to investments to improve agricultural productivity, and the Bank and IFC can be important in expanding the supply and efficiency of agricultural credit. The World Bank Group has numerous instruments it can use for this purpose, including traditional public sector lending and private investments, trade finance and private equity facilities, and risk-mitigation instruments. Effectiveness and efficiency will require careful attention to synergies in the design of financial and agricultural lending, and thus close collaboration between rural and financial sector specialists in the Bank Group.

Access to land and formalization of land rights are thought to contribute to both poverty reduction and improvements in agricultural production and productivity, and the Bank and IFC have been quite active in both—most notably in land administration—in recent years. Evidence of the impacts of these efforts on agricultural productivity is weak, however, particularly for land administration, because these projects do not typically include agricultural productivity as a core objective to be monitored. Going forward, greater emphasis is needed on measuring these impacts to reflect the World Bank Group's increasing focus on production and productivity in the agriculture sector. Given the multifaceted nature of agricultural development, it may be important to coordinate land administration with other support services in some settings to achieve productivity gains.

The Bank has been extensively engaged in building transport infrastructure, including rural roads, and the Bank and IFC have invested in other market infrastructure and logistics, such as storage, ports, forwarders, and trading platforms. Available data point to high average success rates in these projects, though somewhat lower in Sub-Saharan Africa. Given Sub-Saharan Africa's low rates of market access, the Bank and IFC need to continue to seek innovative ways to support the development and maintenance of transport and market infrastructure through both public and private investments.

Finally, the World Bank Group has provided extensive support to clients to improve the broader enabling environment (primarily the World Bank) and access to input and output markets, including through the development of agribusiness linked to small-scale producers, where there is strong engagement by IFC. Appropriate policies and a supportive business environment are critical to agricultural development, and though much progress has been made through liberalization and globalization in the past two-to-three decades, challenges remain. Much greater recognition and coordination of the complementary roles of the Bank and IFC are needed going forward.

All six areas covered in this chapter must function effectively together for success and growth in agriculture.

As figure 1.3 shows, the requirements for successful agriculture are multifaceted, and all six areas covered in this chapter—in addition to others not covered here—must function effectively together for success and growth. It is difficult for farmers to buy inputs unless there are functioning credit institutions to meet their needs. Markets cannot be easily accessed if there are no roads. Farmers may not know about new technologies and improved ways of doing work unless there are good extension services. They may not have the incentive to adopt new, possibly riskier, more productive technologies unless they can be sure that their land rights are secure and they have access to water and inputs. This is part of the reason why the processor business model supported by IFC is successful—it ensures that the multifaceted needs of agricultural development can be effectively addressed.

The IFC and the Bank have complementary roles in agriculture.

More generally, the role of the private sector (including foreign investors) in agriculture has grown in recent years and should continue to grow with the help and support of IFC, complemented by World Bank support to important public functions such as research, policy setting, and the provision of basic infrastructure. The challenges are immense and can best be achieved through effective partnerships within the World Bank Group, with other donors, and with governments, NGOs, and private firms. The China Irrigated Agriculture Intensification Project (Loan II, fiscal 1998), discussed in box 3.13, illustrates the importance of synergies and partnerships in achieving results.

Neither the World Bank Group nor any other donor alone can ensure that support for all areas comes together effectively. The World Bank Group can *contribute* to country efforts that attempt to promote development of the sector. It is not project design complexity (or simplicity) that is relevant per se for producing successful outcomes, however, but the suitability of that design to country and client circumstances and capacity. Chapter 4 discusses these institutional issues.

Chapter 4

EVALUATION HIGHLIGHTS

- The outcomes of Bank Group interventions are inevitably affected by borrower commitment and capacity, and this has tended to disadvantage countries in Sub-Saharan Africa.

- Institutional factors such as staff skills and the extent of coordination also affect outcomes, and both the World Bank and IFC have coordination issues that need to be addressed.

- Coordination across the Bank Group has also been limited, and deeper efforts at donor coordination will be essential.

- Two Bank Group strategic priorities—environmental sustainability and gender mainstreaming—have strong linkages with agriculture and require careful attention in investments and analytic work.

- Strong M&E are necessary to ensure good outcomes and learning and need to be combined with strong and consistent supervision.

Photo courtesy of Curt Carnemark/World Bank.

Institutional Factors

Institutional incentives and capacities, both of clients and in the World Bank Group, are important determinants of project outcomes. This chapter explores these institutional factors, drawing on both country case studies and background literature, supplemented by data and analysis using IEG ratings and country-level indicators (see appendix D).

Factors Specific to Borrowers

Three specific factors were found by the evaluation to be associated with borrower performance and project outcomes,[1] regardless of whether the borrower is a sovereign government or a private company. These are *commitment, capacity,* and the *country governance environment* in which the interventions are carried out.

Capacity and Commitment

The World Bank and IFC treat client capacity and commitment differently in their decision-making processes. IFC's mandate to run a sustainable business model and help develop a sustainable private sector makes assessing the capacity and commitment of agribusiness clients (known as sponsors) an important part of screening and approving investments. The Bank does not formally screen borrowers for capacity and commitment, though its decisions are influenced by its perception of these variables, and countries are less likely to borrow when commitment is weak.

The importance of country capacity and commitment for the development of the agricultural sector is evident in the experience of agriculturally advanced developing countries such as Brazil, China, India, and Vietnam, as documented in country studies, project assessments, and literature (such as ADB 2000 for Vietnam and IEG 2009i for Brazil). Favorable price and trade policies emerged only slowly as these economies liberalized (Anderson 2009; Anderson and Martin 2009; Huang and others 2009; Pursell, Gulati, and Gupta 2009). But for many years these countries committed extensive resources for the development of roads and irrigation infrastructure and for the building of technical capacity through investments in research and agricultural education, reflecting their commitment to agricultural growth.[2] Public agricultural research expenditures in Brazil grew at an annual rate of 9.9 percent between 1976 and 1981 (Beintema and others 2006). On average, Asian countries spent nearly five times the amount spent by countries in Sub-Saharan Africa on agricultural research per hectare over the period 1980–2003 (Alene and Coulibaly 2009). Both India and China dramatically increased their investments in agriculture from the 1950s to the 1980s in an effort to solve their food security problems (Fan and Thorat 2007). India's public spending on agriculture grew some 18 percent annually between 1970 and 1990, and China's public spending on research and development and on irrigation grew at an estimated 19 and 18 percent annually, respectively, between 1950 and 1978.

Transforming and urbanized country borrowers tended to have clear strategic visions for agricultural development that directed Bank resources for agricultural sector development to the areas where they were most needed. The China country study found that the World Bank program largely aligned its agricultural strategy to the priorities specified in China's Five-Year Plans.[3] A strong commitment to revive agricultural production after the socialist era was present in several countries of Central and Eastern Europe. In Azerbaijan, for example, the Farm Privatization Project (fiscal 1997) and the Agriculture Development and Credit Project (fiscal 1999) directly translated the government's agricultural strategy into an implementation program and served as piloting vehicles to adjust strategy as experience was gained.[4]

> Transforming and urbanized country borrowers tended to have clear strategic visions for agricultural development that directed resources where they were most needed.

In Egypt, the Bank's major support in the agricultural sector was for irrigation and drainage, which was in line with the government's goal of ensuring the sustainability of the irrigation systems. In transforming and urbanizing countries, the Bank also engaged the government with nonlending activities in areas where specific technical input was requested—for example, the land-related AAA in China (fiscal 2005–07) and the Egypt agriculture Public Expenditure Review. These countries were thus able to use the Bank support more strategically to develop their agricultural sectors.

In contrast, commitment to agriculture is relatively recent in many countries in Sub-Saharan Africa. Post-independence governments in Sub-Saharan Africa tended to treat the agricultural sector primarily as a source of resources for industrialization. Their actions were in line with the prevailing development paradigm at the time, which viewed industrialization as the road to development, while agriculture was viewed as providing surplus to meet the needs of cities, with imports and food aid filling in when there were shortfalls or emergencies (Eicher 1999; IEG 2007j). Government spending on agriculture remained modest in Sub-Saharan Africa through the 1980s and 1990s, increasing only gradually, at 2.5 percent per year between 1980 and 2002. With the recent (2003) adoption of the Comprehensive Africa Agriculture Development Programme, greater priority is being given to agriculture. The goals of the Regional program are to eliminate hunger and reduce poverty through agriculture, and governments in Sub-Saharan Africa have agreed to increase public investment in agriculture by a minimum of 10 percent of their national budgets and to raise agricultural productivity by at least 6 percent by 2015.[5]

Commitment to agriculture in many Sub-Saharan Africa countries is relatively recent.

Both public and private agricultural research capacity continues to be comparatively weaker in Sub-Saharan Africa (table 4.1; Pardy and others 2006), where agricultural education and training has been neglected (World Bank 2007f). Well-developed education and training systems are the foundation of country research capacity and help develop the technical experts needed to staff government departments and the private sector, as illustrated by the experience of Brazil, China, and India (Fan, Qian, and Zhang 2006; Lele and Goldsmith 1989; Stads and Beintema 2009) and as instructively illustrated by Bonnen (1998) in reviewing the U.S. experience for its relevance to developing countries.

Public and private research capacity continues to be comparatively weaker in Africa, resulting in worse project performance.

The Bank has also invested less in building capacity in public institutions in the agriculture-based economies compared to its support in transforming economies (appendix table D.7). Though training activities supported by Bank projects and through the World Bank Institute can also contribute to capacity building, IEG's recent evaluation of those training efforts (IEG 2008o) found that it is important to embed training in broader programs that address organizational and institutional capacity constraints so that individuals who are trained are able to apply their training in the workplace. That evaluation also found that lack of incentives posed a particular problem to civil service training in low-capacity countries.

Project performance is worse in Sub-Saharan Africa and in agriculture-based economies more generally, in part due to the weaker capacity and inadequate long-term strategic focus. For example, an IEG assessment of three agricultural projects in Tanzania (IEG 2007i) rated the outcome moderately unsatisfactory or worse and the risk to development outcome high in two of them. The assessment

Photo courtesy of Masaru Goto/World Bank.

TABLE 4.1 Agricultural Technical Capacity

A. By WDR typology (average for 1998–2006)

	Agriculture-based	Transforming	Urbanized
Government R&D expenditure as percentage of total agricultural R&D expenditure[a]	51	65	73
Donor R&D expenditure as percentage of total agricultural R&D expenditure[a]	37	10	7
Government and donor share as percentage of total agricultural R&D expenditure	84	72	78
Public agricultural R&D expenditure per capita	1.8	3.4	5.0
Agricultural research intensity (public agricultural R&D expenditures/ agricultural GDP percentage)	0.49	0.57	2.13
Public agricultural research staff per million agricultural laborers	82	225	600
Number of countries[b]	29	25	17

B. In selected countries (average for 1998–2006)

	Brazil	China	India	Indonesia	Phillipines	Tanzania	Burkina Faso
Government R&D expenditure as percentage of total agricultural R&D expenditure	94.3	—	—	47.8	84.9	25.5	38.6
Donor R&D expenditure as percentage of total agricultural R&D expenditure	1.2	—	—	5.8	2.3	55.9	51.3
Government and donor share as percentage of total agricultural R&D expenditure	95.5			53.6	87.2	81.4	89.9
Public agricultural R&D expenditure per capita	6.9	2.2	—	0.8	1.8	1.2	2.2
Agricultural research intensity (public agricultural R&D expenditures /agricultural GDP percentage)	1.6	0.4	0.3	0.2	0.4	0.4	0.7
Public agricultural research staff per million agricultural laborers	379	103	—	98	250	37	50

Sources: www.asti.cgiar.org/data; CGIAR's Agricultural Science and Technology Indicators for the data and evaluation calculations.

Note: R&D = research and development; — = Unavailable.

a. Data are available for only 23 countries.

b. Numbers reported are averages for countries for the years data are available. This row reports the maximum number of countries of each type in this data set.

noted the challenge of sustaining improved processes established with Bank support. It said, "For many years, research has gone through an inefficient cycle of funding fluctuations with donor funds giving temporary support that cannot later be sustained. . . . The evidence over recent years suggests that either the public research system is far too large to be sustained by government or that government has been unwilling to give research in particular, and agriculture more generally, sufficient priority" (pp. 23–24).

The Bank has spent considerable time and resources helping with strategy formulation in the agriculture-based economies. One of the four thrusts of *Reaching the Rural Poor* (World Bank 2003d) is supporting preparation of National Rural Development Strategies. The Rural Strategy Implementation Mid-Term Review of 2007 found that the Bank had supported 54 client countries in completing national and subnational rural development strategies; about 40 percent of these countries were agriculture-based economies. In Mali, the Bank and other development partners helped the Ministry of Rural Development prepare a long-term Master Plan for Rural Development (*Schéma Directeur du Développement Rural*) in 1992 and to update it in 2001. Mali is one of the few countries in Sub-Saharan Africa where 70 percent of Bank projects were focused on agricultural growth and productivity, and strong government commitment appears to have been one reason for this. However, weak capacity, along with adverse agro-ecological conditions, has made the quest for productivity growth challenging and progress slow, especially when contrasted with population growth rates.

IFC's screening process helps to explain why most IFC investments in the past decade have been in Latin America and the Caribbean and Europe and Central Asia and why, even though IFC strategy has emphasized investments in Sub-Saharan Africa, they have not increased as rapidly as expected. Factors that have contributed to the lower level of IFC operations in Sub-Saharan Africa include the paucity of indigenous entrepreneurial capacity, small size of potential investments, difficult business environments (see below), and lack of ready access to markets (as discussed in chapter 3). IFC's F&A commitments in Sub-Saharan Africa have increased in the latter part of this decade, though not as fast as in other Regions and starting from a low base (appendix table D.8).

> The IFC screening process helps explain why most IFC investments in the past decade have been in Latin America and the Caribbean and Europe and Central Asia.

The paucity of indigenous entrepreneurs (AgCLIR: Ghana 2008) and the small size of the potential investments (Liberia 2007) have contributed to IFC's emphasis on plantation and export-crop investments in Sub-Saharan Africa. The IEG evaluation of the disappointing performance of IFC's African Enterprise Fund shows some of the challenges of working with small indigenous entrepreneurs

in Sub-Saharan Africa (IEG-IFC 2004). Consequently, IFC has generally supported foreign sponsors, some of them with experience in sectors other than agribusiness. Most IFC sponsors in Sub-Saharan Africa have larger proportions of self-production and smaller proportions of outgrower contracting (for example, a palm oil producer in Ghana) than in other Regions, where heavy dependence on outgrower contracting is common (such as clients in the Russian Federation and India).

IFC's agribusiness portfolio review confirms that strong client commitment and capacity have underpinned positive outcomes. Forty-two percent of the evaluated projects (64 of 152) were categorized by IEG as investment winners because they have displayed both high DO and high IO. Twenty-two percent of the evaluated projects (34 of 152) were categorized by IEG as investment losers, since they have displayed low DO and/or low IO. The investment winners were larger projects[6] with low project-risk layering (particularly with strong-capacity sponsors in recent commitments), and in more than 85 percent the stated project objectives included the provision of long-term financing, improvement of environmental and social effects, and the strengthening of SME linkages. They have achieved excellent IFC screening and appraisal ratings, underlying IFC's success at identifying clear client commitment and capacity from the beginning.

> Strong client commitment and capacity have underpinned positive outcomes in the IFC agribusiness portfolio.

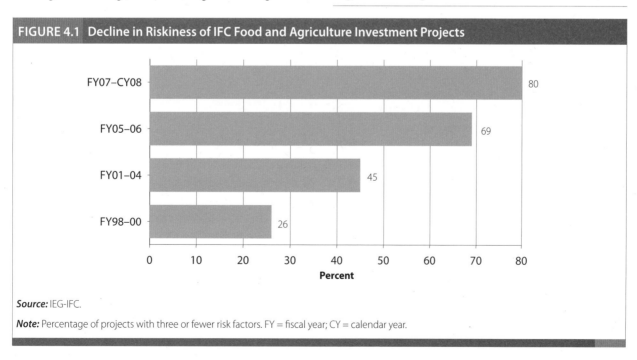

FIGURE 4.1 Decline in Riskiness of IFC Food and Agriculture Investment Projects

Source: IEG-IFC.

Note: Percentage of projects with three or fewer risk factors. FY = fiscal year; CY = calendar year.

The risks[7] of the IFC F&A portfolio have declined in recent years (figure 4.1), in part due to higher-quality sponsors with stronger commitment. The F&A projects present a remarkably low-risk portfolio, partially because IFC has tended to avoid Sub-Saharan Africa. The lower risk profile has also increased the opportunities for IFC to add value for its clients (that is, *additionality*). Other explanations for this risk reduction include: (i) the higher proportion of repeat projects; (ii) the higher quality of IFC's sponsors (with more experience, commitment, and financial capacity); (iii) improved project screening and appraisal quality (partly due to credit review procedures introduced in 2000); (iv) more conservative financial structures at the company level (such as a higher proportion of equity investments and longer loan repayment terms); (v) a higher proportion of expansion projects (instead of new projects); (vi) better sponsor position to compete in their markets; and (vii) an improved business environment in the target markets. Higher sponsor and IFC appraisal quality also seem to drive financial additionality[8] (appendix table D.9).[9]

Larger investments also permit IFC to deliver more forms of additionality, which may also tilt IFC against smaller investments in agriculture-based economies. IFC appears to have achieved more forms of additionality in F&A investments larger than $10 million (its median). The stronger additionality results from the relatively advanced sophistication of IFC's larger clients and their heightened capacity to absorb knowledge and the intense project approval process required for larger investments. For instance, the realization rate[10] for providing long-term financing was 95 percent in larger investments (versus 84 percent in the smaller ones), and 73 percent for delivering market comfort in larger investments (versus 57 percent in the smaller ones) (appendix table D.10).

Countercyclical finance appears to be typical of large-scale F&A investments. Because the credit quality of large agribusiness exporters may sometimes be higher than their sovereign risk, IFC has been able to engage with these companies in times of crisis and indirectly benefit farmers and smaller businesses. For instance, IFC's support for a food company in Argentina has helped it to provide working capital to thousands of its suppliers.

Countercyclical finance appears to be typical of large-scale F&A investments.

Country Governance Environment

Good governance is important for a favorable policy environment and effective implementation of policy agendas (World Bank 2007k). A weak governance environment inhibits dialogue with the government and makes it difficult to design interventions. About half the countries in Sub-Saharan Africa are fragile states or post-conflict countries. The country study for Guinea found that serious governance problems in the Ministry of Agriculture constrained cooperation with the Bank. And in Nepal, a country study found that the Bank has been unable to provide effective support for development of agriculture. In a country where 85 percent of the population depends on agriculture for subsistence and employment, poverty is predominantly a rural issue, and the country's Tenth Plan and PRSP had prioritized agriculture and rural growth, the Bank's failure to support agriculture was a critical gap (IEG 2008h). Among other reasons, the country study and the recent CAE noted the negative impact of the deteriorating political environment and the weakening commitment to reforms.

Agricultural projects were less likely to achieve their objectives in countries with weak governance (where 72 percent were rated moderately satisfactory or better) than in countries with a more favorable governance environment (where 82 percent were rated moderately satisfactory or better). Projects in countries with high levels of corruption—one aspect of weak governance—performed even worse, at 67 percent moderately satisfactory or better.[11]

Agriculture projects were less likely to achieve their objectives in countries with weak governance.

Unfortunately, governance tends to be weakest where the public sector is most needed to support agricultural development. The recent WDR on agriculture (World Bank 2007b) found that governance problems are particularly pronounced in agriculture-based countries, which include some of the lowest-income countries. Governance problems are a major reason why many recommendations in the 1982 WDR on agriculture could not be implemented (World Bank 2007b).

In countries with significant governance problems, the Bank has often attempted to work directly with communities, using a CDD approach. In Nigeria, consistently ranked at or close to the bottom in international comparisons of corruption, IEG's recent CAE noted that although the Bank's strategic objective was to support agricultural intensification and diversification, this support depended on the resolution of fiduciary issues related to earlier Bank investments in Nigerian agriculture. "In light of the failure to resolve these issues, the Bank decided to use a CDD approach to address the issues of agricultural productivity and rural service delivery by preparing the second [currently active] Fadama project" (IEG 2008j, p. 49). The IEG-IFC Nigeria Country Impact Review found that IFC could not engage in the country because of governance issues that negatively affected the business environment. However, CDD investments in rural areas do not always give priority to agricultural development.[12]

> In countries with significant governance problems, the Bank has often attempted to work directly with communities by using CDD projects.

Although IFC's strategies call for policy and regulatory dialogue with government, it has not made significant contributions in this area. IFC strategies state that it is well prepared to contribute to the improvement of regulatory frameworks, land and trade policy, research, and extension, based on its core competences—knowledge, innovation, and the business enabling environment (appendix box D.1). However, it has not done so for two reasons. First, IFC has made minimal use of Business Enabling Environment and Infrastructure advisory service projects linked to agribusiness investments.[13] Second, it has made limited use of its leverage as a part of the World Bank Group, as discussed later in this chapter. These issues

could also explain why IFC has had limited success in moving forward in Sub-Saharan Africa. In addition, IFC has been inconsistent in its treatment of market distortions driven by taxes and export bans in Argentina.[14]

Factors Specific to the World Bank Group

Institutional issues within the Bank Group have also influenced the outcomes of World Bank Group interventions. These include the availability of appropriate skills to support clients effectively, the extent of coordination among different sector units or departments and parts of the World Bank Group, the effectiveness of aid coordination with donors, and the quality of M&E systems. The ability to integrate cross-cutting institutional priorities, such as gender equality and environmental sustainability, has also had implications for agricultural lending.

Bank Performance: Quality at Entry and Quality of Supervision

IEG and QAG data show that Bank projects in Sub-Saharan Africa that were focused primarily on agriculture performed below the Bank-wide average on quality–at-entry ratings (tables 4.2 and 4.3). A review of 12 of these projects found that an overly ambitious project design relative to country capacity was the most important reason for the low rating. These and similar projects in other agriculture-

TABLE 4.2	Ratings Reflecting Performance of the Bank, by WDR Typology and Region							
	Agriculture-focused projects				Nonagricultural projects			
	IEG, Bank supervision		IEG, quality at entry		IEG, Bank supervision		IEG, quality at entry	
Category	N	Percent rated satisfactory	N	Percent rated satisfactory	N	Percent rated satisfactory	N	Percent rated satisfactory
WDR typology								
Agriculture-based	29	**69**	29	62	239	**82**	249	**67**
Transforming	43	88	45	76	305	87	320	80
Urbanized	19	**95**	21	62	364	**93**	389	**83**
Region								
Sub-Saharan Africa	27	**70**	27	**56**	256	**78**	265	**67**
East Asia & Pacific	16	**94**	17	76	133	88	140	81
Europe & Central Asia	25	**100**	25	80	274	**92**	287	**84**
Latin America & Caribbean	11	82	12	**92**	254	**94**	277	**84**
Middle East & North Africa	8	63	8	50	79	89	82	73
South Asia	14	79	14	64	94	86	94	78
All	101	83	103	70	1,090	88	1,145	79

Sources: World Bank data and evaluation calculations.

Note: The numbers in bold are statistically significantly different from the mean of all projects. IEG Bank supervision and quality at entry are rated separately in ICR Reviews, and together make up the Bank performance rating. When quality at entry and Bank supervision are compared across agriculture-focused projects and the nonagriculture projects, both ratings are statistically significantly lower for the former. Across WDR typology, Bank supervision ratings are lower in the agriculture-based economies for the agriculture-focused projects compared to nonagriculture projects.

TABLE 4.3 Quality Assurance Group Ratings for Quality at Entry and Quality of Supervision of Bank Agriculture-Focused Projects, by Typology and Region

	Percent rated satisfactory on QAG QAE ratings						Percent rated satisfactory on QAG QSA ratings			
	N	Adequacy of lessons of experience	N	Adequacy of country and sector knowledge	N	Appropriateness of arrangements for evaluating impact and measuring outcomes	N	Sound design at entry	Borrower commitment	Staff continuity
WDR typology										
Agriculture-based	16	**63**	12	**75**	15	**40**	10	**50**	70	**90**
Transforming	31	**94**	28	93	31	**71**	24	75	71	100
Urbanized	14	**100**	12	**100**		71	7	**100**	71	100
Region										
Sub-Saharan Africa	17	**71**	14	**79**	16	56	11	64	**45**	**91**
East Asia & Pacific	11	**100**	11	100	11	64	8	75	75	100
Europe & Central Asia	16	88	14	88	16	**50**	10	**90**	**90**	100
Latin America & Caribbean	6	100	5	100	6	83	3	67	100	100
Middle East & North Africa	9	89	7	100	9	78	5	**40**	60	**80**
South Asia	8	100	7	100	8	75	7	86	86	100
All	67	88	58	91	66	64	44	88	88	98

Sources: World Bank data and evaluation calculations.

Note: Bold numbers are statistically significantly different from average of the rest. QAE = quality at entry; QSA = quality of supervision assessment.

based economies were also less likely to be rated satisfactory on appropriateness of arrangements for evaluating impact and measuring outcomes (table 4.3). Data from QAG also show lower ratings for Sub-Saharan Africa and agriculture-based economies on some aspects of quality at entry, such as adequacy of reflection of lessons of experience and adequacy of country and sector knowledge (table 4.3).

> Bank agriculture-focused projects in Sub-Saharan Africa were below the Bank average on quality at entry and on quality of supervision.

IEG and QAG data also indicate that the agriculture-focused projects in Sub-Saharan Africa and agriculture-based economies performed below average on quality-of-supervision ratings (tables 4.2 and 4.3). Of the nine projects that were rated unsatisfactory on supervision in agriculture-based economies (mostly in Sub-Saharan Africa), inadequate skill mix and shortage of sector specialists were noted as concerns in about half of them. Rapid turnover of staff, poor M&E, and inadequate attention to pertinent issues were some of the other concerns noted. QAG data also show lower ratings for agriculture-based economies on some aspects of quality of supervision (table 4.3).

The agriculture-focused projects were less successful and had lower Bank performance ratings than nonagricultural projects Bank-wide. The former category also had lower IEG Bank supervision ratings in the agriculture-based economies (see note in table 4.2).

Staff Skills

The Bank's human resources data show a decline in technical staff in agriculture and rural development. Figure 4.2 shows the overall trend in staff mapped to the ARD Network and its distribution among generalist and technical staff. Between 2000 and 2006, the years for which data are available, the number of technical staff trended downward. The decline in technical skills was most pronounced in Sub-Saharan Africa (figure 4.3). However, the overall extent of Bank focus on agricultural productivity does not appear to be directly linked to the number of technical skills (comparing figures 4.4 and 4.5).

Staff skills are likely to affect project design and outcomes. QAG data, for example, indicate that projects rated unsatisfactory on supervision-staff skill mix were less likely to have satisfactory outcome ratings (appendix table D.5) than other projects. Consultants with technical expertise (often Bank Group retirees or experts from other agencies, such as the FAO Cooperative Program) cannot substitute for staff in all functions; the most important are task management,

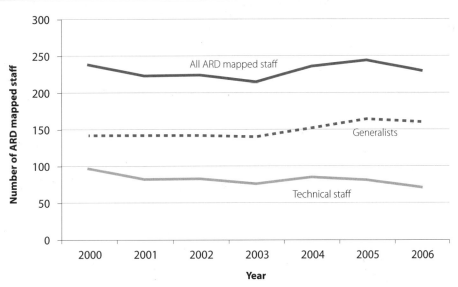

FIGURE 4.2 Trends in Agriculture and Rural Development Staff: Total, Generalists, Technical

Source: World Bank human resources data.

Note: Technical staff include, among others, soil scientists and forestry experts and extension, livestock, agribusiness, and irrigation specialists. Generalist staff include, among others, operations officers, economists, and rural development specialists.

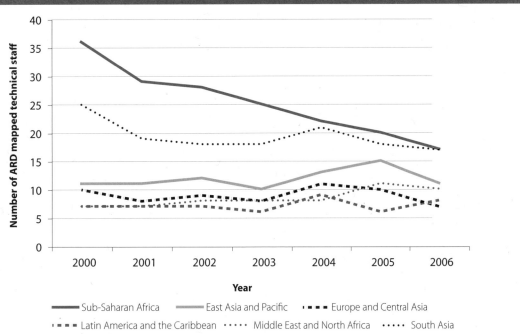

FIGURE 4.3 Trends in Technical Staff, by Region

Source: World Bank human resources data.

Note: Technical staff include, among others, soil scientists and forestry experts and extension, livestock, agribusiness, and irrigation specialists. Generalist staff include, among others, operations officers, economists, and rural development specialists.

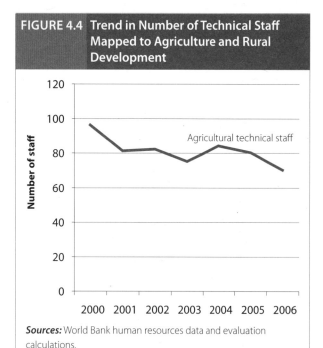

FIGURE 4.4 Trend in Number of Technical Staff Mapped to Agriculture and Rural Development

Sources: World Bank human resources data and evaluation calculations.

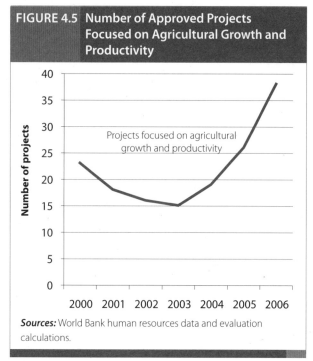

FIGURE 4.5 Number of Approved Projects Focused on Agricultural Growth and Productivity

Sources: World Bank human resources data and evaluation calculations.

continuous client dialogue, and mentoring of new hires (junior and middle level).

There has been a decline in technical staff in agriculture and rural development.

Country directors interviewed for this evaluation raised concerns about staff skills in the sector, including analytic, policy, and client interaction skills. Many emphasized that the skill level necessary to effectively engage with the clients is thinner in the agricultural sector than other sectors. In response to a question about support from sector teams, about half the country directors interviewed expressed some dissatisfaction with the quality of sector support. Specific issues raised included the "lack of skills among agricultural staff to support the sector in an imaginative way," "limited capacity to apply a cross-cutting view," "failure to replace senior, experienced agricultural staff," and "the difficulty to bring in new staff due to the Bank's Human Resources system." Country directors also underlined the need for policy and public finance skills to engage strategically with borrowers in difficult environments. It should also be noted, however, that a number of the country directors commended the advice received from specific agricultural staffers.

Insufficient skills have reduced IFC's opportunity to deliver operational additionality and resulted in a more reactive business development process. IFC's average annual commitments to agribusiness roughly quintupled, from $128

million in fiscal 1998–2000 to $592 million in fiscal 2007–calendar 2008, after remaining relatively flat in fiscal 2001–04. Meanwhile, the number of personnel in CAG only doubled (appendix figure D.1), from 27 people at headquarters[15] in fiscal 2001 to 52 people at headquarters and 15 people in country offices[16] in fiscal 2009. At the same time, only a small number of F&A projects—24 percent, or 32 projects—were expected to address client knowledge and skills (that is, operational additionality; appendix table D.11).

Insufficient skills have reduced IFC's opportunity to deliver operational additionality.

These results were confirmed by IEG evaluation work that found that agribusiness projects lagged behind the rest of IFC on knowledge and innovation. Though the lower additionality may be partly explained by the standardized production technologies and business models typical of the F&A subsectors, and by the capacity of IFC's larger clients to master them, the shortage of industry knowledge in IFC has also been a factor. To increase the impact of its operations in the sector, IFC would require an increase in CAG staff or more efficient investment processes, or both.[17]

The small number of industry specialists retained by CAG and the lack of industry-specific expertise among advisory and Environmental and Social Development Department staff has prevented IFC from consistently

making more meaningful contributions to its clients.[18] This is evident in IEG interviews and in the human resource data. First, industry, technical, and market expertise have been limited and dispersed among industry specialists and economists embedded in investment departments, consultants hired by the advisory teams, and policy specialists working in the Foreign Investment Advisory Services (FIAS).[19] CAG[20] has had, on average, only three industry specialists[21] and one economist over the review period. Other IFC departments along the agribusiness supply chain have only had a few industry specialists (for example, Global Manufacturing Services had a food retail specialist). Second, advisory services and FIAS expertise is even more limited and loosely coordinated with the specialists in investment departments. Third, coordination among these three sources of industry expertise was limited and, according to IEG interviews, confusing to IFC's staff and clients. Furthermore, no network links agribusiness supply-chain specialists across IFC departments, probably because no potential synergies were expected along the supply chains.[22]

> Recent decentralization efforts risk
> exacerbating the skills issues.

Recent decentralization efforts run the risk of exacerbating skills issues. Despite decentralization efforts, CAG's business development process still appears to be more reactive, and staff seem to perceive that organizational incentives favor repeat and larger businesses. A number of recent clients[23] have indicated that they had approached IFC with business proposals (instead of the proposals being initiated by IFC), although the rationale for IFC's Global/Local[24] Initiative (including clustering and the IFC 2010 Initiative) was to position IFC closer to the country and regional markets in order to proactively reach new clients and better serve existing ones. That said, some staff from IFC Regions mapped to CAG are progressively providing part-time support for development and portfolio supervision (and to a lesser extent for transaction processing).[25]

Furthermore, some clients reported that they are now dealing with a larger number of investment staff based in various offices around the world, though they had expected to deal with fewer IFC staff based in their country offices.[26] Looking forward, IEG interviews suggest that these initiatives, intended to increase local presence and brand recognition, may overstretch CAG's already limited technical expertise. In addition, investment officers in country offices appear to report now to one or two extra managers (the investment manager or portfolio cluster managers) in addition to their four traditional managers: the country, industry, and portfolio managers and the industry director. The recent IFC 2013 Initiative[27] is expected to address these organizational issues.

Interdepartmental and Bank-IFC Coordination

Inadequate coordination among the Bank's sector units is a recognized problem. As noted in chapters 1 and 3, a multifaceted approach to development of the sector requires

---

BOX 4.1 IMPROVING COORDINATION BETWEEN THE TRANSPORT AND AGRICULTURAL SECTORS: AN EXAMPLE FROM AZERBAIJAN

The Bank's roads portfolio is assisting Azerbaijan in a major, long-term investment program to upgrade the country's highways. The ongoing Highways II Project (fiscal 2006, IBRD loan plus additional financing in fiscal 2008 and 2009) is providing $675 million. The emphasis is investment in major highways, although about 3 percent of funds go to rural roads.

The agricultural sector would be a beneficiary of such highway projects through reduced costs of transporting inputs and agricultural produce. Yet agricultural development does not appear to have been systematically considered in the planning and implementation of the road rehabilitation program. No sector work was done to assess the roads program in an economywide strategy or to identify road priorities in rural areas. While the government has a list of medium-size and access roads for upgrading, there is no evidence of rigorous analysis to determine how road segments should be prioritized.[a]

Finally, while the Highway Project Unit mentioned "consultation" with the First and Second Agriculture Credit and Development Project units, such interactions are informal and not a structural part of decision making. And the Bank's Azerbaijan highways and rural teams did not have systematic interactions, though they are in the same department.

Source: Azerbaijan country study.

a. A recent development in the appraisal document (May 2009) for the Second Additional Financing for the Second Highway Project notes that the project would select connecting roads for rehabilitation based on the combination of cost-effectiveness and consumer surplus approaches. While this is a promising step, it is still too early to tell how it is being implemented.

that Bank sector units such as transport, finance, and agriculture and rural development approach the agricultural sector in a coordinated manner. Previous evaluations and an ARD survey have documented a lack of such coordination. *World Bank Assistance to Agriculture in Sub-Saharan Africa: An IEG Evaluation* (IEG 2007j) noted that overall coordination between the transport and agricultural sectors was inadequate to strategically develop rural roads. IEG's *2006 Annual Review of Development Effectiveness: Getting Results* (IEG 2006a) noted that the Bank's matrix management structure does not encourage staff to work across sectoral boundaries. ARD's survey on the Agriculture and Rural Development Agenda (World Bank 2005c) reported on concerns among country directors about the lack of interaction between staff from other departments under the matrix management system and the "narrow subsectoral view" taken by many ARD specialists. Inadequate attention to coordination with agricultural sector issues in financial sector projects was raised in chapter 3.

> Inadequate coordination among the Bank's sector units is a recognized problem.

The country studies further document inadequate internal coordination within the Bank. The Azerbaijan country study found that Bank projects tend to operate in "silos." Project managers of even closely related projects are reported to have minimal interaction. Box 4.1 provides one example. The India country study found collaboration between sectors in some projects but not in others.[28] It noted the specific effort that had been made to coordinate irrigation and agricultural activities.

> IFC also has interdepartmental coordination issues and lacks a cross-department strategy that covers the full supply chain.

The creation of the Sustainable Development Network[29] in January 2007 was intended help improve coordination. However, at an IEG session at ARD Week in 2009, Bank staff raised concerns about the inadequate participation of agricultural staff in supervision missions for irrigation projects following the formation of the network. An examination of the staff composition of supervision missions for 26 projects (half approved before and half after 2007) found somewhat declining participation by agricultural specialists, though it is too early to draw a firm conclusion, since many projects are still active.

Interdepartmental coordination issues also exist in IFC, which lacks a cross-department strategy[30] that covers the supply chain from inputs and farms to markets, pro-cessors, retail stores, and consumers.[31] It is challenging for CAG to tackle supply-chain issues when that responsibility is shared by seven investment departments,[32] five advisory business lines,[33] and the World Bank.

IFC investment departments have been working globally in various subsectors of the agribusiness supply chain without a strategic approach to supply chains at the country and regional levels. For example, IFC has invested in Peru in agricultural production, processing, and marketing; input handling, warehousing, distribution, and forwarder services; food processing; and financing.

But all these investments have been developed by various IFC departments without significant coordination with CAG.[34] Worldwide, non-CAG agribusiness investments rose from 26 percent of total agribusiness commitments ($134 million) in fiscal 1998–2000 to 52 percent ($1,581 million) in fiscal 2007–calendar 2008 (appendix table D.12). They generally focused on trade finance during that period, which accounted for 76 percent of all non-CAG commitments. Before 2007, non-CAG investments had focused on retail, infrastructure, information technology, and rural telecommunications. Interviews with IFC's personnel confirm that most of the non-CAG investments have been developed independently of the CAG operations.

IFC's stated objective to link more F&A investments with advisory projects has not been achieved. Indeed, since fiscal 2007 the F&A investment commitments not linked to advisory services have been growing faster than those that are linked. CAG advisory-linked investments committed since fiscal 2007 represent only 8.6 percent of all its projects, or 7.8 percent of its commitments. In contrast, 28 percent of the F&A investment projects (17 percent of commitments) have been linked to advisory service projects over the review period (appendix table D.13). A recent IEG report found that between 2006 and 2008, some 30 percent of all IFC advisory projects were tied to existing investments (IEG-IFC 2009).

> IFC's objective to link more food and agriculture investments with advisory projects has not been achieved.

Coordination between the World Bank and IFC was limited during the evaluation period, despite an increasing emphasis on coordination in their strategy documents.[35] A review of the closed projects supported by the World Bank found little coordination with IFC, and the country studies reveal that relations between the Bank and IFC staff were piecemeal and not systematically coordinated. Where there were complementary operations, they seem to have come about by coincidence rather than as the result of coordinated planning. For example, in Peru a small but growing IFC agribusiness portfolio has assisted in the rapid growth of agricultural exports from the coastal area. These activities seemingly complement Bank projects that have also supported this growth (Irrigation Subsector Project, 1997, Agriculture Research and Extension II, 2006). In India, collaboration between the World Bank and IFC mostly occurred where specific projects offered opportunities. This was the case with the Bank's Uttar Pradesh Water Sector Restructuring Project (fiscal 2002), under which a sugar mill that received IFC funding was involved in providing agricultural services in irrigation areas covered by the project.

Coordination between the Bank and IFC was limited, despite increasing emphasis on coordination in their strategy documents.

Interaction between IFC and the World Bank seems to have been particularly limited in policy dialogue and regulatory reform. IEG interviews reveal that World Bank staff have perceived FIAS, the joint WB-IFC-MIGA Investment Climate Department, as an IFC advisory function. Furthermore, IFC's investment officers have not seen policy and regulation as challenges that can be addressed with the World Bank. The promotion of mango exports from Mali is an example of an opportunity the World Bank Group initially missed but later addressed, though there is still room for some improvement, according to IEG interviews.

In 2005 the World Bank approved a project supporting growth in the export of mangoes and other crops.[36] Discussions between the World Bank and FIAS led FIAS to produce (through an IFC advisory service project) a general report on investment opportunities in these crops, in support of the Bank project, in 2008 (FIAS 2008). IFC has recently approved a second phase of the same advisory service project,[37] and the Bank expects to conduct several forums jointly with FIAS to attract private investors to the sector.

In another example, in Argentina, where IFC has its second-largest agribusiness portfolio, the World Bank is working with the government in a program that seeks to improve existing agribusiness-related infrastructure and research and extension (Programa de Servicios Agricolas Provinciales, approximately $900 million). However, there is no interaction about these interventions between the World Bank and IFC country teams in Buenos Aires.[38]

Interaction has been particularly limited in policy dialogue and regulatory reform.

The limited coordination observed could indicate that there is little overlap in the activities supported by the Bank and IFC apart from the Bank's potential to affect the business environment for the private sector. IFC works mainly[39] with the private sector and is limited in its ability to work directly with small producers because of economies of scale. Hence, as noted in chapter 2, IFC has been absent from many of the agriculture-based economies and the poorer countries in Sub-Saharan Africa where there are fewer large private sector actors. IFC has focused on several relatively large investments in Europe and Central Asia and Latin America and the Caribbean. Both these factors—working only with the private sector and the threshold arising from transaction costs—limit the overlap with the Bank's work in the agriculture sector, particularly with IDA lending.

Where the two organizations overlap they have sometimes competed rather than collaborated.

Where the two organizations do overlap, as in the provision of rural finance, there has sometimes been competition rather than collaboration. A recent project assessment of the Third Rural Finance Project in the Philippines (IEG 2009l) found that "turf" issues affected the approval of the Fourth Rural Finance Project.[40] The assessment noted the need for better coordination between the two organizations and resolution of disputed areas of assigned responsibilities before preparation work on a potential project. The assessment noted: "The Guidelines may need tightening, particularly with respect to mode and timing of coordination and respective policy roles and perhaps even some arbitration process. The Guidelines still seem to leave considerable discretion to staff" (p. 20).

For all of these reasons, areas for collaboration need to be carefully identified based on the expected benefits to both the institutions and their clients. A review of the 25 World Bank projects with the largest agribusiness components found that the Bank is largely supporting the enabling environment for private sector development. IFC is bound by the local business environment, though it does have the Business Enabling Environment and Infrastructure advisory business lines, which could be leveraged by the Bank. In that sense, the work between the Bank and IFC could be more complementary than competitive, and coordination would be important in ensuring greater synergy.[41] Greater collaboration could also be built through support to public-private partnerships.

It appears that efforts at Bank-IFC collaboration in the agricultural and agribusiness sector have picked up re-

cently, which bodes well for the increased emphasis on agriculture going forward, provided there is adequate follow through. The May 2008 Country Partnership Strategy for Brazil mentioned preparation for increased coordination between IFC and the Bank. Likewise the Tamil Nadu Irrigated Agriculture Modernization and Water Bodies Restoration and Management Project (fiscal 2007) sought strengthened collaboration with IFC in the marketing sector. A recent Operations Policy and Country Services (OPCS) document (World Bank 2009d) notes the effort made in the context of the Tajikistan CAS to place IFC in the lead to design the World Bank Group Program for one of three pillars—"Improve business opportunities in rural and urban areas."

Efforts at collaboration in the sector have picked up recently.

Collaboration also appears to be emerging in response to the global food crisis. For example, in Indonesia, the Bank and IFC are reported to be completing a feasibility study on a crop insurance pilot for small-scale maize farmers. Other recent areas of collaboration include the World Bank Group Agriculture Action Plan 2010–12, the World Bank Group's Africa Agriculture-Agribusiness Strategy; advisory work for governments on large-scale land acquisition, within the up-

Photo courtesy of Curt Carnemark/World Bank.

coming sector study on the World Bank rules of engagement in large-scale commercial agriculture; and coverage of rural small and medium-size enterprises by the *Doing Business* report (with financial support from the Gates Foundation). Additionally, CAG represents IFC in the ARD Sector Board, and every quarter it reports jointly with the World Bank to the President of the World Bank Group on the state of the combined response to the food crisis (CAG's report includes the agribusiness activities by IFC's Oil, Gas, Mining, and Chemicals; Global Manufacturing and Services; and Global Financial Markets Departments).

Coordination with Other Donors

A large number of donors provide support to agriculture, particularly in poorer countries. Several donors have increased their support to the agricultural sector in recent years, and there are several new players raising the challenges to effective coordination. These challenges arise because donors are accountable to constituencies in their home countries, which gives them an incentive to support projects and programs that can be attributed to them. This can lead to duplications, fragmentation, and sometimes contradictory donor interventions (World Bank 2007b).

Cofinancing is viewed as one approach to donor coordination. About a quarter of Bank projects in the closed evaluation portfolio were cofinanced. The share contributed by other donors in cofinanced projects was, on average, about one-third of total actual project cost.[42] But there are typically a large number of active donors in a country beyond those cofinancing Bank projects.

The global food crisis has led to renewed interest in partnerships, collaboration, and harmonization. Several IEG reports have drawn attention to the challenge of establishing country leadership of the aid-coordination process (IEG 2001b, IEG-IFC 2003), and PRSP processes have helped somewhat in this regard (IEG 2004d). In addition, since its launch in 2004, the Global Donor Platform for Rural Development has attempted to draft a set of "Joint Donor Principles" for effective assistance in agriculture and rural development (GDPRD 2009). The Global Food Crisis Response Program launched by the Bank Group in May 2008 was articulated in coordination with the United Nations' High-Level Task Force on the Global Food Security Crises. The Bank has also created a new Multi-Donor Trust Fund to facilitate the involvement of partners to support the program.

The global food crisis has led to renewed interest in partnerships, collaboration, and harmonization.

The country studies found that the number of players is smaller in the transforming and urbanized economies than in agriculture-based settings. In Egypt, the country study found that the number of players in agriculture is limited, with the International Fund for Agricultural Development, FAO, and the Bank being the most active. In India, the government decided to limit the number of international development organizations that are active in the country, so the number of other donors that are active in agriculture is relatively small.

The number of players is smaller in the transforming and urbanized economies than in agriculture-based economies.

There are some states where other development partners implement the same types of projects as the Bank. FAO organizes a forum regularly for information exchange among donors engaged in agriculture in India. In China, the Bank's collaboration with other donors was mostly at the individual-project level. In both Azerbaijan and Bulgaria, the country studies found that there was informal collaboration between Bank staff and other donors, based on interpersonal relations rather than formal, structured mechanisms established between the institutions. In Azerbaijan, the country study noted that although the Bank does invite development partners to some key meetings, regular meetings for coordination and planning between agencies would be helpful. In Bulgaria, the most important donor partner is the European Union (EU), and while the Bank did not have a formal mechanism to coordinate with the EU, interviews with staff indicate that coordination was strong in the form of regular meetings and participation in Bulgaria's own donor coordination meetings.

Those poorer economies that are heavily dependent on donor support generally have weaker capacity to coordinate.

The agriculture-based and poorer economies are heavily dependent on donor support and generally have weaker capacity to coordinate. In Nepal, an agriculture-based economy heavily dependent on donor assistance, the country study notes the dominance of donors in designing and implementing programs. In Ethiopia, almost 20 donors were supporting more than 100 agricultural projects in 2005, with high transaction costs and duplication of effort (World Bank 2007b, p. 257). In Nicaragua, significant progress was achieved in formalizing a coordinated approach among donors through the establishment of the sectorwide approach

PRORURAL, which was based on the 2005 Paris Declaration on Aid Effectiveness. But in practice, apart from the Common Fund (Fonda Comun, a smaller group consisting of the aid agencies of the Netherlands, Sweden, Switzerland, the United Kingdom, Norway, Finland, Demark, and Luxembourg), which does meet frequently and coordinates the lending programs of its members, other donors tend to work independently of each other and provide mostly project-based aid. The Bank, too, decided not to pool its lending with other donors in support of PRORURAL, which led to considerable loss of credibility for the institution in the country. In Malawi, inconsistent donor policies and government priorities are reported to have redesigned national food security programs several times (World Bank 2007b). The Mali 2007 CAE (IEG 2007f, p. 10) is instructive in its finding in this regard:

> Still, significant challenges remain to turn Mali's development effort away from being a largely donor-driven process and make it government-owned. One is that the government's capacity to lead the partnership process is weak. The need to spend resources and show results pushes many donors to rely on international expertise instead of investing in local capacity-building. Another difficulty is the presence of a growing number of "non-traditional" donors which operate outside the normal coordination mechanisms, and which provide Mali with large, though frequently unspecified, sums not always on concessional terms. These include China, India, Libya, Saudi Arabia and a number of other countries from the Islamic world. There is also the issue of the Millennium Challenge Corporation (MCC) which plans to invest about $461 million in Mali over a five-year period starting in late 2006 to help stimulate private sector growth. It is not clear, however, that the MCC has adequately taken into account Mali's limited absorption capacity and other donors' assistance programs.

IFC is involved in several of the World Bank's partnerships, but has few opportunities to cofinance with other private sector development institutions.

IFC, as a member of the World Bank Group, is in one way or another involved in several of the World Bank's partnerships with other donors. Beyond this, IFC is working with the International Labour Organization to improve labor practices in Sub-Saharan Africa and is exploring opportunities for synergies with the African Development Bank.

There are few opportunities for IFC to cofinance clients with other private sector development institutions. IFC is the only global investor working with the private sector. In addition, agribusiness investments are typically smaller than those in other sectors. The two top investors are IFC, with a 45 percent market share, followed by the EBRD, with 29 percent. In consequence, only in exceptional cases has IFC coinvested in agribusiness clients with other private sector development institutions, mostly with the EBRD in Europe and Central Asia.

Cross-Cutting Institutional Priorities

The Bank has cross-cutting institutional priorities, such as ensuring environmental sustainability, reducing gender disparity, and maintaining a strong focus on development results. How do these relate to the World Bank Group's activities in the agricultural sector?

Environmental Sustainability

The World Bank's requirement that each project be screened for its environmental impact has been particularly important for the design and implementation of agricultural interventions, because crop production can negatively affect the natural resource asset base on which it depends. Agricultural cultivation can lead to aquifer depletion, habitat encroachment, and misuse of pesticides. It has transformed between one-third and one-half of the earth's land surface, and current practices are threatening long-term sustainability (United Nations 2002).

In the World Bank's evaluation portfolio, about 70 percent of the project appraisal documents mentioned the need to balance agricultural growth and productivity with considerations of environmental sustainability. A review of 51 IEG agricultural project assessments[43] found

positive environmental impact arising from some Bank projects. For example, the China Tarim Basin Project (fiscal 1998) has helped rejuvenate the grasslands and trees in the Tarim Basin, which has contributed to the return of wildlife to the area. Similarly, the Morocco Water Resources Management Project (fiscal 1998) has helped stabilize degraded hillsides. IEG's recent water evaluation (IEG 2010f) also found that watershed management projects with a primary concentration on land management improvements contributed to environmental restoration, though environmental benefits arising from these projects were usually not quantified.

The review of project assessments did not find evidence of failure to comply with environmental safeguard policies, though it should be noted that IEG's recent safeguard evaluation found that reporting on safeguard compliance in project M&E is weak. That said, the safeguard evaluation also found that projects in the agriculture sector do as well as projects in other Bank sectors on environmental and social safeguards. In the review of 51 project assessments, a negative environmental impact was found in only 1 project, in China.[44] In two other projects, in Niger and China, the evaluation questioned the safeguard category applied to the project when it was designed.[45] In four others,[46] project assessments raised environmental concerns but did not document a negative impact.

An assessment of the likely future contribution of recent Bank-supported agricultural projects to adaptation and mitigation of climate change found that the projects have the potential to improve the readiness of countries to deal with the effects of climate change. An analysis of all 212 projects with agricultural activities approved during the period fiscal 2006–08[47] found that 49 percent of the projects included at least one component that could help in adapting to or mitigating the effects of climate change,[48] with a like-

---

BOX 4.2   IFC—SUPPLY-CHAIN ISSUES NEAR THE AMAZON BIOME

A soy-processing and farming project approved in 2004 has faced serious concerns that its expanding IFC-supported activities were contributing to the rapid encroachment into the Amazon biome. The crucial question has been how, beyond the project's own boundaries, supply-chain sustainability is or is not being advanced. In response to the concerns, the client has ensured that forested areas on its own farms and those of pre-financed outgrowers remain. However, the client purchases nearly half of its soy needs from local markets, and it cannot control the practices of these other farmers. For this reason, the client, NGOs, and IFC are working with the soy commodity roundtable and follow the Greenpeace initiative of declaring a moratorium on soy purchases from all deforested land (regardless of whether conversion to agriculture was legal). The results of the initiative are yet to be assessed.

Another IFC investment near the Amazon biome, approved in 2007, that also faced serious environmental concerns has been a failure . IFC withdrew in June 2009 from its investment in this client (a beef- and hide-processing project) because it had built new slaughterhouses (in breach of loan agreements) without convincing evidence on the sustainability of the supply chain from cattle farmers to slaughterhouses.

Source: IEG.

ly greater contribution to adaptation than to mitigation.[49] The Bank could make a substantial further contribution through focused ESW that discussed the links between climate change and agricultural production, because interviews with country directors for this evaluation indicated that many country clients do not to realize the potential impact of climate change on agricultural production. Such ESW is emerging in the World Bank—for example, the report on *Low-Carbon Development: Latin American Responses to Climate Change* (World Bank 2009f).

Within IFC, CAG and the Environmental and Social Development Department are jointly responsible for the environmental sustainability of supply chains. IFC agribusiness projects generally include industrial facilities with limited environmental and social risks (for example, air and water pollution and waste management), but their supply chains pose special concerns. Since 2006, CAG and the Environmental and Social Development Department have addressed sustainable supply-chain management through IFC's Performance Standards,[50] which have been viewed as a key component of IFC's additionality in the sector. The Performance Standards have typically ensured that F&A supply chains do not lead to adverse environmental impacts in areas legally defined as protected (as required in Performance Standard 6, biodiversity conservation), and that child and

forced labor are not a factor (as required in Performance Standard 2,[51] labor and working conditions). Nevertheless, to expand IFC's environmental and social requirements to all material biodiversity aspects can have positive environmental and social ripple effects.[52] Prior to the Performance Standards, supply-chain issues were not addressed in IFC's safeguard policies. For example, mixed results were produced by two F&A projects near the Amazon biome, which were appraised before Performance Standard 6[53] came into effect (box 4.2).

Furthermore, supply-chain sustainability is becoming part of the strategies of global corporations, and consumers in developed countries are keen to purchase goods produced by wholly sustainable F&A supply chains. Therefore, there are also sound business reasons for IFC clients to respond to this preference by ensuring not only the sustainability of their own operations, but also those of their suppliers.

Inadequate management of agribusiness supply-chain issues has been evident in a number of complaints submitted to the compliance advisor and ombudsman by individuals or communities affected by various IFC investments. Out of the 31 projects that received compliance advisor and ombudsman complaints between 1999 and 2009, 6 (19 percent) were in the agribusiness sector, includ-

India

India's Diversified Agricultural Support Project (fiscal 1998) reported that more than one-third of the 20,000 self-help groups formed were women's groups. Similarly, under the Sodic Lands Project, 7,200 women's self-help groups were formed (World Bank 2008m, p. 44). The livelihoods projects have a strong focus on gender, and forming women's self-help groups is one of their main activities. The National Agriculture Technology Project (fiscal 1998) addressed gender issues in extension by including women (30 percent of the membership) in the Agriculture Technology Management Agency (ATMA) governing bodies. Interview information indicates that there was considerable resistance to addressing gender issues when ATMA was introduced. To address this problem, the project concentrated on areas where women play an important role, such as livestock and horticulture. However, interviews with agricultural department staff in charge of extension suggest that despite increased awareness, the attention to gender issues is rather low. In the Tamil Nadu Irrigated Agriculture Modernization and Water Bodies Restoration and Management Project, gender issues were addressed by the agricultural research team from the Tamil Nadu Agricultural University, which developed a rotary weeder suitable for female laborers.

China

In China, though the available information from irrigation projects does not provide strong evidence that gender concerns were systematically addressed, the livestock projects and the poverty-focused projects have a better record. Under the Coastal Resource Management Project, more than 40 percent of participants in project infrastructure and 50 percent of trainees were women; in addition, more than 20 percent of female representatives in village implementation groups were involved in the project. Also, 28,000 women were hired by seafood processing plants during the project, contributing to the economic empowerment of women throughout the project area. Under the Smallholder Cattle Project (fiscal 2000), the China Women's Federations at all levels participated in the selection of project households, and priority was given to women-dominated households. Slightly more than half (54 percent) of trainees were women, compared with a target of 40 percent. The project processing plants employed approximately 1,000 women for beef grading and product packaging.

The primary gender impacts of the Gansu and Inner Mongolia Poverty Reduction Projects (fiscal 1999) were twofold. First, the construction of drinking water facilities in project villages is reported to have reduced the workload of women, permitting time for more economically productive activities. The number of households within 100 meters of a drinking water source increased by 14.5 percent in project villages, against an increase of only 7.2 percent in nonproject villages. Second, project areas witnessed pronounced growth in school completion rates for girls.

Sources: Country studies; World Bank 2008m.

---

ing 4 pre–Performance Standard and 2 post–Performance Standard projects (such as a palm oil producer[54] in Indonesia), a slightly higher proportion than the 13 percent share of the agribusiness sector in all nonfinancial sector projects in the period. Addressing the environmental impacts of agribusiness remains a crucial challenge, especially in light of the heightened concerns about the environmental destruction resulting from weak regulations.

> Inadequate management of agribusiness supply-chain issues in IFC investments has been evident in complaints submitted to the compliance advisor and ombudsman.

Although IFC was an early supporter of commodity roundtables, they have not yet developed internationally accepted standards for supply-chain certification. Commodity roundtables attempt to engage all actors in the industry in agreeing on a set of standards for sustainable production.[55] IFC staff have participated from the outset in roundtable meetings, and IFC advisory services have funded some commodity roundtables' activities,[56] which have included environmental audits of biodiversity, energy, and water conservation. Additionally, IFC is providing financial support (through grants funded by the Global Environment Facility) to the newly created Biodiversity and Agricultural Commodities Program for including biodiversity issues in roundtable discussions. IFC has recently provided financial support to the Business and Biodiversity Offsets Program, a partnership of NGOs, the private sector, and governments working on market-based mechanisms to support biodiversity conservation.

Furthermore, Performance Standard 6 requires, where possible, that the client demonstrate sustainable management of renewable natural resources[57] through an appropriate system of independent certification. Therefore, commodity

TABLE 4.4   Percentage of Projects Rated Good for Monitoring and Evaluation in the ICR Review Database

Category	Closed agriculture-focused projects with information on M&E	
	Number of observations	Percentage with good M&E
Region		
Sub-Saharan Africa	16	25
East Asia & Pacific	14	57
Europe & Central Asia	14	29
Latin America & Caribbean	10	30
Middle East & North Africa	6	33
South Asia	10	30
All Regions	70	34
WDR typology		
Agriculture-based	15	**13**
Transforming	36	**47**
Urbanized	**12**	**33**

Sources: World Bank data and evaluation calculations.

Note: M&E quality is considered good for projects rated substantial or high for M&E by IEG and for projects where comments in the ICR review database indicated that M&E quality was substantial, high, or good. M&E quality was not considered good where it was rated modest or poor and where the comments indicated that it was poor, weak, or not good. Projects for which the ICR review had no comments or ratings for M&E were excluded. The numbers in bold are statistically different from the mean for all Regions.

roundtables need to develop rigorous certification systems to prove sustainability of the F&A production along the entire supply chain. Once they are developed, IFC could refer to roundtable certification in project-specific environmental and social requirements, and possibly in the future update of Performance Standard 6, and promote their use as global standards to seek to shift F&A commodity markets toward sustainable production.

Reducing Gender Disparity

Women are important agricultural producers and agents of food and nutritional security. In many parts of the world, such as Sub-Saharan Africa, they provide about half of the agricultural labor force and produce most of the food crops consumed by the family (IEG 2007j; van Koppen 2009). However, social structures and norms constrain their access to agricultural services, extension, credit, and land (World Bank, FAO, and IFAD 2009).

The World Bank adopted a gender and development mainstreaming strategy in 2001 and issued a revised Operational Policy and Bank Procedures statement in 2003. A recent IEG evaluation (IEG 2010b) found that the Bank's progress in mainstreaming gender issues in lending

TABLE 4.5   Association between Project Outcome and Quality Assurance Group Ratings Related to M&E

Rating category	Percentage with ratings of satisfactory among agriculture-focused projects in the evaluation portfolio assessed for quality of supervision	
	IEG outcome rating	Sustainability rating
Quality or candor of reporting		
0	50	30
1	85	76
Performance and progress monitoring		
0	43	33
1	80	67

Sources: World Bank data and evaluation calculations.

Note: QAG quality of supervision assessment rating: 0 = unsatisfactory; 1 = satisfactory.

operations and analytical work has been mixed, though it recognized the success of ARD's recent *Sourcebook on Gender in Agriculture* (World Bank, FAO, and IFAD 2009) in increasing attention to gender issues in agriculture. A recent joint study by the World Bank and IFPRI across three countries—Ethiopia, Ghana, and India—also reports similar mixed findings on mainstreaming (World Bank and IFPRI 2010).

This evaluation looked at gender integration at the project and country sector levels. In the sample portfolio examined by IEG, more attention was given to gender issues during design than during implementation.[58] Of the 11 countries covered by case studies, only 2—India and China (box 4.3)—recorded achievements on gender in the agricultural sector (such as enhanced women's access to extension services and credit). In the other nine, the attention to gender was limited. In some of these countries, such as Guinea, achievements on gender in the sector were limited because agricultural lending itself was very limited. In Peru, project documents acknowledged slow achievements on gender, but with some recent improvement in progress. In Azerbaijan, where women are about half of the country's agricultural labor force, the Bank's program was largely neutral (project components neither promoting nor discouraging women's participation). In Mali, which has one of the worst and most persistent gender situations in the world, the attention to gender issues in a variety of projects was too limited to have a significant effect, and it was also minimal in Egypt, Jordan, Nepal, and Nicaragua.

IFC is tracking the gender impact of its agribusiness operations but needs to broaden its range of indicators.[59] Unlike other IFC units, the tracking of gender in agribusiness is limited to the number of women employed. Preliminary figures show that 14 percent of client companies' employees in agriculture and forestry are women. This is an inadequate indicator. Other gender indicators—such as female wages, number of females in top management or on boards of directors, and local purchases from female-owned businesses—are not yet covered by CAG.

Monitoring and Evaluation and Data Systems

The World Bank emphasizes the importance of monitoring progress toward achieving project objectives as part of day-to-day management as well as the advantages of learning lessons from evaluations of selected projects.[60] All closed projects in the evaluation portfolio were examined for their M&E. M&E performance of the agriculture-focused projects is shown in table 4.4. About a third of the projects had good M&E.

By Region, Sub-Saharan Africa had the lowest percentage of projects with good M&E, and East Asia and the Pacific had the highest (table 4.4). Bivariate analysis found that projects with good M&E quality were more likely to have satisfactory outcome and sustainability ratings (appendix table D.4). A challenge in the subsector analysis, reported in chapter 3, was the difficulty of attributing results to Bank efforts because of M&E shortcomings. A review of lessons in the ICR review database for all closed projects with some agricultural activities also found that M&E is more frequently mentioned than any other issue in ICR reviews, and the need to improve M&E was noted in about one-third of the projects.

The Sub-Saharan Africa Region had the lowest percentage of projects with good M&E, East Asia and the Pacific had the highest.

QAG data on quality of supervision show a high positive association between "good" M&E and project performance (table 4.5). QAG assessments have noted numerous problems with M&E, including lack of baseline indicators, delays, lack of specific modalities for community-level M&E, vague performance indicators, overly optimistic status assessments, lack of application of indicators following a restructuring, and simply insufficient attention overall to M&E.

Problems with project M&E were also flagged in the completion reports for closed projects in the sample portfolio. The most commonly mentioned issues were design flaws, such as project development objectives that are too broad to be measured, poorly designed indicators (including missing indicators, mismatch between objectives and indicators, and output indicators that do not measure outcome), lack of baseline data, and lack of a management information system. Weak country capacity was mentioned as a problem in Afghanistan, Georgia, Ghana, and the Philippines.

Problems with project M&E were also flagged in the completion reports for closed projects.

The main weaknesses found in the country studies included design of agricultural productivity indicators, questions about the generally satisfactory carry-through of objectives into indicators, delays, and weaknesses in livestock indicators. The India country study found weak M&E across all irrigation projects. Baselines were rarely collected before the project began. While some indicators, such as crop production, tended to have existing baseline data,

data on beneficiaries and incomes were collected only after the project had started. In some cases (as in China) there were methodological problems, such as choice of control area and lack of randomness in sampling respondent farmers.[61] The country study for India suggests that Bank staff do not have adequate incentives to ensure adequate data generation to achieve a results-based focus. In India, the U.K. Department for International Development has proposed a technical group to try to improve the standards of M&E in agriculture.

The China country study found that most projects monitored a reasonable range of indicators related to agricultural production, poverty, and environmental goals. However, baselines were not established, which made it difficult to measure incremental gains. Moreover, it was difficult to access the survey reports on which project evaluations were based. For one illustrative case, the Sustainable Coastal Development Project (fiscal 1998), the ICR did not indicate that there was a baseline. The reviewers found that comparing the figures in the ICR with growth rates nearby suggested that the project beneficiaries did not perform any better than nonproject comparators. The ICR found that no arrangements appeared to have been made for an M&E system to be designed or for a baseline to be carried out.

The Bank's data systems have weaknesses that constrain strategic planning of support for the agricultural sector. As noted in chapter 3, from the Bank's coding and monitoring systems it is difficult to track the total amount of support from the institution for land, rain-fed agriculture, and rural finance activities. DPLs present their own M&E challenge. The poor quality of outcome indicators in agriculture-focused DPLs makes it difficult to assess the program's influence on the performance of the sector. Thirty-five percent of the interventions reviewed did not have performance indicators. Of those that did, only half included quantitative indicators, but the link between the intervention and the agricultural result was often tenuous.

Weaknesses in the Bank's data systems constrain strategic planning of support for the agriculture sector.

IFC's M&E activities have expanded significantly in the past few years; however, they have not captured the effects on poverty of IFC's agribusiness investments. In late 2005, IFC launched a Development Outcome Tracking System, coordinated by a newly established Development Effectiveness Unit, to monitor the development performance of its projects. In 2006, IFC began piloting Project Comple-

tion Reports, an evaluation system for advisory services. The impact evaluation of an asparagus producer discussed in chapter 3 shows that tools other than those typically used for M&E are needed to understand the poverty effects of agribusiness investments.

IFC has expanded its M&E activities, but a recent evaluation identified some shortcomings.

A recent IEG evaluation (IEG-IFC 2008a) found that IFC should achieve better coverage of its portfolio in reporting on results and improve the quality of data in M&E. These recommendations also apply to CAG's operations. IFC's M&E activities broadly cover the range of its activities, from project-level M&E to aggregate performance monitoring by country, region, sector, industry, and client group. The results of these activities (and those discussed earlier) are intended to generate learning that feeds into IFC's strategies and ongoing operations and to provide a basis for rewarding good staff performance, with the ultimate goal of stronger long-term development results.

Summary and Implications Going Forward

The lessons of experience reveal a number of factors that affect investment outcomes and that the World Bank Group will need to consider carefully as it expands its focus on agriculture.

- **First, outcomes of both Bank and IFC interventions are inevitably affected by borrower commitment and capacity—capacity to implement projects, to set strategies, to design and implement policies for a good business environment, and to fund and use research, including that generated in international institutions such as those of the CGIAR. In countries with relatively weak capacity, the Bank Group needs to set realistic objectives, while also allocating resources for capacity building. Where commitment is weak, the Bank may need to limit lending while using ESW to highlight issues and raise awareness, and IFC, in coordination with the Bank, may need to step up advisory services to build capacity in the private sector.**

- **Second, World Bank Group institutional factors—such as staff skills and the extent of coordination among sector departments, between the World Bank and IFC, and with other donors—can also affect project outcomes. Both the Bank and IFC will need to focus on staff capacity in agriculture, and greater efforts are needed to exploit synergies among sectors (such as agriculture, finance, and** transport) and within the World Bank Group (for example, in helping clients improve the business environment or in setting up public-private partnerships in infrastructure or agricultural research). Given the enormous challenges in the agricultural sector, it will also be critical to deepen donor coordination efforts, as has been a focus in the context of the global food crisis. Building on the gains achieved by transforming and urbanized economies, the World Bank Group could help facilitate partnerships between countries to encourage south-south knowledge exchange.

- **Two of the World Bank Group's strategic priorities— environmental sustainability and gender mainstream-** ing—have strong linkages with agriculture and deserve careful attention in investments and analytic work.

- **Strong M&E—including realistic objectives, well-specified performance indicators, good baseline data, and timely monitoring—is an important ingredient in ensuring good outcomes and needs to be combined with strong and consistent supervision.** Expanded use of impact assessment can promote learning and inform the design of future interventions. Better data are also needed to track Bank Group activities in agriculture as a whole and in various subsectors, because current coding and tracking systems are inadequate for that purpose.

Chapter 5

Summary and Recommendations

This evaluation of agriculture and agribusiness addresses a critical challenge for the World Bank Group.

The recent food and financial crises, the continuing challenges of poverty reduction, and the expected doubling of food demand by 2050 have put increasing pressure on developing countries to enhance agricultural productivity, and on the World Bank Group to assist proactively in that effort. During the decade from June 1997 to July 2008 (fiscal years 1998–2008), the period coved by this evaluation, the World Bank Group provided $23.7 billion in financing for agricultural and agribusiness activities in 108 countries, as well as nonlending services and support for important global and regional programs and partnerships in the agricultural sector.

Only a share of World Bank interventions that included support for agricultural activities focused on improving agricultural growth and productivity in poor, agriculture-based economies. The Bank's strategy shifted in the early 1990s from a narrower focus on agriculture to a broader one encompassing poverty and rural development, and this led to a broader definition of objectives in lending to the rural sector and a less direct focus on food production and agricultural productivity. IFC investments focused on agribusiness growth and development but were concentrated primarily in urbanized and transforming economies in Latin America, Eastern Europe, and Central Asia.

Project ratings against stated objectives in World Bank agricultural lending have been about the same as those for lending in other sectors, with Europe and Central Asia performing better than average and Sub-Saharan Africa notably worse. Similarly, IFC investments in agribusiness had above-average development outcome ratings in Latin America and the Caribbean and Europe and Central Asia but have been weak in Sub-Saharan Africa. Many countries—particularly transforming and urbanized economies—have benefited from the exposure to improved management practices and production technologies that come with Bank Group interventions. But it has been more difficult for countries in Sub-Saharan Africa to benefit commensurately. Not only is the environment for agricultural development less favorable in Sub-Saharan Africa's agriculture-based economies—with poor road and market infrastructure, underdeveloped financial sectors, difficult business environments, a shortage of indigenous entrepreneurs, and higher weather-related and disease risks—but country capacity and governance have been weaker as well.

Sustainability of World Bank-supported activities remains a concern. Efforts at cost recovery for extension services and irrigation have generally met with limited success, and financing of research remains problematic, particularly in agriculture-based economies. Inadequate government budgets and lack of skilled personnel have contributed to weak follow-up of Bank activities in these settings.

Institutional limitations within the World Bank Group have inhibited its contribution to agricultural development. Until recently the Bank and IFC lacked a focused strategy that prioritized agricultural growth and productivity. Potential synergies among sectors such as transport, finance, and agriculture and between the World Bank and IFC have not been fully exploited. Skills gaps need to be addressed. These factors may have contributed to the recognized weaknesses in World Bank project outcome and project quality at entry and supervision in Sub-Saharan Africa and may also constrain implementation of the recent Agriculture Action Plan 2010–12. IFC has also lacked an adequate number of industry specialists and a network linking agribusiness supply-chain specialists across departments to match the rapid growth in its agribusiness commitments. Recent IFC decentralization efforts risk exacerbating this situation by further stretching scarce industry expertise.

M&E continues to be weak in both investment lending and DPLs, and the Bank's data and coding systems do not effectively track all agricultural activities. Reporting on outcomes and results is incomplete in both the Bank and IFC, which constrains project effectiveness and inhibits institutional learning.

Analytical work is a critical tool to identify issues and inform both policy advice and financing. The Bank's agricultural AAA has been of sound quality, and the lending that it informed had better outcomes, yet little agriculture-related AAA has been done in some IDA countries over several years. IFC advisory services have been largely supply driven and have lacked a focus on relevant agribusiness subsectors. Few advisory services leveraged outcomes by linking with investments.

Finally, gender and environment are cross-cutting World Bank Group priorities, and agriculture and agribusiness could make a strong contribution to gender empowerment and environmental sustainability. In the Bank, greater attention has been paid to gender issues during the design of projects than in their implementation. In IFC, the tracking of gender in agribusiness is limited to the number of women employed, which is an incomplete indicator. With regard to environment, projects supported by the Bank appear to be in compliance with the Bank's environmental safeguards, but reporting on safeguards within the institution is weak. IFC's Performance Standards have had limited range and could go further along the full supply chain. Inadequate management of agribusiness supply-chain issues has been evident in the number of complaints submitted to the compliance advisor and ombudsman addressing the concerns of individuals or communities affected by various IFC investments.

Recommendations

The overarching recommendation of this review is:

To get the most from recent increases in financing for agriculture and agribusiness, the World Bank Group needs to increase the effectiveness of its support for agricultural growth and productivity in agriculture-based economies, notably Sub-Saharan Africa.

The agriculture-based economies, particularly those of Sub-Saharan Africa, are where the needs are greatest and success has been most elusive. Other countries and Regions also have important needs that the Bank Group should continue to support, given that the increased demand for global food production also has to be met. However, greater effectiveness in the poorest countries is the most critical challenge. The findings of this evaluation point to specific recommendations in three areas.

I. Synergies and complementarities

In the areas that drive productivity, such as irrigation and drainage, agricultural research and extension, access to credit, access to land, transport infrastructure, and the policy environment, complementarities and synergies are key drivers

Photo courtesy of Arne Hoel/World Bank.

of effectiveness. To take better advantage of these complementarities:

1. Step up *IFC's engagement in Sub-Saharan Africa,* including supporting public-private partnerships and adapting the integrated trader-processor model for more effective use with small-to-midsize indigenous companies in the agriculture-based economies.

2. Set up a *knowledge network* linking agriculture and agribusiness supply-chain specialists across the Bank Group to strengthen communication and collaboration among sector departments within the Bank and IFC, as well as across the Bank Group.

3. Work with partners to ensure that CGIAR research and other *global and regional efforts* are translated into benefits on the ground, and facilitate partnerships among countries to encourage south-south knowledge exchange.

II. Knowledge and capacity building

Experience points to the importance of capacity and how analytical work can highlight issues and raise awareness—particularly when capacity is weak:

1. Ensure sufficient quantity and quality of *Bank AAA and IFC advisory services in agriculture-based economies,* link them closely to lending, and use them to build counterpart commitment and to address constraints along the production chain.

2. Establish mechanisms to confirm ex ante if *project M&E frameworks* are adequate—with clear, relevant, and realistic objectives; a thorough cost-benefit analysis; appropriate indicators; and adequate baseline data.

3. Review the *human resource base and skill gaps* (also in light of the increased lending), and develop and implement a strategic plan to enhance the technical and policy skills of Bank and IFC staff working in the agriculture sector, particularly in agriculture-based economies.

III. Efficiency and sustainability

The impact of increased resource flows into agriculture will depend on the efficiency of resource use and the financial, social, and environmental sustainability of investments:

1. Increase Bank Group support to *medium-term expenditure planning* to help ensure the adequacy of funding for operations and maintenance, and work with clients to ensure *sustainable financing*—including cost recovery where appropriate—for irrigation, transport, and research and extension services.

2. Take stock of experience in water management and crop technologies in *rain-fed areas* to inform future Bank Group support.

3. Ensure that *gender concerns* are adequately mainstreamed and monitored in World Bank and IFC agriculture operations.

4. Expand the application of *IFC Performance Standards* to material biodiversity and other environmental and social aspects along the supply chain for primary suppliers (and for secondary suppliers, to the extent the client has leverage), and enhance IFC support to the development and application of internationally accepted commodity certification systems.

Appendixes

Evaluation Methodology and Instruments

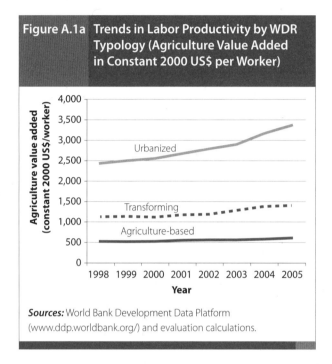

Figure A.1a Trends in Labor Productivity by WDR Typology (Agriculture Value Added in Constant 2000 US$ per Worker)

Sources: World Bank Development Data Platform (www.ddp.worldbank.org/) and evaluation calculations.

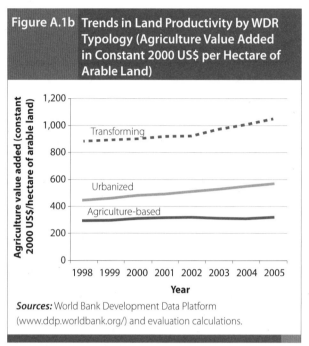

Figure A.1b Trends in Land Productivity by WDR Typology (Agriculture Value Added in Constant 2000 US$ per Hectare of Arable Land)

Sources: World Bank Development Data Platform (www.ddp.worldbank.org/) and evaluation calculations.

World Bank Methodology

The evaluation considers the Bank's International Development Association (IDA) and International Bank for Reconstruction and Development (IBRD) lending and nonlending activities over the 11-year period from fiscal 1998 to 2008. It seeks to answer the following evaluation questions:

- *Strategy:* What strategic approach has the World Bank taken toward agriculture and agribusiness, how has it evolved, and how has it influenced the choice of activities?

- *World Bank engagement and results:* What have been the trends in World Bank lending and investment and nonlending and advisory activities? What have been the results of these activities at both the project and country levels?

- *Drivers of results:* What sector-specific constraints has the World Bank faced, and how have they been addressed? To what extent do institutional factors, whether in client countries or in the World Bank Group, contribute to outcomes?

In seeking to answer these questions, the study used several sources of information and analyses: a portfolio review, country reviews, literature reviews, stakeholder interviews, and additional analyses, including regression analysis and impact assessments.

Portfolio Review
Population Analysis

The population analysis was done on three sets of data: the evaluation portfolio, including the closed evaluation portfolio; Quality Assurance Group quality-at-entry (QAE) and quality-of-supervision (QSA) assessments on all projects in the evaluation portfolio; and analytical and advisory activity (AAA) products.

The evaluation portfolio: IEG identified a portfolio of 633 projects funded by the IBRD and IDA that were approved between fiscal years 1998 and 2008 and had agricultural activities. The agricultural activities were identified according to the codes used by the Agriculture and Rural Development Department (ARD) to report on lending trends in the sector. The agriculture codes are grouped within two sectors:

agriculture, fishing, and forestry; and industry and trade. The subsectors under the former are: agricultural extension and research; animal production; crops; forestry; irrigation and drainage; and general agriculture, fishing, and forestry. Subsectors under the industry and trade sector are agricultural marketing and trade and agro-industry. The portfolio, referred to as the *evaluation portfolio*, covers 101 countries and includes 5 regional projects (all in Sub-Saharan Africa).

The evaluation portfolio was analyzed for trends in lending (for both investment operations and development policy loans [DPLs]) and project objectives (see appendix B: "Analysis of Objectives"). Project Appraisal Documents or Staff Appraisal Reports were used as the source for statements of objectives.[1] Among the objectives coded were: increasing agricultural growth and productivity; improving food security, promoting economic growth, and development in general; reducing poverty; improving macroeconomic stability; promoting environmental sustainability; promoting private and public sector roles; promoting local community participation (through demand-driven approaches, for example); providing infrastructure and social services; providing credit and rural financial services; and mitigating the impacts of drought, floods, and other emergencies.

Appendix table B.2 provides frequencies of the objectives identified and the extent of their overlap with the objective of increasing agricultural growth and productivity. Appendix table B.3 includes details on distribution of the evaluation portfolio by Region, country-income level, *World Development Report* (WDR) typology,[2] country capacity, time period, ARD Sector Board or non-ARD sector board oversight, lending instrument type, and percentage of projects aiming to increase agricultural growth and productivity. Appendix table B.4 also provides IEG ratings for projects in the evaluation portfolio that were closed and rated (as of December 2, 2008) and aimed at increasing agricultural growth and productivity.

Subsector analysis was undertaken in six areas—irrigation and drainage, research and extension, credit, land, roads and marketing infrastructure, and market and agribusiness. Subsector analysis involved desk reviews of relevant ongoing and closed projects in the evaluation portfolio and a review of relevant literature, including previous IEG evaluation findings. The work identified patterns in activities, their outcomes, and factors affecting performance in the subsectors. Details on analyses and summaries of results in these subsectors are provided in chapter 3. Appendix C explains how the subsector portfolios were identified.

QAG assessments. Among the 633 projects in the evaluation portfolio, 135 projects were assessed for QAE, and 81

were assessed for QSA by QAG. Sixty-seven of the 135 and 44 of the 81 projects aimed to increase agricultural growth and productivity in their objectives. Appendix tables B.5 and B.6 provide QAG QSA and QAE ratings by category. Appendix tables D.5 and D.6 provide information on the relationship between QAG QSA and QAE ratings and IEG ratings.

Analysis of AAA products. The Bank's database does not have a complete record of all AAA carried out. Hence, the AAA portfolio was identified from three sources. AAA approved between fiscal years 1998 and 2008 was downloaded from the Project Portal on June 4, 2009, using a search for all AAA identified with the major sector "agriculture, fishing, and forestry." These were supplemented with AAA identified by IEG's economic and sector work (ESW) study (IEG 2008n) that were managed by the ARD Sector Board and were approved between fiscal years 2000 to 2006. The final step added AAA with agricultural codes approved between fiscal 2000 to 2008, which were downloaded from the World Bank's database on April 2, 2009. This provided a AAA cohort of 1,432 products, of which 1,110 were active or closed and 322 had a status of "dropped" or "n.a." Descriptions of the AAA products and details on costs associated with them are in appendix B. Results of AAA analyses are mostly reported in chapter 2.

Sample Analysis

A randomly selected sample of 84 closed and ongoing projects was intensively reviewed to get detailed information on the various factors of performance. The sample of 84 projects is referred to as the *sample portfolio*. Specific care was taken to account for supplemental projects in the drawing of the sample. During fiscal 1998–2008, 633 agricultural projects and 47 supplemental loans or credits were approved. The World Bank's data system does not recognize supplemental loans or credits as additional projects when tallying the total number of projects approved in a given year, but the amount of supplemental loans or credits approved in each fiscal year is counted toward the total commitment amounts recorded for that year.

To select the sample, IEG included supplemental loans or credits as projects if the parent project was approved before fiscal 1998. If the parent project was approved during the study period (1998–2008), it was already part of the evaluation portfolio, so the supplemental was not counted as an additional project. This exercise yielded a total of 645 projects from which the sample of 84 projects was drawn, the sample size necessary for a 95 percent confidence level and 10 percent margin of error.[3]

Documents Reviewed for the Sample Portfolio

A template was developed to systematically extract information from the sample portfolio to address the evaluation questions. Several documents were used as sources of information, including Project Appraisal Documents, Implementation Completion Reports (ICRs), Public Expenditure Reviews, Country Assistance Strategies (CASs), Poverty Reduction Support Papers (PRSPs), and CAS Completion Reports.

Project analysis. A detailed analysis of the Project Appraisal Documents or Staff Appraisal Reports of the 84 sample projects was conducted to answer specific questions as laid out in a template. Some of the questions in the template included whether analytical work, policy dialogue, technical advice, project lessons, and the like on agricultural issues informed project design and whether improved technologies were disseminated. A detailed systematic analysis of the ICRs of the 38 projects among the 84 that had ICRs (as of July 29, 2008) was also conducted.

Country-level analysis. The Bank's CASs for the 51 countries served by the sample portfolio were examined to assess the Bank's strategic approach to the development of the agricultural sector in client countries. Two CAS documents were reviewed for each country (based on availability) to trace changes over time: the one closest to the start date of the evaluation period, fiscal 1998, and the one closest to the end date of the evaluation period, fiscal 2008. A total of 93 CASs were reviewed. In addition, 33 CAS reviews that covered the evaluation period were also reviewed to extract information relevant to the evaluation questions.

Counts of the documents reviewed for the evaluation portfolio are presented in table A.1, and counts of the documents reviewed for the 51 countries in which the sample portfolio falls are presented in table A.2. Table A.3 presents country-level reviews.

AAA analysis. A sample of AAA was evaluated for quality and effectiveness in the context of the country case studies done as background for the evaluation. Results of this analysis are in appendix B ("Main Findings from IEG Assessment of AAA on Agriculture in 14 Countries").

DPL analysis. A random sample of 10 of the 22 countries that had agriculture-focused DPLs was used to analyze DPL performance. The review examined whether the agricultural reforms in these DPLs influenced agricultural growth and productivity.

Country Reviews

Country reviews involved country case studies and assessments of CAEs and project assessments.

Country studies. Eleven countries were selected as country case studies for the evaluation. Nine of these were randomly selected, and two of the largest Bank borrowers in the agricultural sector (India and China) were purposely selected. Countries where there has been very limited Bank intervention (lending and AAA), countries with populations below a million, and countries with active conflict were excluded when making the random selection. The nine countries were: Azerbaijan, Bulgaria, Egypt, Guinea, Jordan, Mali, Nepal, Nicaragua, and Peru. The 11 country studies represent more than one-third of total World Bank agricultural lending during the evaluation period.

A template was developed and applied across all countries to extract information systematically on the evaluation questions. Each country study entailed an intensive desk review of relevant Bank and non-Bank literature, the portfolio of Bank agricultural projects, CASs, PRSPs (where relevant), and eco-

TABLE A.1	Documents Reviewed for the 101 Countries Covered by the World Bank Evaluation Portfolio by WDR Typology				
WDR typology	Objective analysis on the evaluation portfolio	Regression analysis on the closed evaluation portfolio	QAE carried out on projects	QSA carried out	AAA[a]
Agriculture-based	203	74	34	24	203
Transforming	231	88	60	37	353
Urbanized	129	52	24	14	206
Not classified	70	29	17	6	101
Total	633	243[b]	135	81	1,110

Source: World Bank data.

a. AAA products are from any country/Region where the AAA was carried out and not only from the 101 countries in the evaluation portfolio.

b. Twelve of the 243 were "not rated" on outcome because they had either been canceled or did not become effective. Regression analysis was carried out on the 231 rated projects.

TABLE A.2 Documents Reviewed for the 51 Countries Covered by the Sample Portfolio by WDR Typology

WDR typology	Appraisal documents	Completion reports	Public Expenditure Review	CAS	PRSP	CAS Completion Report	Poverty Assessments
Agriculture-based	20	11	21	30	13	9	17
Transforming	36	13	17	30	9	13	25
Urbanized	16	9	10	24	3	8	20
Not classified	10	5	6	9	4	3	7
Total	84	38	54	93	29	33	69

Source: World Bank data.

nomic and sector work (ESW). Field visits were carried out in eight of the countries, and for the remaining three countries, telephone consultations with field-based Bank staff and other relevant stakeholders were carried out.

Country Assistance Evaluations and Project Assessments. Fifty-seven Country Assistance Evaluations (CAEs) and 51 project assessments of agricultural projects were reviewed by IEG. Thirty-eight of the project assessments covered projects during the evaluation period (fiscal 1998–2008); six project assessments covered projects outside the evaluation period, but they were part of three cluster assessments that included projects within the evaluation period. The three cross-country cluster assessments, which covered 10 projects with specific themes—research and extension, rural finance, and farm restructuring—were conducted in fiscal 2008 to gather project-specific experiences. These included: the Latin America and the Caribbean Agricultural Research and Competitive Grant Schemes Cluster Project Performance Assessment Report (IEG 2009i), which included an assessment of the Nicaragua Agricultural Technology and Rural Education Project (C3371), Peru Agricultural Research and Extension Project (L4519), Colombia Agriculture Technology Development Project (L3871), and the Brazil Agricultural Technology Development Project (L4169); the Europe

and Central Asia Cluster Project Performance Assessment Report (IEG 2010a), which included an assessment of the Armenia Agricultural Reform Support Project (C30350 and C30351) and the Georgia Agricultural Development Project (C29410); and the Rural Finance Cluster Project Performance Assessment Report, which included assessments of the Moldova Rural Investment and Services Project (C36680 and C36681), Romania Rural Finance Project (APL) (L46020), Vietnam Rural Finance Project (C2855), and Philippines Third Rural Finance Project (L4413).

Literature Reviews

Bank and non-Bank literature was reviewed to gain an understanding of the complexities of the agricultural sector in various countries and Regions and the Bank's role. The review was also used to support findings emerging from the portfolio review and the county reviews. This evaluation also drew on sector and subsector reviews and progress reports by ARD, as well as a previous ARD interview survey of country directors (World Bank 2005c).

The evaluation also built on previous IEG studies including: *World Bank Assistance to Agriculture in Sub-Saharan Africa* (IEG 2007j); *Country Assistance Evaluation Retrospective: OED Self-Evaluation* (IEG 2005a); *The Development Potential of Regional Programs: An Evaluation of World Bank*

TABLE A.3 Country-Level Reviews and Other IEG Country-Level Reports by WDR Typology

WDR typology	Country studies	Project Performance Assessment Reports	CAEs	Nª
Agriculture-based	3 (Guinea, Mali, Nepal)	22	17	19
Transforming	3 (China, Egypt, India)	19	22	22
Urbanized	4 (Azerbaijan, Bulgaria, Jordan, Peru)	8	14	17
Not classified	1 (Nicaragua)	2	4	6
Total	11	51ᵇ	57	64

Source: World Bank data.

a. N = Total number of countries where relevant fieldwork was carried out by IEG in the context of various reports over the evaluation period (fiscal 1998–2008).

b. Additional Project Performance Assessment Reports were reviewed for subsector reviews when available.

Support of Multicountry Operations (IEG 2007b); *A Decade of Action in Transport: An Evaluation of World Bank Assistance to the Transport Sector, 1995-2005* (IEG 2007a); *Using Knowledge to Improve Development Effectiveness: An Evaluation of World Bank Economic and Sector Work and Technical Assistance, 2000–2006* (IEG 2008n); *An Impact Evaluation of India's Second and Third Andhra Pradesh Irrigation Projects: A Case of Poverty Reduction with Low Economic Returns* (IEG 2008e); *Using Training to Build Capacity for Development: An IEG Evaluation of Project-based and WBI Training* (IEG 2008o); *Environmental Sustainability: An Evaluation of World Bank Support* (IEG 2008b); *Climate Change and the World Bank Group, Phase I: An Evaluation of World Bank Win-Win Energy Policy Reforms* (IEG 2009c); *Water Management in Agriculture: Ten Years of World Bank Assistance* (IEG 2006e); *Water and Development: An Evaluation of World Bank Support, 1997–2007* (IEG 2010f); *Evaluating a Decade of World Bank Gender Policy, 1990–1999* (IEG 2005b); *Gender and Development: An Evaluation of World Bank Support, 2002–08* (IEG 2010b); *The World Bank's Country Policy and Institutional Assessment: An Evaluation* (IEG 2010g); and *Impact Evaluations in Agriculture: An Assessment of the Evidence* (IEG 2010c).

Stakeholder Interviews

Bank staff and managers, both at headquarters and field-based, were interviewed during country studies and project assessments on various aspects of the Bank's support to the agricultural sector in client countries. In addition, 23 previous and current country directors covering 28 randomly selected countries responded to a structured interview designed to get their feedback on the Bank's contribution to agricultural development and the institutional factors that determine it.

Additional Analysis

To assess performance of the evaluation portfolio, all closed projects that were rated and posted by IEG as of December 2, 2008,[4] were added, resulting in a total of 243 projects in the *closed evaluation portfolio*. IEG ICR reviews of the closed evaluation portfolio were reviewed. Of the 243 projects, 231 had a valid rating on overall outcome and 202 projects had a valid rating on sustainability and risk to development outcome. The data were matched with Country Political and Institutional Assessment indicators and country income-level data (based on the 2007 gross national income [GNI] per capita, calculated using the *World Bank Atlas* method).[5] Regression analysis was undertaken on the rated projects in the closed evaluation portfolio to explain differences in overall outcomes and sustainability (see appendix table D.1 for details on variables used in the regressions, tables D.2 and

D.3 for regression results, and table D.4 for bivariate relationships between several explanatory variables and project outcomes). Impact studies of the Peru Irrigation Subsector Program (fiscal 1997) and the Malawi Community-Based Rural Land Development Project (fiscal 2004) were also carried out and informed this evaluation (IEG 2009f, g).

In addition, the evaluation drew on the Agricultural Science and Technology Indicators of the Consultative Group on International Agricultral Research (CGIAR) to measure agricultural technical capacity within countries. These indicators were particularly useful in exploring the differences in technical capacity among agriculture-based, transforming, and urbanized economies. World Bank ARD human resources data were also analyzed for reporting on staff skills.

IFC Methodology

The methodologies are based on five building blocks.

Portfolio Review

To describe International Finance Corporation (IFC) agribusiness operations and to evaluate sector strategies, IEG has adopted an agribusiness supply-value chain approach from farmers to markets. IEG has also rated and evaluated in-depth IFC projects in the food and agriculture sector (F&A), carried out by the Agribusiness Department (CAG) and by its joint ventures with other IFC investment departments. For projects earlier than 2002, this report has also drawn on earlier IEG-IFC work, because it had evaluated projects approved in fiscal 1990–2001.

The supply-value chain evaluation approach is a concept from business management that was first described and popularized by Michael Porter in his 1985 bestseller, *Competitive Advantage: Creating and Sustaining Superior Performance*. In a supply-value chain of activities, products pass through, gaining some value. The value-chain constitutes a good base for identifying the most critical constraints preventing the materialization of development opportunities in a holistic way, and not merely shifting the constraint from one link to another. This evaluation approach is similar to the one used by IEG-IFC in 2003 and by the EBRD (2008).

The investment projects in the F&A sector have been desk reviewed using IEG's Mini Expanded Project Supervision Report (Mini XPSR) framework, and IEG's additionality framework. IEG's risk intensity framework has been used to determine how the risk profile of the investment projects in the F&A sector has shifted over the review period (IEG-IFC 2008c). There were 275 stand-alone and parent projects; repeat and subprojects such as B–loans (see endnote 13), loan increases, risk management/swaps, and rights issues were not counted as stand-alone or parent projects. Of these 275 projects, 152 were evaluated in this study; the lending amounts of the repeat and subprojects were aggregated into the parent project. Included in the 152 evaluations were 42 projects that were evaluated for risk intensity and IFC's additionality, although it is too early to evaluate them in depth. The balance of 123 projects was not evaluated because 40 Africa Enterprise Fund and Small Enterprise Fund projects had already been evaluated by IEG and discontinued, and because 83 projects were either non-F&A projects or not carried out by CAG joint ventures.

To compare the performance of the F&A projects with the performance of IFC projects worldwide, IEG has drawn on the results of the XPSRs. IFC's evaluation system for investment operations is based on self-evaluation. Investment staff prepare XPSRs for a random, representative sample of projects. IEG-IFC then undertakes an independent review of the project's performance and the XPSR's assigned ratings (and adjusts them if needed) to ensure that the prescribed evaluation guidelines and criteria are applied consistently.

The advisory services projects have been desk reviewed using IEG's project completion report framework. Because this system was only introduced in 2006, IEG has focused much of its effort to date on the evaluative substance of the project completion reports (IEG-IFC 2009), on the sufficiency of evidence, and on the correct application of the rating guidelines (supplemented with selective field validation).

IFC and IEG are working on plans to establish a rigorous advisory self-evaluation system validated by IEG, similar to the one used for investment projects (XPSR system). There were 205 stand-alone advisory service projects over the review period. Of these 205 projects, 81 were not evaluated, because prior to 2006, the records of advisory service projects were not systematically collected or stored centrally. Therefore, IEG has evaluated 124 projects in the aggregate: 97 projects were evaluated for this specific agribusiness study and 27 projects had been previously evaluated by IEG within a pilot program across business lines. To compare the performance of the agri-

business advisory projects with the performance of the IFC advisory projects worldwide, IEG has drawn on the ratings of a previous IEG evaluation (IEG-IFC 2009).

Counts of the documents reviewed for the 42 countries in which the evaluation portfolio falls are presented in table A.4.

Corporate and Sector Strategies

IEG has used expert judgment, in addition to its in-house expertise, to examine the relevance and degree of implementation of the various IFC strategies along the supply-value chain. The team also reviewed project and strategy information and evaluation results produced by other donors (multilateral and bilateral), both information in the public domain and information made available upon request.

To evaluate sector-level performance, IEG also used the established European Bank for Reconstruction and Development (EBRD) Evaluation Department evaluation methodology, which was applied to the evaluation of the EBRD's Agribusiness Operations (OPER No: PE07-378S–June 2008). The methodology has been adjusted by IEG to allow for the equivalence between EBRD's system and IEG's XPSR rating system (following results of joint project evaluation), and for the IFC's sector objectives set out in the agribusiness development plan.

This methodology assesses four components of IFC's performance in the agribusiness sector: relevance, efficacy, efficiency, and role and contribution. First, it assesses relevance by considering the degree to which IFC agribusiness sector investment projects have stated the objectives set out in the agribusiness development plan. Second, efficacy is measured by considering the degree of IFC project-development success achieved in targeting the policy objectives (weighted by the development outcome [DO] rating). Third, efficiency is evaluated by considering the degree of IFC project financial success (weighted by the projects business success rating). Finally, role and contribution are measured by considering the degree of success IFC had in providing value added to its projects (weighted by the role and contribution rating). The IFC investment projects

TABLE A.4	Documents Reviewed for the 42 Countries Covered by the IFC Evaluation Portfolio		
Country typology	XPSRs and minis	Advisory services	Risk intensity
Agriculture-based	12	14	12
Transforming	46	41	46
Urbanized	108	40	108
Not classified	28	30	28
Total	194	125	194

Source: IEG.

were rated in accordance with the following scale: highly successful (1–1.9), successful (2–2.9), mostly successful (3–3.9), mostly unsuccessful (4–4.9), unsuccessful (5–5.9), and highly unsuccessful (6).

Impact Evaluation

The study has carried out an impact evaluation of an IFC investment in an asparagus producer and processor in Peru, to assess its impact on poverty and gender issues. IEG used three different methodological approaches: (i) time trend analysis, which compares the affected districts over time; (ii) industry analysis, which compares the affected industries within relevant districts with the nonaffected industries within the same districts; and (iii) counterfactual analysis (quasi-experimental method), which compares the change in affected districts with those in a set of comparable districts. This is the first time that an IFC investment has been evaluated through quasi-experimental methods.

The evaluation used two sources of information: (i) employment information provided by the client and (ii) data collected annually by the National Institute of Statistics and Information at the individual and household levels. Households from 9 out of the 10 districts involved are represented in the sample. Moreover, the wide data coverage, in terms of locations and survey topics, has allowed IEG to construct a counterfactual scenario, thereby enabling the analysis to compare impacts with and without the project over time. The national poverty line is defined roughly as $1,000 dollars per person per year. However, the range of incomes and expenditures for "nonpoor" is quite large; those directly above the poverty line are still relatively poor. The legal working age in Peru is 16; therefore, the individual-level analysis includes only individuals above the working age.

To evaluate what changes are likely to have been brought about by the asparagus producer, IEG sought to identify through propensity score matching methods the counterfactual districts (control group) that were similar in every important dimension to the districts where the producer was active (treatment group). The counterfactual districts were identified in two steps: (i) the dataset was restricted to districts along the coast and (ii) the dataset was further restricted to districts that were similar in their geography (for example, distance to a river), welfare factors, and labor variables. Subsequent tests have demonstrated that the identified counterfactual district was statistically similar, except for nonpoor nonwage income.[6]

The propensity-score matching method weighs covariates based on how well they identify the set of districts that send workers to the producer. These weights are applied to other districts to identify districts that match the producer with respect to the selected covariates. Statistically, this is done by regressing a binary variable indicating a district that is affected by the firm on the set of district-level characteristics thought to identify such districts. All districts are included in the regression. This regression is done at the district level; each observation represents a district. The estimation includes observations before the previous firm released control of the farm and packing plant, in order to find comparable districts at baseline. The resulting coefficients are then used to predict similarity to the producer's districts to construct a propensity score for all districts. The propensity score is used to match beneficiary districts to the counterfactual districts along key dimensions at baseline. Details on the merits of propensity-score matching and the mechanics of how matches are determined are described in Dehejia and Wahba (2002) and in the seminal work by Heckman, Ichimura, and Todd (1998).

Country Reviews

Owing to the concentrated nature of IFC commitments, seven countries were purposively sampled. The objective was to examine the impact of IFC operations in three

TABLE A.5	Country-Level Reviews and Other IEG-IFC Country-Level Reports by WDR Typology			
Country typology	Country-level reviews	Country Impact Review	Agriculture XPSRs	Total number of countries where relevant field work was carried out by IEG in the context of various reports over the evaluation period (fiscal 1998–2008)
Agriculture-based	2	0	4	2
Transforming	2	4	4	6
Urbanized	2	5	18	7
Not classified	1	0	6	1
Total	7	9	32	16

Source: IEG.

country subsets defined by the intensity of IFC operations: (i) large IFC operations, Argentina and Peru; (ii) small-to-negligible IFC operations, Egypt, Ghana, Nicaragua, and Nigeria; and (iii) midsize IFC operations, India. The study also drew on the most recent IEG country impact reviews of IFC's operations in Indonesia, Nigeria, and Ukraine, as well as on earlier IEG-IFC country evaluations. Table A.5 provides the count of the country-level reviews and other IEG country-level reports.

CAG Human Resource Data

CAG human resource data from 2001 to 2008 were provided by the IFC Human Resources Department and analyzed for trends.

Literature Reviews

IEG reviewed research and databases related to private sector development produced by the World Bank Group, academia, think tanks, and multilateral institutions. IEG also drew on three evaluations of IFC's food and agriculture operations: an evaluation of IFC's investments in the food and agribusiness sector, an evaluation of IFC's experience in the agricultural production sub-sector; and an evaluation of IFC's experience in the agricultural processing and storage sub-sector.

Stakeholder Interviews

The study team has conducted approximately 300 interviews, both in headquarters and in the countries visited, with IFC and World Bank staff, clients (both current and past), donors' representatives (multilateral and bilateral), and representatives of other stakeholders, including the business community, government, and nongovernmental Organizations (NGOs).

Limitations

Although every effort has been made to collect information, certain limitations on study coverage persist, including availability of some information and IEG-IFC's budget for this study. For instance, prior to 2006, advisory service operation records were not systematically collected and stored centrally. As a result, information pertaining to a number of early advisory assignments was collected for this study on a best-effort basis, and evaluative judgments were made based on all available data.

The scope of this study has not included programs that have been previously evaluated by IEG: (i) investments through the Africa Enterprise Fund and the Small Enterprise Fund; (ii) technical assistance provided by the Africa Project Development Facility; and (iii) technical assistance provided by the African Management Service Company. The Africa Enterprise Fund was evaluated by IEG in 2004 with the report "An Evaluation of IFC's Investments through the Africa Enterprise Fund" (IEG-IFC 2004). The Africa Project Development Facility and the African Management Service Company were evaluated by IEG in 2003. Furthermore, the scope of the study has not included other IFC interventions that may have a direct or indirect impact on agriculture, such as infrastructure, gas, mining, and chemicals; financial services; retail; and forestry, unless their focus is on agriculture or agribusiness sectors.

Description and Performance of the Evaluation Portfolio

World Bank Group Lending to Agriculture

TABLE B.1 Total World Bank Lending to Agriculture, 1998–2008

Details of agricultural lending	1998–2008
Total World Bank lending (all sectors, US$ billions)	243.1
Lending to projects with agricultural components (US$ billions)	45.2
Lending to projects with agricultural components (as a percentage of total World Bank lending)	20
Agricultural lending[a] (US$ billions)	18.1[b]
Agricultural lending (as a percentage of lending to projects with agriculture components)	40
Agricultural lending (as a percentage of total World Bank lending)	7

Source: World Bank data.

a. Agricultural activities were identified according to the codes used by ARD to report on lending trends in the sector. "Agriculture" comprises components with any of the following codes: agricultural extension and research; animal production; crops; forestry; irrigation and drainage; general agriculture, fishing, and forestry; agricultural marketing and trade; and agro-industry. Agricultural lending consists of the dollar amounts assigned to these subsectors.

b. An additional $3.8 billion was committed by the World Bank in fiscal 2009.

FIGURE B.1 Trends in World Bank Lending to Agriculture, Fiscal 1998–2008

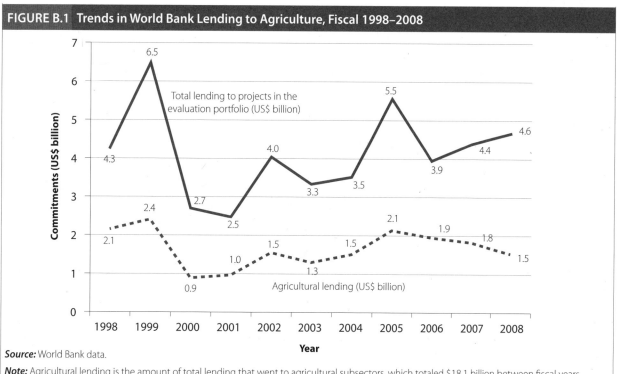

Source: World Bank data.

Note: Agricultural lending is the amount of total lending that went to agricultural subsectors, which totaled $18.1 billion between fiscal years 1998 and 2008.

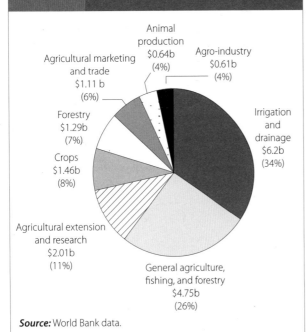

FIGURE B.2a Distribution of Agricultural Lending by Subsector, Fiscal 1998–2008

- Animal production $0.64b (4%)
- Agro-industry $0.61b (4%)
- Agricultural marketing and trade $1.11 b (6%)
- Forestry $1.29b (7%)
- Crops $1.46b (8%)
- Agricultural extension and research $2.01b (11%)
- Irrigation and drainage $6.2b (34%)
- General agriculture, fishing, and forestry $4.75b (26%)

Source: World Bank data.

Note: The commitments exclude those to supplemental projects that are not included in the evaluation portfolio. The definition of agricultural and nonagricultural lending is based on the Bank's formal subsector and sector coding system.

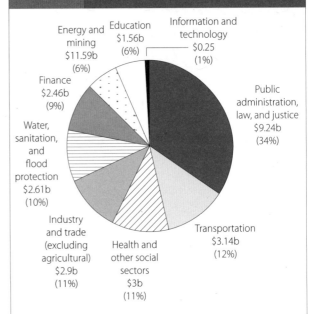

FIGURE B.2b Distribution of Nonagricultural Lending in Projects in the Evaluation Portfolio, Fiscal 1998–2008

- Energy and mining $11.59b (6%)
- Education $1.56b (6%)
- Information and technology $0.25 (1%)
- Finance $2.46b (9%)
- Water, sanitation, and flood protection $2.61b (10%)
- Industry and trade (excluding agricultural) $2.9b (11%)
- Health and other social sectors $3b (11%)
- Public administration, law, and justice $9.24b (34%)
- Transportation $3.14b (12%)

Source: World Bank data.

Note: The commitments exclude those to supplemental projects that are not included in the evaluation portfolio. The definition of agricultural and nonagricultural lending is based on the Bank's formal subsector and sector coding system.

Analysis of Objectives

Objective statements of the 633 projects in the evaluation portfolio were used to identify the largely agricultural projects; that is, the projects that were focused **directly** or **indirectly** on agricultural growth and productivity. The spirit of the objective, whether it could directly or indirectly contribute to agricultural growth and productivity, was taken into account in identifying the projects. The coding was done in the following manner:

Agricultural growth and productivity codes

0. No direct or indirect relationship to agricultural growth and productivity.

1. Directly related to agricultural (crop) growth and productivity.

2. Livestock (including avian-flu projects, pastoral activities, and fodder production).

3. Fisheries and aquaculture.

4. Agriculture and livestock.

5. Contributing to agricultural productivity through the overall program that has an objective of increasing agricultural productivity.

6. Implicitly contributing to agricultural productivity (for example, those aiming to improve agricultural policy).

7. Regain the potential of agricultural sector/restoring and strengthening farming activities.

8. Implicit but not clear if contributing to agricultural productivity; for example, increasing access to productive assets or increasing productive investments or re-establishing production levels, but "agriculture" is not mentioned.

9. Agriculture, livestock, and fisheries or aquaculture.

All projects coded 1, 2, 3, 4, 5, 6, 7, and 9 were included among projects aiming to increase agricultural growth and productivity. Those coded 0 and 8 were excluded. To ensure quality and consistency, all 633 objectives were coded by the same team member. To check whether agricultural productivity projects were coded properly, a random check was done by other team members. The codes were also verified by country study team members for projects in the sampled countries. Objectives of the projects in the sample portfolio of 84 projects were independently categorized by another team member, and provided an additional check since this coding was compared to that carried out on the 633. As chapter 2 showed, the projects that aimed at increasing agricultural growth and productivity had a large share of their commitments (65 percent) in agricultural activities, indicating that they adequately represent the largely agricultural projects. These are referred to as "agriculture-focused" projects in this evaluation.

Projects generally had more than one objective. Other objectives that were coded included:

1. General economic growth or development.

2. Poverty alleviation.

3. Targeting poor or vulnerable groups (such as women, small farmers, and those affected by HIV/AIDs).

4. Environmental sustainability.

5. Food security.

6. Control and mitigation of drought, flood, avian-flu, and other emergencies.

7. Credit, rural finance, and subsidies.

8. Promotion of private and public sector roles.

9. Promotion of local participation (including community demand-driven approaches, promotion of good governance, local capacity building, decentralization).

10. Provision of infrastructure and social services.

Table B.2 shows the frequency of these objectives and extent of overlap with the agricultural growth and productivity objective. When a project had these objectives as well as the objective of increasing agricultural growth and productivity, it was included among agriculture-focused projects. When there was no overlap, the project was considered nonagriculture focused. Distribution of the evaluation portfolio by agriculture-focused projects and nonagriculture focused projects is provided in table B.3. Forty-six percent of the projects in the evaluation portfolio (41 percent in commitments) were agriculture-focused. Figure B.3 shows the trend in percentage of these projects. Tables B.4 and B.5 show the performance of the portfolio based on IEG and QAG ratings for the agriculture-focused projects.

TABLE B.2	Objectives in the Evaluation Portfolio and Their Overlap with the Objective of Improving Agricultural Growth and Productivity					
Objective	Number of projects	Number overlapping	Mean (N=633)	Standard deviation	Correlation coefficient	Percent overlapping[a]
Agricultural growth and productivity	292	292	0.461	0.499	1.000	100
Food security	23	14	0.036	0.187	0.057	61
Credit, rural finance, and subsidies	60	33	0.095	0.293	0.058	55
Promoting private- or public-sector participation	181	93	0.286	0.452	0.067[b]	51
Flood, drought, avian flu, other emergencies	78	37	0.123	0.329	0.010	47
Environmental sustainability	170	73	0.269	0.444	−0.039	43
Economic growth and development	272	113	0.430	0.495	−0.080[b]	42
Targeting poor or vulnerable groups	204	81	0.322	0.468	−0.089[c]	40
Transport	65	25	0.103	0.304	−0.052	38
Encouraging local participation	264	101	0.417	0.493	−0.134[d]	38
Poverty alleviation	274	100	0.433	0.496	−0.169[d]	36
Provision of public infrastructure (including transport)	204	66	0.322	0.468	−0.191[d]	32
Macroeconomic stability	102	30	0.161	0.368	−0.147[d]	29

Sources: World Bank data and evaluation calculations.

a. This is 100*(column 2/column 1).

b. The pair-wise correlation coefficient between the dummy variable for that objective and that of increasing agricultural growth and productivity is statistically significant at $p \leq 0.10$.

c. The pair-wise correlation coefficient between the dummy variable for that objective and that of increasing agricultural growth and productivity is statistically significant at $p \leq 0.05$.

d. The pair-wise correlation coefficient between the dummy variable for that objective and that of increasing agricultural growth and productivity is statistically significant at $p \leq 0.01$.

TABLE B.3	Distribution of Agriculture-Focused Projects across Categories (among the 633 in the evaluation portfolio)				
Category	Number of observations	Number of agriculture-focused projects	Percent of agriculture-focused projects[a]	Total commitments to all projects (US$ million)	Percent of commitments to agriculture-focused projects
Region					
Sub-Saharan Africa	193	78	40	11,471	32
East Asia & Pacific	97	40	41	8,670	38
Europe & Central Asia	122	77	63	5,834	58
Latin America & Caribbean	106	34	32	6,373	28
Middle East & North Africa	35	22	63	1,999	68
South Asia	80	41	51	10,286	48
All Regions	633	292	46	44,633[b]	41
Country-income level					
Agriculture-based, 20 lowest income	97	38	39	6,229	27
20 lowest income	111	41	37	7,228	24
Low income	299	140	47	16,566	35
Middle income	334	152	46	28,067	45
20 highest income	95	40	42	7,549	47
WDR 2008 typology					
Agriculture-based	203	91	44	10,583	37
Transforming	231	115	50	21,780[g]	45
Urbanized	129	54	42	10,053	39
Not classified[c]	70	32	46	2,217	38
IDA-IBRD commitments[d]					
IDA	421	193	46	22,314	35
IBRD	212	99	47	22,318	47
Country governance capacity[e]					
Low capacity	272	129	47	14,483	36
High capacity	361	162	45	30,149	44
Time period[f]					
Fiscal 1998–2001	205	112	58	15,666	50
Fiscal 2002–08	428	180	42	28,966	36
Sector board					
ARD	370	240	65	20,829	69
Non-ARD	263	51	19	23,803	16
Lending instrument type					
Investment	506	256	51	29,535	49
Development policy	127	35	28	15,098	27

a. (100* column 3/column2).

b. Amount excludes $553.5 million that went to supplemental projects.

c. These include the five regional projects.

d. Projects with both IDA and IBRD funding were considered IDA when they were mainly funded by IDA resources, and IBRD when they were mainly funded by IBRD resources.

e. Country governance capacity is high/good for countries with an average public sector management and institutions rating greater than 3.18 (the average for all countries in the Country Policy and Institutional Assessment data set, for the period 1998–2007).

f. Time period is based on fiscal year of project's approval; the second period has seven years, the first period has four years.

g. When China and India are excluded, the total commitments to transforming economies are $11,835 million.

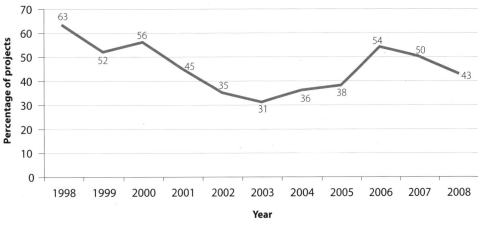

FIGURE B.3a   Trend in Percentage of Agriculture-Focused Projects in the Evaluation Portfolio

Sources: World Bank data and evaluation calculations.

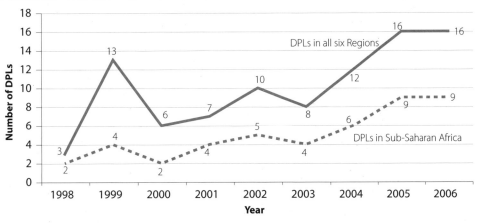

FIGURE B.3b   Trends in Number of DPLs in All Regions and in Sub-Saharan Africa in the Evaluation Portfolio

Sources: World Bank data and evaluation calculations.

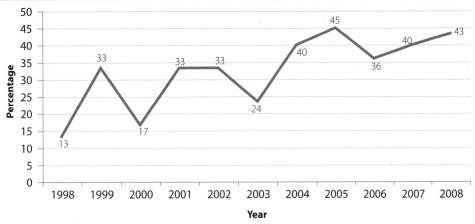

FIGURE B.3c   DPLs in the Africa Evaluation Portfolio as a Percentage of Projects in the Region

Sources: World Bank data and evaluation calculations.

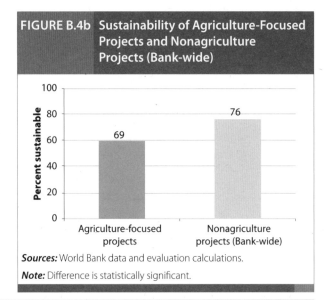

FIGURE B.4a Overall Outcome Performance of Agriculture-Focused Projects and Nonagriculture Projects (Bank-wide)

Sources: World Bank data and evaluation calculations.

FIGURE B.4b Sustainability of Agriculture-Focused Projects and Nonagriculture Projects (Bank-wide)

Sources: World Bank data and evaluation calculations.

Note: Difference is statistically significant.

TABLE B.4a Performance of Agriculture-Focused Projects in the Closed Evaluation Portfolio

Category	Number of projects	Satisfactory overall outcome	Satis-factory sustaina-bility[a]	Satisfactory borrower performance	Satis-factory quality at entry	Satis-factory Bank supervision	"Good" M&E quality[b]	Affected by political factors[b]	Affected by external factors[b]
Region									
Sub-Saharan Africa	27	**56**	64	**59**	**56**	**70**	25	**52**	**4**
East Asia & Pacific	16	88	67	**88**	77	**94**	**57**	18	6
Europe & Central Asia	24	**96**	82	**88**	80	100[c]	29	28	8
Latin America & Caribbean	10	80	73	71	**92**	82	30	0[c]	14
Middle East & North Africa	8	63	71	25	50	63	33	38	**0[c]**
South Asia	14	79	54 [d]	79	64	79	30	29	21
All Regions	99[e]	77	69	72	70	83	34	30	9
Country income level									
Agriculture-based,									
20 lowest income	12	**42**	**30**	**50**	**50**	**50**	**0[c]**	28	8
20 lowest income	13	**38**	**27**	**46**	54	**59**	**0[c]**	46[f]	8
Low income	57	**67**	**49**	67	62[g]	**71**	25[g]	**41**	12
Middle income	42	**84**	**82**	76	75[g]	**92**	40[g]	22	6
20 highest income	13	**92**	**92**	81	**86**	93	14	25	**0[c]**
WDR 2008 typology									
Agriculture-based	29	**62**	56[h]	**59**	62	**69**	**13**	**52**	7
Transforming	43	84[i]	73	75	76	88[i]	**47**	29	11
Urbanized	19	84 [i]	78	**83**	62	**95**	33	**9**	9
Not classified	8	75	71						
Other categorizations									
IDA	65	71	**60**	71	65	77	29 [g]	34	11
IBRD	34	**88**	**85**	74	**79**	**94**	44 [g]	23	5
Investment	81	79	68	73	68	86 [g]	34	25	9
DPL	18	67	75	67	78	72[g]	33	**50**	6
Low capacity	44	75	64	67	72	82	29	37	9
High capacity	55	78	73	77	68	84	38	24	8
ARD	74	80	68	71	67	86	**38**	27	6
Non-ARD	25	68	71	74	78	77	18	37	15

Note: See table notes at the end of table B.4b.

TABLE B.4b Performance of Agriculture-Focused Projects, by Time Period

Category	Number of projects	Percent								
		Satis-factory overall outcome	Satis-factory sustaina-bility[a]	Satisfactory borrower performance	Satis-factory quality at entry	Satis-factory Bank supervision	"Good" M&E quality[b]	Affected by political factors[b]	Affected by external factors[b]
Time period (fiscal years)									
1998–2001	**100**	**80**[g]	**65**	**75**	**67**	**83**	—	—	—
2002–08	26	65[g]	56	64	71	78	—	—	—

Note: The data analysis for table B.4a is based on data downloaded from the World Bank database on December 2, 2008. Data analysis for table B.4b is based on data downloaded on May 05, 2010, for comparison of ratings for projects over two time periods (fiscal 1998–2001 and fiscal 2002–08). The total number of agriculture-focused projects rated for overall outcome in this data set is 126. Bolded cells are percentages that are statistically significantly different from the mean for all Regions ($p \leq 0.10$).

a. See appendix table D.1 for definition of sustainable projects.

b. Based on comments in the ICR review database, where political factors include lack of government will or support caused by factors such as change of government or political appointments or delays in fulfilling counterpart funding obligations. For M&E quality, the percentages reported exclude observations where the ICR reviewer did not have any comment or rating on M&E. M&E quality is good for projects rated substantial or high for M&E and for projects with comments that indicated that M&E quality was substantial, high, or good.

c. T-test statistic not provided.

d. Statistically below mean of Regions other than South Asia.

e. The number of projects with ratings on overall outcome for agriculture-focused projects is 99. For other ratings, the number of projects changes depending on availability of data for that rating. For example, sustainability ratings are available for 90 projects and borrower performance ratings for 104 projects. The maximum number of agriculture-focused projects in the closed evaluation portfolio is 105.

f. Statistically significantly higher than the mean of countries other than the 20 lowest-income countries.

g. Statistically significantly different from each other.

h. Statistically significantly below nonagriculture-based economies (that is, below transforming and urbanized ratings).

i. Statistically above mean for agriculture-based economies.

TABLE B.5 Percentage of Projects Rated Satisfactory on Selected Quality-of-Supervision Assessment (QSA) Ratings for Projects Assessed by the World Bank Quality Assurance Group (QAG)

| | All projects that were assessed for QSA, among the 633 projects | | | | | |
| | | Percent | | | | |
	Number of observations (N)	Sound design at entry[a] (N=81)	Borrower commitment[a] (N=81)	Satisfactory borrower and stakeholder ownership (N=77)	Satisfactory staffing (N=81)	Satisfactory staff continuity (N=81)
Region						
Sub-Saharan Africa	27	56[b]	70	92	88 [b]	93
East Asia & Pacific	13	77	69	92	100[c]	92
Europe & Central Asia	17	**94**	**88**	100 [c]	100 [c]	100[c]
Latin America & Caribbean	8	71	86	83	100 [c]	100[c]
Middle East & North Africa	9	**30**	70	80 [d]	90 .	100[c]
South Asia	7	86	86	100[c]	100[c]	100[c]
All Regions	81	68	77	92	95	96
Country income level						
Agriculture-based, 20 lowest income	15	60	80	100[c]	93	100[c]
20 lowest income	19	58	74	95	89[e]	100[c]
Low income	43	63	79	95	92	95
Middle income	38	72	74	90	98	98
20 highest income	11	100[c,f]	82	100[c]	100[a]	100[c]
WDR 2008 typology						
Agriculture-based	24	**54**	83	96	96	92
Transforming	37	73	76	89	95	100[c]
Urbanized	14	86[e]	64	92	100[c]	93
Country governance capacity						
Low capacity	41	69	78	88[h]	93	100[h]
High capacity	40	68	75	**97[h]**	98	93[h]
Time period						
Fiscal 1998–2001	57	68	67 [h]	89[h]	95	96
Fiscal 2002–08	24	67	100[h,c]	100 [h,c]	96	90
Sector board						
ARD	54	69	76	92	96	100 [h,c]
Non-ARD	27	67	78	92	93	89[h]
Objective						
Agriculture-focused	44	73	73	88[h]	98	98
Nonagriculture-focused	37	62	81	**97[h]**	92	95

Note: Satisfactory are those rated highly satisfactory and satisfactory when the four-point scale was used (on fiscal 2000 QSA, QSA4, and QSA5 forms) and those rated highly satisfactory, satisfactory, and moderately satisfactory when the six-point scale was used (on QSA6 and QSA7 forms). The four-point scale on fiscal 2000 QSA, QSA4, and QSA5 forms was: 1= highly satisfactory, 2=satisfactory, 3=marginal, 4=unsatisfactory, n.a.=not applicable; the six-point scale on QSA6 and QSA7 was 1=highly satisfactory, 2=satisfactory, 3=moderately satisfactory, 4=moderately unsatisfactory, 5=unsatisfactory, 6=highly unsatisfactory.

(N= #) is number of observations that are available for that rating. Numbers in bold type are statistically significantly different from mean value for the 81 or 44 projects (or as indicated with a letter, depending on the type of test done) at (p ≤ 0.10).

a. These ratings are based on yes/no responses.

b. This is statistically significantly lower than the mean for non-African countries.

	Agriculture-focused projects among those assessed for QSA				
	Percent				
Number of observations (N)	Sound design at entry[a] (N=43)	Borrower commitment[a] (N=41)	Satisfactory borrower and stakeholder ownership (N=47)	Satisfactory staffing (N=44)	Satisfactory staff continuity (N=44)
11	64	**45**	82	100[c]	91[b]
8	75	75	88	100[c]	100[c]
10	**90**	**90**	100[c]	100[c]	100[c]
3	67	100[c]	100[c]	100[c]	100[c]
5	40[d]	60	60[d]	80[d]	80[d]
7	86	86	100[c]	100[c]	100[c]
44	73	88	88	98	98
5	60	60	100[c]	100[c]	100[c]
6	67	50[e]	83	100[c]	100[c]
21	71	71	90	96	95
23	74	74	85	100[c]	100[c]
5	100[c,f]	80	100[c]	100[c]	100[c]
10	**50**	70	90	100[c]	90[g]
24	75	71	83	100[c]	100[c]
7	100[c,e]	71	100[c]	100[c]	100[c]
			100[c]		
21	71	81	80[h]	95	100
23	74	65	95[h]	100[c]	96
37	76	68[h]	85	97	100[h]
7	57	100[h,c]	100[c]	100[c]	86[h]
39	74	72	89	97	100[h]
5	60	80	75	100[c]	80[h]
—	—	—	—	—	—
—	—	—	—	—	—

c. P-statistic was not provided.

d. Statistically significantly lower than the mean for Regions other than the Middle East & North Africa.

e. Statistically significantly higher than the mean of nonurbanized countries.

f. Statistically significantly higher than the mean for countries other than the 20 highest-income countries.

g. Statistically significantly lower than the mean of nonagriculture-based countries.

h. Statistically significantly different from each other.

TABLE B.6	Percentage of Projects Rated Satisfactory on Selected QAE Ratings for Projects Assessed by QAG

	All projects that were assessed for QAE, among the 633 projects					
	Percent					
	Number of observations (N)	Bank inputs and processes (N=135)	Strategic relevance and approach (N=135)	Adequate reflection of lessons of experience (N=134)	Adequacy of country and sector knowledge (N=125)	Appropriateness of arrangements for evaluating impact and measuring outcomes (N=133)
Region						
Sub-Saharan Africa	42	79	90	**76**	90	68
East Asia & Pacific	22	91	91	91	100 [b,c]	68
Europe & Central Asia	24	92	96	92	91	67
Latin America & Caribbean	14	79	86	86	92	85
Middle East & North Africa	17	**65**	82 [d]	88	93	76
South Asia	16	100 [b,e]	100 [b,e]	100 [b,e]	100 [b]	75
All Regions	135	84	91	87	94	71
Country income level						
Agriculture-based, 20 lowest income	16	69 [f]	88	**69**	91	56 [f]
20 lowest income	22	73 [g]	91	**73**	90	64
Low income	60	82	93	80 [i]	91	66
Middle income	75	85	89	**92** [i]	96	76
20 highest income	17	82	94	100 [b,h]	100 [b]	82
WDR 2008 typology						
Agriculture-based	37	79	88	**71**	90	55
Transforming	60	85	93	**92**	95	77 [j]
Urbanized	24	92	92	100 [b,k]	100 [b,k]	79
Country governance capacity						
Low capacity	57	77 [l]	88	81 [l]	**85** [l]	67
High capacity	78	**88** [l]	94	**91** [l]	100 [l,b]	74
Time period						
Fiscal 1998–fiscal 2001	58	81	91	**78**	**85**	**56**
Fiscal 2002–fiscal 2008	77	86	92	**93**	**99**	**83**
Sector board						
ARD	81	80 [l]	89	88	95	66 [l]
Non-ARD	54	89 [l]	94	85	92	**79** [l]
Objective						
Agriculture-focused	67	79 [l]	90	88	91	**64**
Nonagriculture- focused	68	88 [l]	93	85	96	**79**

Note: Rated satisfactory = Projects rated highly satisfactory and satisfactory when the four-point scale was used (QAE0, QAE4 and QAE6 forms) are considered satisfactory, those rated highly satisfactory, satisfactory, and moderately satisfactory when the six-point scale was used (QAE7 and QAE8 forms) are considered satisfactory. The four-point scale on QAE0 form was: 1= highly satisfactory, 2=satisfactory, 3=marginal, 4=unsatisfactory, n.a.=not applicable; for QAE4 and QAE6 it was 1= highly satisfactory, 2=satisfactory, 3=marginally satisfactory, 4=unsatisfactory, n.a.=not applicable; for QAE7 and QAE8 it was 1=highly satisfactory, 2=satisfactory, 3=moderately satisfactory, 4=moderately unsatisfactory, 5=unsatisfactory, 6=highly unsatisfactory. Bolded areas are statistically significantly different from mean of all Regions.— = Not applicable.

Agriculture-focused projects that were assessed for QAE

	Number of observations (N)	Percent				
		Bank inputs and processes (N=67)	Strategic relevance and approach (N=67)	Adequate reflection of lessons of experience (N=67)	Adequacy of country and sector knowledge (N=58)	Appropriateness of arrangements for evaluating impact and measuring outcomes (N=66)
	17	71	76 [a]	**71**	79 [a]	56
	11	82	91	100 [b,c]	100 [b]	64
	16	88	94	88	88	50 [b]
	6	83	100 [b]	100 [b]	100 [b]	83
	9	56 [d]	89	89	100 [b]	78
	8	100 [b,e]	100 [b]	100 [b]	100 [b]	75
	67	79	90	88	91	64
	6	50 [f]	67 [f]	67 [f]	50 [f]	17
	7	57 [g]	71 [g]	71 [g]	75	29
	26	73	85	81 [i]	81 [i]	60
	41	83	93	93 [i]	**97 [i]**	66
	10	80	100 [b]	100 [b]	100 [b]	70
	16	69	75 [i]	**63**	75 [j]	**40**
	31	77	94	94 [j]	93	71 [j]
	14	86	93	100 [b,i]	100 [b,k]	71
	38	55 [i]	89	83	**80 [i]**	57
	29	**76 [i]**	89	92	100 [i,b]	68
	33	82	85	**76 [h]**	79 [i]	**50 [i]**
	34	76	94	100 [i,b]	100 [i,b]	**76 [i]**
	56	61 [i]	88	89	78 [i]	63
	11	100 [b,i]	100 [b]	82	94 [i]	70
	—	—	—	—	—	—
	—	—	—	—	—	—

a. Statistically significantly lower than the mean for non-Africa regions.

b. No p-value provided.

c. Statistically significantly higher than the mean of non-East Asia and Pacific Regions.

d. Statistically significantly lower than the mean for non-Middle East and North Africa Regions.

e. Statistically significantly higher than the mean of non-Sub-Saharan Africa Regions.

f. Statistically significantly lower than the mean for nonagriculture-based 20 lowest-income countries.

g. Statically significantly lower than the mean of non-20 lowest-income countries.

h. Statistically significantly higher than the mean for non-20 highest-income countries.

i. Statistically significantly lower than the mean for nonagriculture-based countries.

j. Statistically significantly higher than the mean for nontransforming countries.

k. Statically significantly higher than the mean of nonurbanized countries.

l. Statistically significantly different from each other.

n. Statistically significantly lower than the mean of non-Europe and Central Asia Regions.

Description of AAA Data

A total of 1,432 analytic and advisory activities approved between fiscal 2000 and fiscal 2008 were identified as related to agriculture, fishing, and forestry. Of these, 322 had a status of "dropped" or "n.a.." Of the remaining 1,110 AAA, 773 (70 percent) were ESW, 337 (30 percent) were nonlending technical assistance, and 682 (78 percent) were country-specific; 248 (22 percent) were Regional or global AAA. About half (48 percent)[1] of the Regional AAA was on Sub-Saharan Africa (compared to 27 percent of country-specific AAA that was on countries in Sub-Saharan Africa). The distribution of AAA and its trend by WDR country typology can be seen in table B.7 and figure B.5.

Dropped AAA

Agriculture-based countries were more likely to have their AAA dropped than transforming and urbanized countries taken together (25 percent of AAA approved in agriculture-based economies was dropped, compared with 19 percent of that approved in transforming and urbanized countries, taken together).

Cost of AAA

Cost information is available for two-thirds of the 1,110

TABLE B.7	Number of World Bank AAA Related to Agriculture, Fishing, and Forestry, Fiscal 2000–08						
	Number						
WDR country typology	AAA initiated	AAA active and closed	ESW active and closed	Technical assistance active and closed	AAA dropped[b]	ESW dropped[b]	Technical assistance dropped[b]
Agriculture-based	272	203	152	51	69 [25]	51 [25]	18 [26]
Transforming	429	353	231	122	76 [18]	56 [20]	20 [14]
Urbanized	265	206	151	55	59 [22]	40 [21]	19 [26]
Not classified	139	100	70	30	39 [28]	25 [26]	14 [31]
Regional/global AAA[a]	327	248	169	79	79 [24]	39 [19]	40 [34]
Total	1,432	1,110	773	337	322 [22]	211 [21]	111 [25]

Sources: World Bank data and evaluation calculations.

Note: AAA includes ESW and technical assistance. Brackets [ ] indicate percentage of AAA initiated that was dropped within that country typology/grouping.

a. These were done on the world as a whole or on several countries, and therefore did not fit into the three-world typology of countries.

b. Dropped AAA is that with status "dropped" (317) or status of "n.a." (5).

FIGURE B.5	Trends in Number of Agriculture-Related AAA over the Evaluation Period, by WDR Typology (3-year moving average)

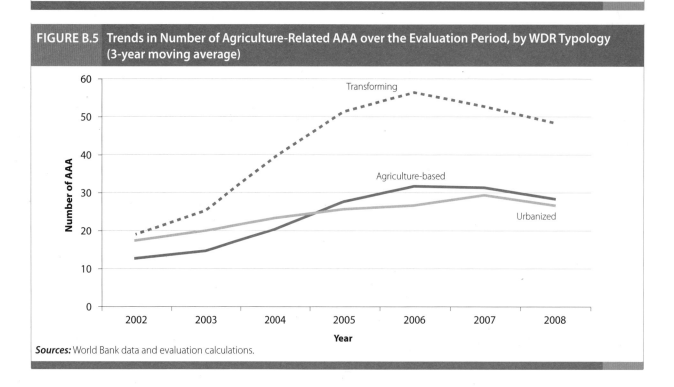

Sources: World Bank data and evaluation calculations.

AAA products. The total amount spent was $151,695,000, of which $116,868,000 (77 percent) was from the Bank budget and $44,827,000 was from trust funds. ESW accounted for 77 percent of the total, technical assistance for 23 percent. Total average AAA unit cost (Bank budget plus trust funds) was $204,000, but the cost varied greatly depending on country type. The unit cost in IDA countries was $180,000, significantly below the average cost of AAA undertaken in IBRD and IBRD/IDA blend countries ($223,000 and $256,000 respectively). In agriculture-based countries it was $185,000, in transforming countries $233,000, and in urbanized countries $193,000. Across the Regions, it was $191,000 in Sub-Saharan Africa, $220,000 in East Asia and the Pacific, $202,000 in Europe and Central Asia, $196,000 in Latin America and the Caribbean, $221,000 in the Middle East and North Africa, and $226,000 in South Asia.

Linkage between Policy Dialogue, AAA, and Lending

From the ESW Evaluation (IEG 2008n)

The ESW evaluation (IEG 2008n) found that two-thirds of a sample of loans examined were preceded by ESW[2] that could have informed the loans. Country-specific ESW had more effects than global and regional ESW on lending (based on task team leaders' ratings of importance of the ESW).[3] Core diagnostics, particularly Public Expenditure Reviews and Country Economic Memoranda, had more effect on DPLs and on CASs than on other products. Across the Regions, Sub-Saharan Africa had the lowest share of loans preceded by ESW. Shares were 36 percent for Sub-Saharan Africa, 50 percent for Latin America and the Caribbean, 56 percent for the Middle East and North Africa, 59 percent for South Asia, 70 percent for Europe and Central Asia, and 83 percent for East Asia and the Pacific.

Based on task team leaders' views, the ESW had positive impacts on (was useful to) the loans. Examples of task team leaders' views of usefulness of ESW to loans included the following:

- Loan would not have happened without the ESW.

- More time would have been needed to prepare the loan.

- Quality of loan would have been compromised if ESW had not been done.

The ESW evaluation also found that loans preceded by ESW had better overall QAG QAE ratings (and subratings, including adequacy of country and sector knowledge underpinning the project).

From this Evaluation

This evaluation found that, in general, less than one-half (49 percent) of the projects in the sample portfolio were informed by World Bank ESW. However, when lessons from other World Bank projects are considered, two-thirds of all projects (67 percent) were informed by World Bank ESW or lessons from World Bank projects. Across the WDR typology, fewer of the projects in agriculture-based economies (50 percent) were informed by World Bank ESW or lessons from World Bank projects than was the case in transforming economies (75 percent) (table B.8).

Among the 84 projects in the sample portfolio, 37 were rated for overall outcome and 33 were rated for sustainability.[4] T-tests showed that projects that were informed by World Bank ESW or technical assistance (policy dialogue, advice, and assistance), and World Bank AAA or lessons from World Bank projects, were more likely to be rated satisfactory than projects that were not informed by these activities (table B.9). QAE data also revealed that projects with a satisfactory rating on adequacy of country and sector knowledge had better QAE performance and were more likely to be sustainable than projects with a nonsatisfactory rating on adequacy of country and sector knowledge (appendix table D.6).

Main Findings from IEG Assessment of AAA on Agriculture in 14 Countries

An assessment was also undertaken on a random sample of 31 pieces of AAA on agriculture from 14 countries to evaluate the results achieved by AAA. By measuring each prod-

TABLE B.8	Percentage of Projects Reported as Informed by AAA, Technical Assistance, and Other Projects in their Design (in the Sample of 84 Projects)			
WDR country typology	World Bank AAA	World Bank projects	World Bank AAA or projects	All AAA (including non-Bank)
Agriculture-based (N=20)	40	10	**50**	45
Transforming (N=36)	53	22	**75**	58
Urbanized (N=18)	50	17	67	50
All (including not classified) N=84	49	18	67	52

Sources: World Bank data and evaluation calculations.

Note: Bolded cells are statistically different from mean (67 percent).

TABLE B.9	Relationship between AAA, Technical Assistance, and Lessons from Other Projects and Project Outcomes, among the 84 Projects in the Sample Portfolio That Were Rated for Overall Outcome and Sustainability				

Was project informed by the following?	N	Percentage rated satisfactory on overall outcome	N	Percentage rated sustainable
World Bank ESW				
Yes	15	**93**	15	**87**
No	22	**77**	18	**67**
World Bank ESW and/or project lessons				
Yes	18	**94**	17	82
No	19	**74**	16	69
Non-World Bank ESW				
Yes	8	88	8	75
No	29	83	25	76
All ESW				
Yes	17	**94**	17	82
No	20	**75**	16	69
Policy dialogue, advice, technical assistance				
Yes	23	**91**	23	74
No	14	**71**	10	80
ESW and technical assistance				
Yes	26	**92**	26	77
No	11	**64**	7	71

Source: Evaluation portfolio.

Note: Bolded cells are statistically significantly different from each other.

uct against a series of indicators, statements can be made on what leads to a results-rich piece of AAA and what could be done in the Bank to ensure that more results are achieved from AAA. Indicators are grouped into four general categories: results, strategic relevance and ownership, technical quality, and dissemination and sustained dialogue. A four-point rating scale was used: high, substantial, modest, and negligible.

Summary Findings
Technical Quality

Based on the sample, the quality of ARD AAA is rated between substantial and high. The Bank has put in place a thorough and systematic process that ensures this outcome.

Given that the Bank is an important repository of global knowledge on development, the fact that only about two-thirds of the studies drew on examples from within the Region or across Regions to illustrate a point indicates that an important area is not being fully exploited.

Recommendations provided in AAA reviewed by this evaluation usually fell short of best practice. Only 10 reports provided specified actions to be taken by specified actors. Only

one report produced a matrix of recommendations that included what changes should be made, who should make those changes (what organization), and when they should be made. None described how such changes could be undertaken. None discussed the sequencing of changes.

Strategic Relevance and Ownership

Strategic relevance and ownership measures are slightly below substantial. Over 85 percent of the products addressed issues that had been identified as development constraints in earlier work or in policy dialogue with clients. And a full 77 percent of products were delivered in time to affect relevant policy decisions by the government.

There is no evidence from the sample that demand-driven AAA produces better results than supply-driven AAA.

Ownership appears to be an important ingredient in overall results achieved. Seven studies with low results also had low ownership.

Dissemination and Sustained Dialogue

Inadequate dissemination and dialogue are limiting results. In this assessment, the score for dissemination and sustained dialogue is rated modest. Only seven studies scored well across all measures, and those same studies also scored well on results.

Lack of translation of reports is a problem. Only 10 of 22 reports were translated into the local language, and the results show that reports that are translated have consistently higher results scores than those that are not.

Identifying the best interlocutors is sometimes an issue, because the organizational structure in the Bank tends to match sectoral units with sectoral ministries in a country.

But the dialogue needs to be carried to core ministries such as finance or planning, where national policy decisions are often made. This highlights the necessity of the country director sustaining the policy dialogue.

Overall Results

AAA, and particularly ESW, makes an important contribution to the Bank's knowledge base and reputation. However, the analysis here indicates that the results of AAA related to ARD are modest, and modifications to the way AAA is done could enhance results.

IFC Strategy and Interventions

BOX B.1 AGRIBUSINESS IN IFC STRATEGIC DIRECTIONS (2000–04)

- **2000–02**: Food industry, agriculture, or agribusiness was not mentioned.
- **2003**: Agribusiness was mentioned in the context of sustainability, environmental, and social issues.
- **2004**: Agribusiness mentioned as part of the "IFC against AIDs" program.

Source: IFC.

BOX B.2 AGRIBUSINESS IN IFC STRATEGIC DIRECTIONS (2005–06)

Fiscal 2006: "Differentiating IFC through Sustainability" includes Agribusiness Sector Strategy as an opportunity for IFC to increase business volume and development impact. Examples mentioned:

- Best management practices for commodities
- Animal welfare program to address humane treatment of animals
- Food quality management systems required by world markets
- Promotion of cleaner and more energy-efficient processes, renewable energy sources (ethanol, cogeneration), and good practices regarding the conservation of natural resources.

Focus on "balance between the need to secure increased food production and the need to safeguard finite resources. The debate is also relevant to IFC's mission of poverty alleviation as, too often, poverty correlates with the degradation of natural resources."

- Expand IFC agribusiness support "outside of the Latin America and Caribbean Region into East Asia and Eastern Europe. IFC uses linkages programs with small and medium-size enterprises to further develop agribusiness and is looking to replicate the program in up to nine new agribusiness linkage projects through PEP Africa."
- Agribusiness mentioned as growth area for IFC in Africa, South Asia, the Russian Federation, Ukraine, and Latin America and Caribbean.

Fiscal 2007: "IFC will engage in countries and sectors where there is a perception that economic development and sustainability concerns may diverge. The objective is to help the private sector define sustainable solutions that will be of value due to their demonstration impact and ability to be replicated."

Source: IFC.

Fiscal 2008: A growth plan guided by IFC's five strategic priorities including "since 2007, agribusiness….These priorities remain equally relevant today, with some additional areas of emphasis, in particular including agribusiness as a focus sector as part of the frontier markets priority"

"**Agribusiness.** In many poorer developing countries, agriculture is the principal source of overall economic growth and agricultural growth is the cornerstone of poverty reduction. Human population growth, improved incomes, and shifting dietary patterns are increasing the demand for food and other agricultural products. International trade is increasing rapidly, bringing with it a set of regulatory frameworks and requirements whose implementation requires local capacity. At the same time, however, the natural resource base underpinning agricultural production is under threat, with growing threats to genetic diversity and the degradation of land and water resources. How to lever these shifts so that the sector continues to improve its efficiency in an environmentally sustainable and socially inclusive way is a major challenge for most developing countries."

Systematic/Programmatic Approaches:
"Greater use of financial intermediaries combined with advisory services to address a specific sector …. such as agribusiness"

Fiscal 2009:"Recognizing its critical role in poverty reduction and environmental and social sustainability, IFC last year made Agribusiness an explicit part of its frontier focuses. IFC extends its impact beyond its direct investments (which increased to $628 million in fiscal 2007 from $456 million in fiscal 2006), by using its convening power to promote global public goods, such as the 'Better Management Practices' for commodities launched in fiscal 2004. In 2006, IFC's agribusiness portfolio companies reached 538,295 farmers and employed 138,893 workers.

Wholesaling and Cross Sector Approaches—combining financial sector and industry expertise to enable wholesaling through local banks and agribusiness trading companies.

"In agribusiness, besides risk mitigation, IFC is providing additionality through its expertise in the safety, environmental, and social standards that are now critical to export markets; through linkage programs that help integrate farmers into global supply chains; and through innovative agricultural wholesale products that target smaller agricultural companies."

Source: IFC internal documentation.

TABLE B.10   IFC'S AGRIBUSINESS COMMITMENTS, BY REGION AND STRATEGY PERIOD ($1 MILLION)

	Strategy period				
	Fiscal 1998–2000	Fiscal 2001–04	Fiscal 2005–06	Fiscal 2007–calendar 2008	Total
Region			Funding (US$)		
Middle East & North Africa	9	22	45	259	335
South Asia	0	35	30	276	341
Sub-Saharan Africa	33	55	63	260	411
East Asia & Pacific	36	153	97	174	460
Europe & Central Asia	115	291	353	612	1,370
Latin America & Caribbean	326	504	402	1,345	2,577
Worldwide	0	0	0	135	135
Grand total	520	1,059	990	3,061	5,629
Average per year	173	265	495	1,224	2,157
	Percent				
Middle East & North Africa	2	2	5	8	6
South Asia	0	3	3	9	6
Sub-Saharan Africa	6	5	6	8	7
East Asia & Pacific	7	14	10	6	8
Europe & Central Asia	22	27	36	20	24
Latin America & Caribbean	63	48	41	44	46
Worldwide	0	0	0	4	2
Grand total	100	100	100	100	100

Source: IEG.

Seven IFC investment departments have made significant commitments in different links of the agribusiness supply-value chain (see table C.1):

- Agribusiness (CAG) (58 percent): $3.2 billion in 116 projects in the food and agriculture (F&A) subsectors.

- Global Financial Markets (23 percent): $1.3 billion in 84 projects. Largely in trade finance guarantees ($1.15 billion, or 20 percent) in 551 transactions through 79 investee banks. Additionally, $113 million in five banking and microfinance projects, and $56 million in four CAG joint-venture projects.

- Global Manufacturing and Services (12 percent): $701 million in 58 projects. They are largely grocery and distribution projects ($629 million), followed by F&A projects ($65 million), two pharmaceutical/warehousing projects, and three agribusiness department projects.

- Oil, Gas, Mining, and Chemicals (2.5 percent): $138 million in seven projects. They are agrichemical/fertilizer projects.

- Infrastructure (2.2 percent): $124 million in five projects. Two common transport carriers, one warehouse, and a port terminal. In addition, four agribusiness department warehouses and a joint venture with CAG for a port terminal.

- Private Equity and Investment Funds (2 percent): $115 million in three CAG joint-venture projects. They include one agricultural farming and production project and two nonprimary production investments.

- Global Information and Communication Technologies (ICT) (0.1 percent): $8 million in two projects in rural telecommunications, plus an access to markets project in preparation. Additionally, ICT has committed $440 million in 17 telecommunication projects that may have unintended positive impacts in the agribusiness chain.

Source: IEG.

IFC has focused on four livestock subsectors: (i) slaughtering and processing (45 percent), (ii) poultry farming (37 percent), dairy (15 percent), and aquaculture and fishing (2 percent). The slaughtering and processing investments generally support large companies that rely on farmers for the supply of cattle or pigs. These processing companies may be involved in genetics, supply of breeding stock, and feed mills. The poultry investments support large, integrated companies that usually own the hatchery, feed mill, and slaughterhouse, and that may resort to contract farming or to own the breeding and broiler-growing farms. The dairy investments support integrated processors that used contract farming to procure milk. Finally, the IFC investments in aquaculture have largely been confined to supporting shrimp farming companies, although it has also supported a few fish farming projects.

IFC has committed about 15 percent of total commitments ($824 million) in projects supporting the livestock sector. The Europe and Central Asia Region has dominated, with 55 percent of investment commitments, followed by Latin America and the Caribbean (32 percent). The countries that received the largest share of investments were the Russian Federation (17 percent), Croatia and Ukraine (14 percent each), and Turkey (10 percent). Only 5 projects of 59 were located in agriculture-based economies (Madagascar, Tanzania, Uganda).

For example, IFC has invested in a company in Turkey to help it diversify its meat processing business by establishing an integrated turkey processing operation to produce value added turkey-based products for the domestic market. The project has benefited consumers (increased consumer surplus), farmers (120 contract farmers provide most of the bird supply), and employees (300 additional direct employees). The company was the pioneer in commercial turkey production in the country, and its success has been emulated by three other meat producers.

Source: IEG.

In early 2003, IFC was still quite reluctant to invest in Ukraine. It considered Ukraine too unstable and too risky to conduct transparent private business. Although IFC had a comprehensive donor-funded technical assistance program employing over 100 local and international staff, it had invested only about $15 million in four projects since Ukraine gained its independence from the Soviet Union in 1991.

As IFC was beginning to focus on additionality, CAG identified a project in Ukraine that was to become a path breaker in many directions, a model for additionality and interdepartmental collaboration, and provide significant capital gains for IFC. In the spring of 2003, joining forces with the IFC Kyiv office, CAG staff began discussions with the owner of a poultry producer. This producer was a relatively new company (established in 1998), run by a progressive agricultural engineer, and it wanted to expand its farms and hatcheries, build a feed plant to process sunflower, expand its distribution network, and modernize its business processes and logistics.

In addition to providing long-term financing (a $20 million loan for six years with two years grace periods, and $6 million in quasi-equity), IFC expected to contribute to the business in many ways. Based on its global experience in the poultry industry, IFC was providing assistance in developing a business plan (including the diversification of grandparent stocks to reduce disease risk), identifying critical bottlenecks, suggesting a corporate reorganization, consolidating its assets, and going through international audits. IFC was also going to help create a state-of-the-art sunflower feed mill (the first in Ukraine) with a technology used only in Spain and France, thus reducing production costs significantly (project #21071).

IFC's contribution in the environmental area was also significant: while IFC's environmental staff was satisfied with company practices, they recommended additional improvements in water treatment, refrigeration systems, and occupational safety. They were pleased with the forthcoming attitude of the sponsor.

IFC expected its investment to benefit consumers with a cost reduction of about 20 percent, generate about 30 new small businesses (retail outlets that were spun off), provide employment to 460 new franchises, and secure employment for about 3,100 workers (2,900 in rural areas) in existing and additional jobs in the otherwise unsustainable production units acquired by the company.

Even before the project was committed and funds disbursed, the company began working on the suggested improvements. In the meantime, IFC brought in a Swedish company to review and make recommendations to improve the safety of production processes. The company implemented the consultants' Hazard Analysis and Critical Control Point recommendations under an advisory project (#522511), as well as improving all three of its wastewater facilities beyond local requirements and IFC guidelines. In addition, the company was able to reduce its costs to among the lowest levels in the world.

IFC soon followed with a second project (#24011), providing $60 million for its own account and syndicating an additional $39 million. The cost of the second project was estimated at $260 million and entailed major expansion of production and distribution facilities. It would build on the rapid and successful implementation of the first project, doubling total poultry output, creating a new processing plant in one of the poorest regions of Ukraine, and entering into cooked and semicooked products. IFC also supported its second investment with another advisory project to analyze waste fermentation and carry out a biogas feasibility study (#523169).

The success of the second project came quickly. The company wasted no time in implementing the physical and environmental elements of the project, and became an internationally respected company. Soon, it was listed at the London Stock Exchange with a valuation that was multiples of the value it had when IFC engaged with the company only a few years earlier.

The final step was to prepay IFC loans in full, including IFC's quasi-equity, with IFC making an attractive capital gain on its investment (December 2006). IFC had accomplished the true mission of a development institution: it had made itself redundant.

Through its investment, IFC had contributed to the emergence of an efficient, transparent, environmentally conscious company in a frontier country. In the process, IFC was able to provide additionality in all of its forms: providing long-term financing, mobilizing funds, contributing to business strategy, improving corporate governance and environmental and social practices, and promoting downstream small and medium enterprises.

In its turn, the company helped IFC to understand (i) that Ukraine presented many opportunities, which enabled IFC to ramp up its investment program to reach, within three years, the maximum allowed by IFC risk management; (ii) that genuine collaboration between its investment and advisory teams could lead to significant gains in additionality. IFC proceeded to build similarly successful agribusiness projects based on the combined efforts of investment and advisory teams.

Source: IEG.

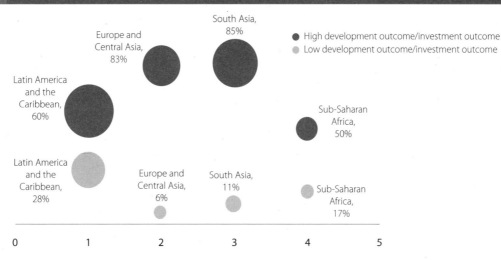

Source: IEG.

Note: The size of the circles indicates the number of evaluated projects (Latin America & Caribbean, 30 high development outcome/investment outcome and 14 low development outcome/investment outcome; Europe and Central Asia, 19 and 2; South Asia, 24 and 3; Sub-Saharan Africa, 6 and 2). Sub-Saharan Africa does not include the outcomes of 22 Africa Enterprise Fund projects, which were evaluated by IEG in 2004 (IEG-IFC 2004).That evaluation found that their performance was generally poor, and the program has been phased out (see IFC methodology in appendix A). If the outcomes of these 22 projects were included in the ratings for the Region, Sub-Saharan Africa outcomes could be worse than 50 percent.

TABLE B.11   IFC—Investment Project Ratings by WDR Typology

	IFC agribusiness investments	
WDR typology	Development outcome (%)	Investment outcome (%)
Agriculture-based countries	77.4	87.1
Transforming countries	87.6	94.0
Urbanized countries	79.4	77.1
Not classified	86.4	95.7
Grand total	81.6	82.0

Source: IEG.

Note: Percentage of high DO/IO and low DO/IO projects.

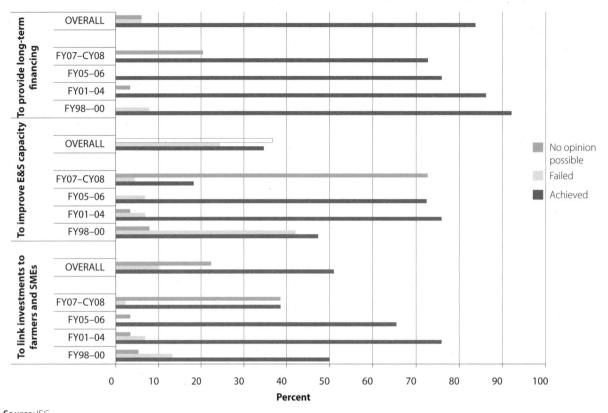

FIGURE B.7 Major IFC Stated and Achieved F&A Investment-Project Objectives, Overall and by Strategy Period

Legend:
- No opinion possible
- Failed
- Achieved

Source: IEG.

Note: E&S = environmental and social; FY = fiscal year; CY = calendar year.

TABLE B.12 IFC's Advisory Service Expenditures, by Strategy Period and Business Line ($1)

Advisory Services Total Donor Funding by Business Line and by Strategy Period

Strategy periods	Corporate Advice	Environmental and Social Sustainability	Access to Finance	Business Enabling Environment	Infrastructure	Grand total
F Y 98–00	5,747,293	86,150	798,655	68,000	0	6,700,098
F Y 01–04	9,113,604	596,400	80,520	0	1,986,313	11,776,837
FY 05–06	19,088,674	1,743,896	1,800,000	0	0	22,632,570
FY07–CY08	31,393,152	8,851,856	5,357,000	4,248,757	570,500	50,421,265
Total	65,342,723	11,278,302	8,036,175	4,316,757	2,556,813	91,530,770
FY98–00	86%	1%	12%	1%	0%	100%
FY01–04	77%	5%	1%	0%	17%	100%
FY05–06	84%	8%	8%	0%	0%	100%
FY07–CY08	62%	18%	11%	8%	1%	100%
Total	71%	12%	9%	5%	3%	100%
FY98–00	9%	1%	10%	2%	0%	7%
FY01–04	14%	5%	1%	0%	78%	13%
FY05–06	29%	15%	22%	0%	0%	25%
FY07–CY08	48%	78%	67%	98%	22%	55%
Total	100%	100%	100%	100%	100%	100%

Source: IEG.

Note: FY = fiscal year; CY = calendar year.

The five IFC advisory service business lines have contributed to the sector with a wide range of projects:

- **Corporate Advice** (71 percent): $65 million in 149 projects in areas such as corporate governance, linkages to farmers, feasibility studies, export programs, sector reviews, land reform, livelihood programs, farming, and processing.

- **Sustainability** (12 percent): $11 million in 40 projects in areas such as bamboo, animal production and processing, sugar, other foods, biofuels, biodiversity, supply chain, and cleaner technology.

- **Access to Finance** (A2F) (9 percent): $8 million in 11 projects in areas such as credit lines, cotton lending, farm financing, agriculture insurance, warehouse receipts, and grassroots entrepreneurs.

- **Business Enabling Environment** (BEE) (5 percent): $4 million in 9 projects in areas including fisheries, investment climate reform, land markets, knowledge management, regional logistics assessments, technical and quality standards for agro-export industry, and partnerships.

- **Infrastructure** (2.8 percent): $3 million in 2 irrigation assignments.

Source: IEG.

These are the major IFC advisory service contributions to some agribusiness subsectors:

- Bamboo/Wood/Forestry (10.6 percent): $9.7 million in 22 assignments, mostly to strengthen supply chain, assist small and medium enterprises, and emphasize sustainability.

- Finance (8.8 percent): $8 million in 11 projects for agricultural insurance development ($3 million); agricultural industrial financing ($2 million); and the balance for post-harvest, grassroots entrepreneur, and farm financing.

- Other Food (7.5 percent): $6.9 million in 20 assignments involving grape, potato, kiwi, breadfruit, seaweed, honey, banana, asparagus, and tomato, among others.

- Fruits & Vegetables (5.9 percent): $5.4 million in 4 assignments to strengthen supply chain, mostly in Ukraine.

- Animal Production and Processing (5 percent): $4.6 million in 28 assignments to further activities such as fisheries, shrimps, crayfish, aquaculture, marine culture, animal and reptile farms, and processing.

- Sugar (0.9 percent): $4.5 million in 2 assignments, a sugarcane management and a cogeneration project (Global Environment Facility externally fired, combined-cycle sugar mill cogeneration, $4.2 million).

- Dairy (3.9 percent): $3.6 million in 10 assignments, mostly to strengthen the dairy farmer supply chain.

- Coffee, Cocoa, Tea (3.8 percent): $3.4 million in 7 assignments to support value chain for sustainable coffee, cocoa, and tea.

- Horticultural (1.4 percent): $1.34 million in 6 assignments to develop exports, primarily roses and ornamental plants.

- Vegetable Fats & Oils (0.8 percent): $0.8 million in 2 assignments in sustainability of olive and palm oil operations.

- Beverages (0.8 percent): $0.8 million in 7 assignments to develop linkages and transfer technology in winery, mineral water, and fruit juices projects.

- Other (47 percent): $43 million in 92 assignments that include subsector and feasibility studies, business plans, and linkages assessments.

Source: IEG.

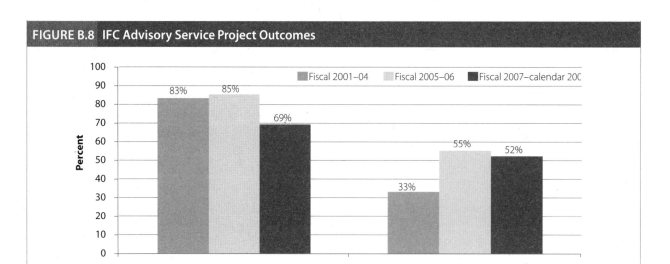

FIGURE B.8 IFC Advisory Service Project Outcomes

Source: IEG.

Note: Percentage of high development effectiveness and role and contribution.

TABLE B.13 IFC Advisory Service Project Ratings by WDR Typology

WDR typology	IFC agribusiness advisory services	
	Development effectiveness (%)	Role and contribution (%)
Agriculture-based countries	70.9	74.0
Transforming countries	68.8	42.3
Urbanized countries	85.3	48.3
Not classified	76.7	73.3
Grand total	76.4	52.0

Source: IEG.

Note: Percentage of high development effectiveness and role and contribution.

FIGURE B.9 IFC Advisory Service Project Outcomes by Region

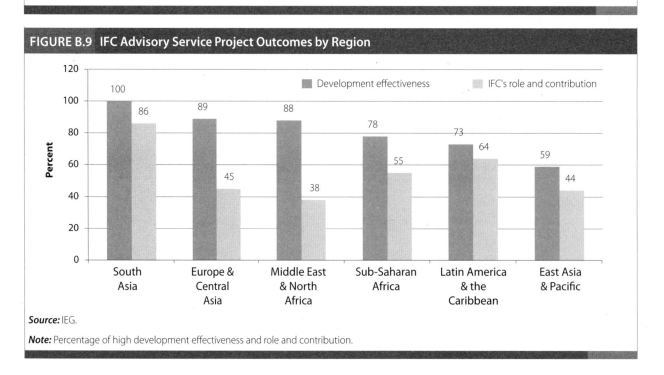

Source: IEG.

Note: Percentage of high development effectiveness and role and contribution.

Identification of Subsector Portfolios

The subsector analysis involved desk reviews of project documents for the relevant portfolios and reviews of IEG evaluations, including Project Performance Assessment Reports, and the literature. The analysis also drew on information from country studies where possible.

For irrigation and drainage, research and extension, market and agribusiness (which included, to some extent, the enabling environment), the portfolios were identified using Operational Policy and Country Services (OPCS) sector codes.

From the 633 projects in the evaluation portfolio, 173 were identified that had irrigation and drainage activities, with an allocation of $6.3 billion. For research and extension, 160 projects were identified, with an allocation of $2 billion. For market and agribusiness, 109 projects were identified, with commitments of $1.3 billion: $0.9 billion for agricultural marketing and trade activities and $0.4 billion for agribusiness activities. Figures C.1, C.2, and C.3 show the regional distribution of irrigation and drainage, research and extension, and marketing and agribusiness commitments, respectively.

For the credit, land, and roads and marketing subsectors, the portfolio was identified as described below.

Access to Land and Formalization of Land Rights

The Bank does not have a sector code to track land administration and policy projects. While there is a thematic code for "land" projects, it covers both land administration and land management projects; the latter are essentially natural resources management projects. Projects in the land subsector were therefore identified using data maintained by the Land Administration and Policy Thematic Group. During the evaluation period, 168 land projects were approved, of which 41 were stand-alone land projects with total commitments of $1.84 billion.

Access to Credit

The Bank does not have a sector code to track agricultural credit or rural finance. Therefore, the subportfolio of projects addressing rural finance or agricultural credit was identified by selecting projects that had one of the eight agricultural

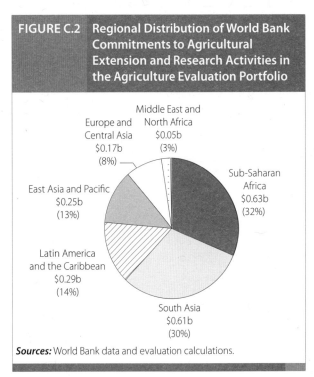

FIGURE C.1 Regional Distribution of World Bank Commitments to Irrigation and Drainage Activities in the Agriculture Evaluation Portfolio

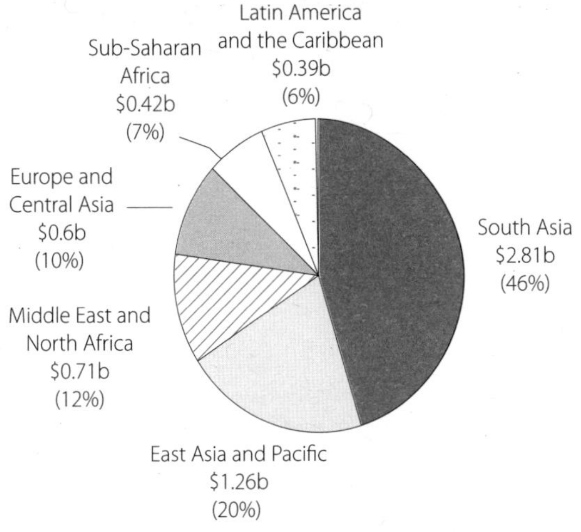

Latin America and the Caribbean $0.39b (6%)
Sub-Saharan Africa $0.42b (7%)
Europe and Central Asia $0.6b (10%)
Middle East and North Africa $0.71b (12%)
East Asia and Pacific $1.26b (20%)
South Asia $2.81b (46%)

Sources: World Bank data and evaluation calculations.

FIGURE C.2 Regional Distribution of World Bank Commitments to Agricultural Extension and Research Activities in the Agriculture Evaluation Portfolio

Middle East and North Africa $0.05b (3%)
Europe and Central Asia $0.17b (8%)
East Asia and Pacific $0.25b (13%)
Latin America and the Caribbean $0.29b (14%)
South Asia $0.61b (30%)
Sub-Saharan Africa $0.63b (32%)

Sources: World Bank data and evaluation calculations.

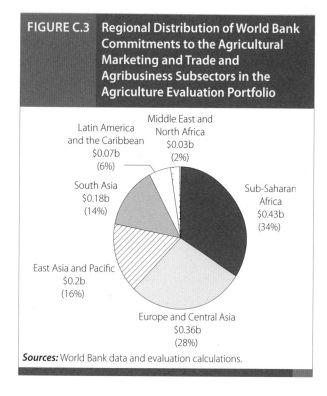

FIGURE C.3 Regional Distribution of World Bank Commitments to the Agricultural Marketing and Trade and Agribusiness Subsectors in the Agriculture Evaluation Portfolio

Middle East and North Africa $0.03b (2%)

Latin America and the Caribbean $0.07b (6%)

South Asia $0.18b (14%)

East Asia and Pacific $0.2b (16%)

Sub-Saharan Africa $0.43b (34%)

Europe and Central Asia $0.36b (28%)

Sources: World Bank data and evaluation calculations.

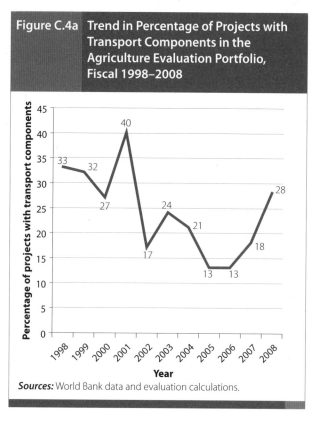

Figure C.4a Trend in Percentage of Projects with Transport Components in the Agriculture Evaluation Portfolio, Fiscal 1998–2008

Sources: World Bank data and evaluation calculations.

sector codes and included one of the following three OPCS finance sector codes: banking, micro and SME finance, and general finance, resulting in a total of 81 projects, with total rural finance or credit commitments of $1.8 billion.

Roads and Marketing Infrastructure

The roads and marketing infrastructure subsector was identified as all projects in the evaluation portfolio that allocated some funds to a transport subsector code (roads and highways; ports, waterways, and shipping; aviation; railways; and general transportation), yielding a total of 149 projects with total transport commitments of $3.1 billion. Figure C.4a provides the percentage of projects in the evaluation portfolio with transport components over the evaluation period. Figure C.4b shows the distribution of the $3.1 billion across the Regions.

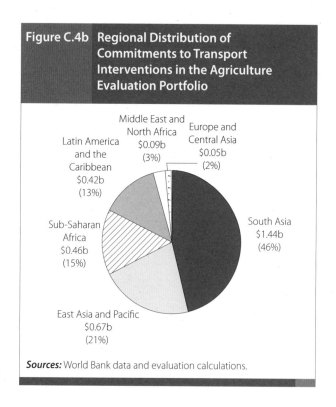

Figure C.4b Regional Distribution of Commitments to Transport Interventions in the Agriculture Evaluation Portfolio

Middle East and North Africa $0.09b (3%)

Europe and Central Asia $0.05b (2%)

Latin America and the Caribbean $0.42b (13%)

Sub-Saharan Africa $0.46b (15%)

East Asia and Pacific $0.67b (21%)

South Asia $1.44b (46%)

Sources: World Bank data and evaluation calculations.

IFC Agribusiness Activities

Supported by IFC's advisory and investment projects, the client is reaching out with extension services to almost 9,000 coffee farmers throughout Central America, helping them to achieve the quality and productivity standards required to compete internationally. Their coffee production is purchased by an international coffee processor, which is also paying 50 percent of the advisory project cost. This signals that the client values the project because at the time of its approval, IFC was not generally requiring clients to pay for these services (the pricing policy was introduced in January 2007). The client has also received an IFC loan for $25 million to be on-lent to the farmers to cover their working capital needs. As a consequence of the improved production technologies, the coffee-processor brand is paying the client farmers a fixed premium of $12.50 per 100 kilograms (quintal) over the market price (expected market range $80-$150 per quintal).

The project's emphasis on a supply-value chain approach, linking the trader client with farmers and the marketer through extension, is potentially a model that IFC could replicate. This is particularly appropriate for companies that rely on large numbers of small farmers (in commodities such as cocoa, coffee, and milk). The client and the coffee processor are interested in replicating the model in countries such as Indonesia, Kenya, Tanzania, Uganda, and Vietnam. Other companies are also interested in replicating the program.

Source: IEG.

IFC invested $10 million in a yogurt manufacturing plant in Stupino, the largest agricultural district in the Moscow region, for a subsidiary of one of Europe's largest dairy cooperatives. The total project cost was estimated at $33.5 million.

A company agreed to invest on the understanding that IFC would provide the advisory work to improve the dairy farmers' output quality and reliability. The factory started production in 2000 and has a capacity of 28,000 tons.

IFC leveraged its investment with an advisory service program to establish a commercially viable outlet for local farmers' raw milk output. It contributed in the following areas:

- Land privatization and farm reorganization
- Support to small-scale farmers in the Russian Federation's dairy sector in animal husbandry, on-farm investments, modern transportation, and hygienic collection systems.

Source: IEG.

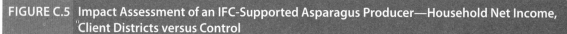

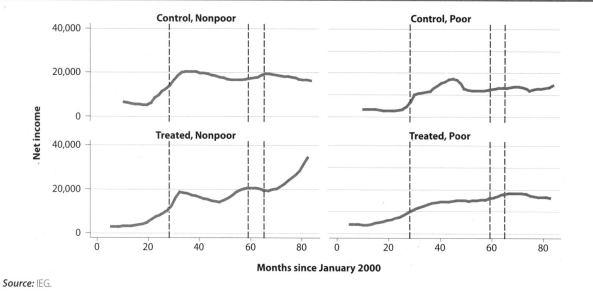

FIGURE C.5 Impact Assessment of an IFC-Supported Asparagus Producer—Household Net Income, Client Districts versus Control

Source: IEG.

Note: The figure depicts the movement in net income for both treated and control districts, both before (until month 60) and after the intervention.

BOX C.3 AN EXAMPLE OF A TYPICAL IFC INVESTMENT IN A PROCESSOR, FACILITATING ACCESS TO MARKETS

The subject is a vertically integrated IFC client in Ecuador with operations in trading and shipping bananas, producing cardboard boxes and plastics, importing fertilizers, dairy farming and processing, forestry, cattle ranching, and renewable energy. IFC has invested in the client three times, in 1999 ($15 million), in 2003 ($15million), and in 2008 ($48 million). These investments have helped the company to improve the competitiveness of its diversified operations.

Ecuador is the largest banana producer in the world, and bananas are one of the country's leading exports (~30 percent of non-oil exports). Banana exports are the primary source of income for over one million farmers and for people in rural communities. Therefore, it becomes critical to improve the competitiveness of the industry, particularly in view of high competition in the world banana markets, real exchange-rate appreciation, and stress on the country's current account.

- **Banana productivity improvement**: Productivity has increased from 1,600 boxes to 2,300 boxes per hectare (roughly a 44 percent increase). To achieve this productivity jump, the company converted the banana variety from Vallery to Williams. It has also extended the productivity gains to the poorly managed plantations that it had acquired from relatively large producers (> 80 hectare). For instance, the company's own production costs were $2.4 per box. The acquired farms, in comparison, had been selling at $3.2 per box and barely making a profit. The acquisition of these plantations also brought benefits to over 1,000 employees (for example, in health, pensions, and training) who had worked for the previous owners.

- **Taxes and contributions**: The client's subsidiaries pay an average of $12 million per year (~50 percent of company's EBITDA[a]) in export taxes, import duties on raw materials, taxes on assets, municipal contributions, and value added tax.

- **Employment:** The company is the main source of employment in Los Rios province; it employs roughly 7,200 full-time agricultural workers and 3,100 full-time industrial workers. Its personnel receive medical insurance, life insurance, a pension fund, bonuses based on company performance, and elementary education and academic scholarships (for their families as well).

- **Farmer benefits**: The company procures 40 percent of its banana needs from 400 independent growers (some of them under year-long contracts), to whom it provides fertilizer advances and technical assistance. It also purchases part of its raw milk requirements from more than 1,800 independent farmers, the vast majority of whom are rural families with one-to-four dairy cows in areas where there are limited production alternatives. It has been providing financial and technical

(Box continues on the following page

BOX C.3 *(continued)*

assistance to these independent dairy producers to improve productivity and sanitary standards and to disseminate best practices.

- **Environmental and social benefits**: The client is the first company in Ecuador to achieve Rainforest Alliance certification in all its banana plantations; its forestry plantations are certified with the Smartwood seal (Forest Stewardship Council), and it has more than 1,000 hectares with the EuroGap seal.

- **Community contributions**: The company's foundation has focused on the improvement of the educational system in rural areas. It supports economically disadvantaged students, provides quality educational programs, and contributes toward the educational infrastructure. It supports 3,100 elementary students in a network of 33 public and public schools (only 26 percent of the children have parents working in the company). It supplies shoes, cofinances textbooks, and provides breakfast. Training materials developed by the foundation are shared with NGOs and the public sector. Capacity building is provided to municipal governments and county boards for the enforcement of children's rights.

Source: IEG.

a. Earnings before interest, taxes, depreciation, and amortization.

BOX C.4   IFC—CREATING A MARKET FOR SMALL-SCALE SUGAR FARMERS IN INDIA

- IFC invested $15 million to help a client expand one of its existing sugar mills and build two new ones in the state of Uttar Pradesh in India. The total project cost was estimated at $105 million. It has increased the number of farmers selling to the client by 46,000.

- In addition, IFC is providing advisory services to enhance sugarcane productivity in the company's catchment area around its four sugar plants in Central Uttar Pradesh. The advisory project has the potential to impact 200,000 sugarcane farmers who are directly linked with the company's sugar operations.

- The increase in sugarcane productivity in the catchment area is critical to making its operations sustainable, so that it can optimally use its installed crushing capacity and sell at competitive prices.

Source: IEG.

Determinants of Project Performance

Econometric Analysis

Purpose

The purpose of the econometric analysis is to explain the factors associated with satisfactory performance of projects in the evaluation portfolio.

Methodology

Regression analysis was used to explain determinants of project performance measured by IEG's ratings of overall outcome and sustainability of projects in the agricultural evaluation portfolio. IEG's ICR reviews assess Bank–supported projects on a number of dimensions. Three dimensions are assessed for overall outcome: the extent to which the project's objectives were met, whether those objectives were efficiently achieved, and whether the objectives were, and continue to be, relevant to the client's development priorities and Bank's country strategy and whether the project's design was relevant to the stated objectives.

The ratings are assigned on a six-point scale: highly satisfactory (no shortcomings), satisfactory (minor shortcomings), moderately satisfactory (moderate shortcomings), moderately unsatisfactory (significant shortcomings), unsatisfactory (major shortcomings), and highly unsatisfactory (severe shortcomings). Satisfactory projects are those with an overall outcome rating of moderately satisfactory or better. Unsatisfactory projects are those rated moderately unsatisfactory or lower. Sustainable projects are those with a sustainability rating of highly likely or likely or those with a risk to development outcome rating of moderate or negligible to low. Unsustainable projects are those with a sustainability rating of highly unlikely, unlikely, or uncertain, or those with a risk to development outcome rating of significant or high.

Dprobit models[1] were run on the whole sample of projects that had these ratings as well as on disaggregated samples, depending on whether the projects were agriculture-focused or not (tables D.2 and D.3). The variables associated with satisfactory performance of agriculture-focused projects are meant to provide guidance on how to improve performance of agricultural projects, and hence the productivity of agriculture. A probit specification was preferred over an ordered or generalized ordered probit (which models a movement from each rating on the six-point scale to the next rating), mainly because Bank documents generally categorize performance of projects based on this cutoff. There is also potential subjectivity between ratings that are adjacent to each other (for example, moderately satisfactory versus satisfactory or moderately satisfactory versus moderately unsatisfactory). This subjectivity is minimized when the ratings are collapsed into satisfactory versus unsatisfactory categories.

Explanatory variables for project performance included other ratings that the ICR reviewer gave to the project on borrower and Bank performance. Generally the ICR reviewer is supposed to judge borrower and Bank performance independent of the overall outcome of the project, except in cases where the constituent subratings fall in different categories. For example, Bank performance is a combination of the rating on quality at entry and Bank supervision. When one of these is in the satisfactory range and the other is in the unsatisfactory range, IEG guidelines prescribe that if the overall performance rating is satisfactory, the Bank supervision rating should be moderately satisfactory, except when Bank performance did not significantly affect the particular outcome. This would introduce some endogeneity in the Bank performance variable, albeit small if such inconsistencies are rare. In the closed evaluations, this occurred 45 times (19 percent of the projects), and IEG guidelines were applied in 31 cases (13 percent), hence it is unlikely to have caused any serious endogeneity problem.

Explanatory variables included country-level variables such as the country's overall capacity to govern as measured by the average rating on the public sector management and institutions cluster of the Country Policy and Institutional Assessment criteria and country income level. The indicators under the public sector management and institutions cluster include property rights and rule-based governance; transparency, accountability, and corruption in the public sector; quality of public administration; quality of budgetary and financial management; and efficiency of revenue mobilization (see IEG 2010g, an evaluation of the World Bank's Country Policy and Institutional Assessments). Therefore, the marginal effects of this variable can be used to reflect the relationship between good governance and project outcomes. Other project-specific variables, such as project aims or project approaches (for example, whether the project was driven by community demand or had a community-based approach, or whether the project was financed using development policy lending or investment lending), were also included as explanatory variables. Table D.1 describes the variables that were included in these regressions and how they were constructed. Table D.2 provides results of regression models that explain overall outcome ratings, and table B.3 provides results of the regression that explain project sustainability ratings. Table D.4 shows the bivariate relationships between performance (project overall outcome and sustainability ratings) and the factors that are expected to influence performance.

To show robustness of results, a number of specifications are reported:

- The basic model estimated on agriculture-focused projects (tables D.2 and D.3: Model 1-Dprobit)

- Separately including quality-at-entry and Bank supervision ratings (the two ratings that make up Bank performance) for the above model, which also partly eliminates any artificially created endogeneity problem described above (tables D.2 and D.3: Model 2-Dprobit)

- The basic model estimated on all projects in the evaluation portfolio (tables D.2 and D.3: Model 3-Dprobit)

- Including Regional dummies in a regression of all projects in the evaluation portfolio (tables D.2 and D.3: Model 4—Sub-Saharan Africa is the baseline—Dprobit)

- Multivariate probit models, where project outcomes, borrower performance, and Bank performance are assumed to be endogenously (jointly) determined. Borrower performance is explained by: (i) weak government commitment to the project, measured by whether the project was reported by the ICR reviewer to be negatively affected by political factors (such as a change of government during or just before implementation that negatively affected

implementation of the project or if the project was delayed or cancelled due to lack of political will or commitment); (ii) weak capacity of the client government or implementing agency (that is, if the ICR reviewer noted that the project underestimated the weak capacity of the government or the implementing agency in relation to complexity of the project); and (iii) a negative external factor such as political strife or economic or other crises that were reported by the ICR reviewer. Bank performance is explained by the same factors and by whether the project had the same task team leader from project appraisal to the ICR writing stage. These variables were guided by comments made by the ICR reviewers on projects in the closed evaluation portfolio and on availability of data (tables D.2 and D.3: Model 5—multivatiate probit with robust standard errors, clustered at country level).

Results

The results show that Bank and borrower performance are the most significant factors positively associated with satisfactory overall performance of agriculture-focused projects, as well as all projects in the evaluation portfolio. Borrower performance is also a significant factor determining sustainability of projects. Weak government commitment, weak capacity of the borrower or the implementing agency in relation to project complexity, and negative external factors, in turn, are statistically significant in explaining borrower performance. Weak capacity of the borrower or the implementing agency in relation to project complexity is also statistically significant in explaining Bank performance (tables D.2 and D.3; lower part of Model 5).

The results also show that projects in countries with better governance are more likely to be rated satisfactory on overall outcome. Country income levelinfluences sustainability of projects (table D.3). South Asia and East Asia and the Pacific, Regions with the largest percentage of irrigation commitments, had projects that were the least likely to be sustainable when all the other variables are taken into consideration.

Variable	Number of observations (in the closed evaluation portfolio)	Mean (in the closed evaluation portfolio)	Description
Project overall outcome was rated satisfactory (Yes=1, No=0)	231	0.77	Satisfactory = 1 if IEG rating of overall outcome was highly satisfactory, satisfactory, or marginally satisfactory. Satisfactory = 0 if IEG rating of overall outcome was highly unsatisfactory, unsatisfactory, or marginally unsatisfactory (that is, according to IEG six-point scale, converted to a dummy variable)
Project was rated sustainable (Yes=1, No=0)	202	0.73	Sustainable = 1 if IEG rating of sustainability was highly likely or likely, or risk to development outcome rating was moderate or negligible to low. Sustainable = 0 if IEG rating of sustainability was highly unlikely, unlikely, or uncertain, or risk to development outcome rating was significant or high
Borrower performance was rated satisfactory (Yes=1, No=0)	241	0.74	Satisfactory defined according to IEG six-point scale, converted to a dummy variable as for project overall outcome
Bank performance was rated satisfactory (Yes=1, No=0)	239	0.83	Satisfactory defined according to IEG six-point scale, converted to a dummy variable as for project overall outcome
Quality at entry was rated satisfactory (Yes=1, No=0)	239	0.74	Satisfactory defined according to IEG six-point scale, converted to a dummy variable as for project overall outcome
Bank supervision was rated satisfactory (Yes=1, No=0)	232	0.88	Satisfactory defined according to IEG six-point scale, converted to a dummy variable as for project overall outcome
Project aimed at promoting community-driven development (CDD) (Yes=1, No=0)	243	0.32	If the objective statement says that local participation was encouraged—for example, through CDD approaches
Project aimed at improving food security (Yes=1, No=0)	243	0.05	If the objective statement specifically mentioned food security as an objective or implicitly mentioned it, say, through promotion of nutrition
Public sector management and institutions/governance rating	243	3.18	The average rating of indicators in the public sector management and institutions cluster of the Country Policy and Institutional Assessment for the country, in the year when the project was approved (obtained from the World Bank Country Policy and Institutional Assessment database). This rating is made up of five governance indicators: property rights and rule-based governance; transparency, accountability, and corruption in the public sector; quality of public administration; quality of budgetary and financial management; and efficiency of revenue mobilization (IEG 2010g)
Project targeted poor/vulnerable/ marginalized people or areas (Yes=1, No=0)	243	0.40	If the objective statement indicated that poor people, tribal and minority groups; women; small farmers; youths; unemployed youths; vulnerable people, such as those affected by war, floods, HIV-AIDS, and drought (including when war- or flood-affected areas were targeted); landless and neediest people; and poor, remote, marginalized, or low-income places, regions, or villages were targeted or if equity was mentioned as an objective but no group was mentioned as a target
Low-income country (Yes=1, No=0)	243	0.45	Based on the 2007 gross national income (GNI) per capita, calculated using the World Bank Atlas method. The groups are: low income, $935 or less; lower-middle income, $936–$3,705; upper-middle income, $3,706–$11,455; and high income, $11,456 or more. Low-income countries were classified as low-income countries, while the lower-middle and upper-middle (and one high-income country, the Slovak Republic) countries were classified as middle-income countries

(Table continues on the following page.)

	Number of observations (in the closed evaluation portfolio)	Mean (in the closed evaluation portfolio)	
TABLE D.1	**Description of Variables Used in Regression Analyses** (*continued*)		
Variable			Description
Development policy lending (Yes=1, No=0)	243	0.33	If the lending instrument type is development policy lending, the variable = 1, if lending instrument type is investment, the variable = 0
Weak government commitment (Yes=1, No=0)	243	0.30	If comments in the ICR review database indicated that political factors (such as change of government during or just before implementation) affected implementation of the project or if the project was delayed or cancelled due to lack of political will or commitment
Project in country with high corruption at the time of project appraisal (Yes=1, No=0)	243	0.36	High corruption = 1 if the rating on the accountability, transparency, and corruption indicator was below 2.91 (the average for projects in the ICR review database over the period 1998–2007)
Negative external factors (Yes=1, No=0)	243	0.16	If project was affected by political strife or economic or other crises or if emergencies led to delay or cancellation of the project or if the project was implemented during or following a time of civil or political unrest (based on comments in the ICR review database)
Weak capacity (Yes=1, No=0)	243	0.18	If project underestimated weak capacity of the client government or implementing agency in relation to complexity of the project and this negatively affected the project (based on comments in the ICR review database)

TABLE D.2 Factors Explaining Overall Outcome Ratings of Projects

Variable	Agriculture-focused projects		All projects in the closed evaluation portfolio		
	Model 1	Model 2	Model 3	Model 4	Model 5
Borrower performance satisfactory (Yes=1, No=0)	0.474[a]	0.590[b]	0.571[b]	0.593[b]	2.423[b]
Bank performance satisfactory (Yes=1, No=0)	0.868[b]	—	0.558[b]	0.555[b]	2.128[b]
Quality at entry satisfactory (Yes=1, No=0)	—	0.222[b]	—	—	—
Bank supervision satisfactory (Yes=1, No=0)	—	0.176[a]	—	—	—
Project aimed at promoting CDD (Yes=1, No=0)	0.054	0.034	0.134[c]	0.129[c]	0.898[b]
Project aimed at improving food security (Yes=1, No=0)	−0.328	−0.357[a]	−0.450[c]	−0.457[b]	−1.399[b]
Project targeted poor/vulnerable/marginalized people or areas (Yes=1, No=0)	0.0003	−0.132[a]	−0.024	−0.019	−0.126
Public sector management rating (measure of country governance)	0.167[a]	0.074	0.092[a]	0.095[a]	0.510[a]
Low-income country (Yes=1, No=0)	0.082	0.012	0.022	0.068	0.185
Development policy lending (DPL)	−0.2273	−0.4273	−0.158[c]	−0.140[c]	−0.726[b]
East Asia & Pacific				−0.005	
Europe & Central Asia				0.047	
Latin America & Caribbean				0.061	
Middle East & North Africa				0.101	
South Asia				0.075	
Borrower performance					
Weak government commitment					−0.528[b]
Weak capacity					−0.667[b]
Negative external factors					−0.465[c]
Bank performance					
Weak government commitment					−0.296
Weak capacity					−0.925[b]
Negative external factors					−0.045
Same task team leader					0.189
Number of observations	**85**	**85**	**231**	**231**	**231**
Pseudo R2	0.7416	0.6701	0.6237	0.6344	—
Likelihood ratio test of rho21 = rho31 = rho32 = 0, chi2(3) = 51.1014 Prob > chi2 = 0.0000					
/atrho21					−0.411[a]
/atrho31					−0.359
/atrho32					0.927[b]
rho21					−0.389[c]
rho31					−0.344
rho32					0.729[a]

Source: World Bank data.

Note: For Models 1 and 2, only the DPLs that are agriculture-specific were included in the model., Marginal effects reported for Models 1–4 and coefficients for Model 5. Model 5 specification includes constant terms for the three equations: overall outcome; borrower performance; and Bank performance.

a. Marginal effect is statistically significant at $p <= 0.10$.

b. Marginal effect is statistically significant at $p <= 0.01$.

c. Marginal effect is statistically significant at $p <= 0.05$.

TABLE D.3	Factors Explaining Sustainability Ratings of Projects				
	Agriculture-focused projects		All projects in the closed evaluation portfolio		
Variable	Model 1	Model 2	Model 3	Model 4	Model 5
Borrower performance satisfactory (Yes=1, No=0)	0.334[b]	0.481[c]	0.509[c]	0.538[c]	1.739 b
Bank performance satisfactory (Yes=1, No=0)	0.460[d]	—	0.128	0.153	−0.007
Quality at entry satisfactory (Yes=1, No=0)	—	0.109	—	—	
Bank supervision satisfactory (Yes=1, No=0)	—	0.081	—	—	
Project aimed at promoting CDD (Yes=1, No=0)	−0.185	−0.193	−0.021	−0.025	−0.072
Project aimed at improving food security (Yes=1, No=0)	0.285[d]	0.271[d]	0.054	0.010[d]	0.232
Project targeted poor/vulnerable/marginalized people or areas (Yes=1, No=0)	0.189	0.115	0.132[d]	0.144	0.480[b]
Public sector management rating (measure of country governance)	0.055	0.012	0.043	0.017	0.146
Low–income country (Yes=1, No=0)	−0.470[c]	−0.491[c]	−0.166[d]	−0.256[c]	−0.559[d]
Development policy lending (DPL)[a]	—	—	0.141[d]	0.101	0.499[b]
East Asia & Pacific				−0.255[d]	
Europe & Central Asia				−0.213	
Latin America & Caribbean				−0.232	
Middle East & North Africa				−0.056	
South Asia				−0.274[b]	
Borrower performance					
Weak government commitment					−0.403[b]
Weak capacity					−0.819[c]
Negative external factors					−0.382
Bank performance					
Weak government commitment					−0.341
Weak capacity					−0.960[c]
Negative external factors					0.007
Same task team leader					0.012
Number of observations	**78**	**78**	**202**	**202**	**202**
Pseudo R2	0.4085	0.3712	0.2984	0.3236	—
Likelihood ratio test of rho21 = rho31 = rho32 = 0, chi2(3) = 50.0057 Prob > chi2 = 0.0000					
/atrho21					−0.044
/atrho31					0.142
/atrho32					1.128[c]
rho21					−0.044
rho31					0.141
rho32					0.810[c]

Source: World Bank data.

Note: Marginal effects reported for Models 1–4 and coefficients for Model 5. (Model 5 specification includes constant terms for the three equations:overall outcome; borrower performance; and Bank performance).

a. DPLs were dropped in Model 1 and 2 due to perfect colinearity.

b. Marginal effect is statistically significant at p <= 0.10.

c. Marginal effect is statistically significant at p <= 0.01.

d. Marginal effect is statistically significant at p <= 0.05.

TABLE D.4 Comparison of IEG Ratings and QAG QSA Ratings for All Projects in the Evaluation Portfolio Assessed for QSA and for Agriculture-Focused Projects

Variable: 1 = satisfactory 0 = unsatisfactory	All projects in the closed evaluation portfolio			
	Overall outcome	Sustainability	DF/dx in overall outcome bivariate regression	DF/dx in sustainability bivariate regression
Borrower performance=1	94	86	0.674[a]	0.567[a]
Borrower performance=0	26	30		
Bank supervision=1	85	80	0.640[a]	0.535[a]
Bank supervision=0	21	26		
Quality at entry=1	88	79	0.396[a]	0.220[a]
Quality at entry=0	48	57		
Good governance=1 (project in country with good governance)[b]	82	77	0.161[a]	0.125[a]
Good governance=0	72	66		
Project with good M&E=1	93	88	0.196[a]	0.187[a]
Project with good M&E=0	73	69		
Same task leader=1	86	84	0.139[c]	0.159[c]
Same task leader=0	73	68		
Investment lending	82	72 n.s.	0.143[c]	−0.032
Development policy lending	68	75 n.s		
ARD Sector Board=1	83	71	0.103[d]	−0.046
ARD Sector Board=0	72	75		
Middle-income country	82	81		
Low-income country	71	64	−0.112[c]	−0.173[c]
Europe & Central Asia Region	89	80 n.s	0.143[c]	0.084
Non-Europe & Central Asia Region	74	72 n.s		
Agriculture-based country	69	69 n.s	−0.136[c]	−0.085
Nonagriculture-based country	83	78 n.s		
Sub-Saharan Africa Region	64	70 n.s	−0.193[a]	−0.050
Non-Africa region	83	75 n.s		
Weak government commitment =1	65	68 n.s	−0.169[a]	−0.068
Weak government commitment =0	82	75 n.s		-
High corruption=1 (project in country with low corruption rating)	67	64	v0.150[a]	−0.137[c]
High corruption=0	82	78		
Negative external factors =1	68	61	−0.103	−0.141
Negative external factors =0	79	75		
Food security was promoted=1	54	67 n.s	−0.246[d]	−0.070
Food security was promoted=0	78	74 n.s		

Sources: World Bank data and evaluation analysis.

Note: For columns 1 and 2 and columns 5 and 6, all differences in percentages are statistically significant except when indicated by n.s. [n.s. means that the items in the pair are not statistically different from each other]. Columns 3 and 4 and 7 and 8 report marginal affects for a bivariate regression of satisfactory outcome or sustainable outcome on the variable indicated.

a. Good governance = 1 if the average rating of indicators in the public sector management and institutions cluster is >3.18 (mean of all countries in the closed evaluation portfolio) in the year the project was approved, and good governance = 0 otherwise.

b. Marginal effect is statistically significant at $p <= 0.01$.

c. Marginal effect is statistically significant at $p <= 0.05$.

d. Marginal effect is statistically significant at $p <= 0.10$.

Agriculture-focused projects			
Overall outcome	Sustainability	DF/dx in overall outcome bivariate regression	DF/dx in sustainability bivariate regression
93	84	0.624[a]	0.575[a]
31	27		
90	79	0.785[a]	0.587[a]
12	20		
93	80	0.507[a]	0.333[a]
42	47		
77 n.s	72 n.s	0.055	0.029
77 n.s	66 n.s		
92	92	0.197[c]	0.311[a]
72	61		
84 n.s	74 n.s.	0.097	0.067
74 n.s	67 n.s.		
79 n.s	75 n.s.	0.123	-0.074
67 n.s	68 n.s.		
80 n.s	71 n.s.	0.117	-0.033
68 n.s.	68 n.s.		
84	82		
67	49	−0.175[c]	−0.332[a]
96	82	0.252[a]	0.171
71	65		
62	56	−0.218[c]	−0.818 m.s^2
84	74		
56	64 n.s	−0.292[a]	−0.070
85	71 n.s.		
63	67 n.s	−0.193[c]	−0.032
83	70 n.s		
66	60	−0.186[c]	−0.160
84	75		
75 n.s	56 n.s.	−0.019	−0.148
77 n.s	70 n.s.		
50	67 n.s.	−0.298*	−0.025
80	69 n.s.		

TABLE D.5 Bivariate Relationships between Selected Explanatory Variables and Satisfactory Overall Outcome and Sustainability of All Projects with Agricultural Components and of Agriculture-Focused Projects

QSA rating 0 = Not satisfactory 1 = Satisfactory	Percentage with satisfactory IEG ratings— all projects rated for QSA					
	Overall outcome rating	Sustainability rating	Borrower performance	Quality at entry	Bank supervision	
Overall QSA rating						
0	**0**	**0**	**0**	50	50	
1	**75**	**62**	**70**	64	80	
Development effectiveness						
0	**0**	**0**	**0**	33	**33**	
1	**77**	**64**	**72**	65	**81**	
Sound design at entry						
0	**45**	**30**	**36**	**36**	**45**	
1	**80**	**69**	**77**	**71**	**89**	
Bank supervision						
0	**33**	**0**	**33**	67	**33**	
1	**74**	**62**	**70**	63	**81**	
Quality/candor of reporting						
0	**53**	**33**	**40**	**47**	**60**	
1	**81**	**70**	**81**	**71**	**87**	
Performance and progress monitoring						
0	**40**	**33**	**50**	50	80	
1	**81**	**67**	**72**	67	78	
Borrower commitment						
0	64	**40**	**50**	64	**64**	
1	75	**66**	**75**	63	**84**	
Borrower and stakeholder ownership						
0	40	40	40	60	60	
1	78	61	70	65	81	
Focus on sustainability						
0	**33**	**17**	**33**	50	**50**	
1	**81**	**67**	**72**	67	**83**	
Staffing						
0	**0**	**0**	**0**	33	**0**	
1	**77**	**64**	**72**	65	**84**	
Supervision staff skill mix						
0	**33**	**33**	**33**	50	**33**	
1	**78**	**64**	**73**	65	**85**	
Country office involvement/contribution						
0	**0**	**0**	25	25	25	
1	**79**	**64**	72	67	85	

Sources: World Bank data and evaluation calculations.

Note: Bolded cells represent statistically significant relationships between QAG QSA and IEG ratings.

– = there were no observations for unsatisfactory Bank supervision.

a. No p-statistic provided, there was only one observation with a nonsatisfactory QSA rating.

Percentage with satisfactory IEG ratings—
agriculture-focused projects that were rated for QSA

	Overall outcome rating	Sustainability rating	Borrower performance	Quality at entry	Bank supervision
	0a	0[a]	0[a]	100[a]	100[a]
	74[a]	62[a]	71[a]	68[a]	71[a]
	0[a]	0[a]	0[a]	100[a]	100[a]
	74[a]	62[a]	71[a]	68[a]	71[a]
	40	**20**	**20**	**20**	**20**
	78	**68**	**78**	**78**	**89**
	–	–	–	–	–
	72	59	69	69	78
	50	**30**	**33**	**50**	**58**
	85	**76**	**90**	**80**	**90**
	43	**33**	57	71	86
	80	**67**	72	68	76
	60	**29**	**40**	60	**60**
	77	**70**	**82**	73	**86**
	25	25	25	50	50
	80	62	72	72	80
	25	**0**	**25**	**50**	**50**
	80	**67**	**72**	**72**	**80**
	0[a]	0[a]	0[a]	0[a]	0[a]
	74[a]	62[a]	71[a]	71[a]	81[a]
	33	33	**33**	**33**	**33**
	76	63	**72**	**72**	**83**
	0	**0**	33	**0**	33
	79	**62**	71	**75**	82

TABLE D.6	Comparison of IEG Ratings and QAG QAE Ratings for All Projects in the Evaluation Portfolio Assessed for QAE and for Agriculture-Focused Projects				
	Percentage with satisfactory IEG ratings— all projects assessed for QAE				
QAE rating 0 = Not satisfactory 1 = Satisfactory	Overall outcome rating	Sustainability rating	Borrower performance	Quality at entry	Bank supervision
Overall QAE rating					
0	75	75	75	75	88
1	81	71	78	71	85
Adequacy of Bank inputs and processes					
0	83	78	78	56	**67**
1	67	71	78	74	**88**
Adequate reflection of lessons of experience					
0	75	**55**	**62**	62	**69**
1	82	**77**	**82**	74	**90**
Adequacy of country and sector knowledge					
0	67	**50**	83	**50**	**67**
1	85	**79**	82	**78**	**91**
Quality and coherence of economic analysis					
0	**43**	50	**43**	**29**	**43**
1	**91**	73	**80**	**77**	**88**
Appropriateness of arrangements to monitor implementation					
0	**67**	**100**	70	**55**	**70**
1	**86**	**69**	84	**79**	**93**
Appropriateness of arrangements for evaluating impact and measuring outcomes					
0	**67**	67	**64**	**61**	**73**
1	**87**	77	**85**	**76**	**92**

Sources: World Bank data and evaluation calculations.

Notes: Bolded cells represent statistically significant relationships between QAG QAE and IEG ratings.

Percentage with satisfactory IEG ratings—agriculture-focused projects that were assessed for QAE				
Overall outcome rating	Sustainability rating	Borrower performance	Quality at entry	Bank supervision
68	100	67	**33**	67
81	76	74	**74**	81
50	100	75	**25**	**50**
84	75	73	**77**	**84**
80	75	60	60	80
79	80	76	72	79
75	75	100	**50**	75
89	87	79	**84**	89
40	60	**40**	**40**	**40**
89	77	**74**	**74**	**89**
60	100	80	**50**	**60**
94	79	82	**88**	94
87	73	62	**57**	69
69	83	81	**80**	87

TABLE D.7   Capacity Building Efforts in Bank Projects, by WDR typology

WDR typology	Number of investment projects that were rated	Percentage that had capacity building components
Agriculture-based	35	40
Transforming	70	**53**
Urbanized	32	**25**
Not classified	17	29
All countries	154	42

Sources: World Bank data and evaluation calculations.

Note: Bolded figures are statistically different from mean of all countries.

TABLE D.8   IFC's F&A Commitments, by Region and Strategy Period

Region	Strategy period				
	Fiscal 1998–2000	Fiscal 2001–04	Fiscal 2005–06	Fiscal 2007– calendar 2008	Total
	$ millions				
Middle East & North Africa	9	0	15	25	49
South Asia	0	17	16	153	186
Sub-Saharan Africa	13	53	54	73	194
East Asia & Pacific	35	136	97	164	432
Europe & Central Asia	72	121	201	483	877
Latin America & Caribbean	256	367	321	526	1,471
World Region	0	0	0	55	55
Grand total	385	694	704	1,479	3,263
Average per year	128	174	352	592	1,246
	Percentage				
Middle East & North Africa	2	0	2	2	2
South Asia	0	2	2	10	6
Sub-Saharan Africa	3	8	8	5	6
East Asia & Pacific	9	20	14	11	13
Europe & Central Asia	19	17	29	33	27
Latin America & Caribbean	67	53	46	36	45
World Region	0	0	0	4	2
Grand total	100	100	100	100	100

Source: IEG.

TABLE D.9 Drivers of IFC Financial Additionality—Regression Analysis

Financial Additionality=1.277-0.198*ApprQ-0.206*Sponsor+.317*FinStru

Regression Statistics					
Multiple R	0.325				
R square	0.106				
Adjusted R square	0.086				
Standard error	0.586				
Observations	140				

ANOVA					
	df	SS	MS	F	Significance F
Regression	3	5.521	1.840	5.356	0.002
Residual	136	46.729	0.344		
Total	139	52.250			

	Coefficients	Standard error	tStat	P-value	
Intercept	1.277	0.092	13.951	0.000	
ApprQ	−0.198	0.107	−1.855	0.066	
Sponsor	−0.206	0.110	−1.872	0.063	
FinStru	0.317	0.103	3.073	**0.003**	

Source: IEG.

TABLE D.10 Distribution of IFC Financial Additionality Realization Rates, Its Forms by Investment Size

Financial additionality	Investment size distribution		
Forms	Large	Small	All
Long-term financing (expected)	78	50	128
Long-term financing (realized)	74	42	116
Long-term financing–realization rate (%)	95	84	91
Fund mobilization (expected)	22	17	39
Fund mobilization (realized)	21	15	36
Fund mobilization–realization rate (%)	95	88	92
Market comfort (expected)	11	7	18
Market comfort (realized)	8	4	12
Market comfort–realization rate (%)	73	57	67
Counter-cyclical finance (expected)	7	0	7
Counter-cyclical finance (realized)	7	0	7
Counter-cyclical finance–realization rate (%)	100	0	100

Source: IEG.

FIGURE D.1   IFC—Number of CAG Personnel (fiscal 2001–calendar 2008), Headquarters and Country Offices

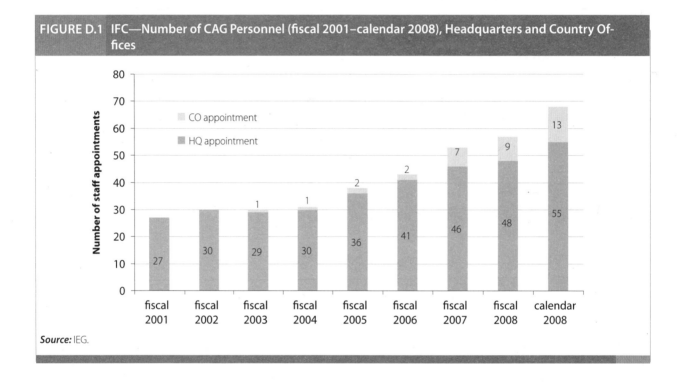

Source: IEG.

TABLE D.1   Operational Additionality in F&A Projects

Modes	Business strategy/ operational knowledge	Supply chain
Expected	32	12
Realized	24	5
Realization rate (%)	75	42

Source: IEG.

TABLE D.12   IFC Agribusiness Commitments, by Department and Strategy Period ($ millions)

Department	Strategy periods				
	FY98–00	FY01–04	FY05–06	FY07–CY08	Total
Agribusiness (CAG)	385	694	704	1,479	3,263
Global financial markets (CGF)	0	—	84	1,196	1,280
General manufacturing (CGM)	114	324	152	112	701
Infrastructure (CIN)	—	24	18	82	124
Private equity funds	—	—	—	115	115
Information technology (CIT)	—	—	—	8	8
Oil, gas, and mining (COC)	20	18	31	69	138
Total	520	1,059	990	3,061	5,629

	Reduce risk FY98–00	Ignore sector FY01–04	Path to E&S impact FY05–06	Growth engine FY07–CY08	Total
Agribusiness (CAG)	74%	66%	71%	48%	58%
Global financial markets (CGF)	0%	0%	9%	39%	23%
General manufacturing (CGM)	22%	31%	15%	4%	12%
Infrastructure (CIN)	0%	2%	2%	3%	2%
Private equity funds	0%	0%	0%	4%	2%
Information technology (CIT)	0%	0%	0%	0%	0%
Oil, gas, and mining (COC)	4%	2%	3%	2%	2%
Total	100%	100%	100%	100%	100%
Share of financial markets, funds, trade finance	0%	0%	9%	43%	25%
Share of retail, infrastructure and rural telecoms	26%	34%	20%	9%	17%
Non-CAG totals	136	365	286	1,581	2,366
Non-CAG share	28%	34%	29%	52%	42%

Source: IEG.

Note: FY = fiscal year; CY = calendar year.

TABLE D.13   IFC Advisory-Linked F&A Investment Commitments, by Year ($ thousands)

Approval fiscal year	Business line	Actual US$	Number of projects
1998	ESS	2,113	1
	CA	23,667	2
1999	CA	8,621	1
2000	CA	1,170	1
2002	ESS	34,505	2
	CA	45,250	4
	A2F	4,333	1
2003	CA	11,591	1
2004	ESS	50,000	2
	CA	53,330	2
2005	CA	45,171	3
2006	ESS	7,245	1
	CA	31,600	2
2007	ESS	120,000	2
	CA	75,000	3
	A2F	3,000	1
2008	ESS	25,000	2
	CA	30,000	1
	A2F	2,000	1
Grand total		573,596	33

Source: IEG.

Note: ESS = environmental and social sustainability; CA = corporate advice; A2F = access to finance.

Endnotes

Management Response

1. http://go.worldbank.org/1R129PSUO0
2. http://go.worldbank.org/ZJIAOSUFU0
3. http://www.gafspfund.org/gafsp/
4. http://www.responsibleagroinvestment.org/rai/
5. http://www.ifc.org/ifcext/agribusiness.nsf/content/palmoil
6. http://www.cgiar.org/changemanagement/pdf/Proposed_Mega_Program_Portfolio_Jul14.pdf
7. http://siteresources.worldbank.org/DEVCOMMINT/Documentation/22553917/DC2010-0004(4)Internal Reform.pdf
8. http://www.ifc.org/ifcext/agribusiness.nsf/Content/AFR
9. http://www.ifc.org/ifcext/devresultsinvestments.nsf/Content/DOTS
10. http://go.worldbank.org/USO9CIWW10
11. http://siteresources.worldbank.org/INTWAT/Resources/ESWWaterManagementRainfed_final.pdf
12. http://worldbank.org/genderinag
13. http://siteresources.worldbank.org/INTARD/Resources/WB_ARD_GandG_Note53_web.pdf
14. http://www.ifc.org/ifcext/sustainability.nsf/Content/EnvSocStandards

Chapter 1

1. Some countries have regional heterogeneity that spans all three categories. For example, India is a transforming economy overall, but some individual states are agriculture-based and some are urbanized. Similarly, though Mexico is an urbanized economy overall, it also has some transforming and agriculture-based states.

Chapter 2

1. Agriculture lending was 6 percent of total IDA/IBRD commitments in 2008 and 8 percent of total commitments in 2009. Even though agriculture lending increased significantly in fiscal 2009, as shown in chapter 1, total IDA/IBRD commitments also increased 1.8 times.

2. In addition, a small amount was provided through trust funds. However, the data are weak, which makes it difficult to estimate the total amount going into agriculture sector development from trust funds. An ongoing IEG evaluation of trust funds will illuminate the role of trust funds in supporting sector development.

3. See appendix B for a description of how the categorization was done.

4. Avian flu interventions were considered among those that aimed at indirectly contributing to the growth and productivity of agriculture by preventing a decline in the animal population.

5. Despite its strategic importance, the record of the Bank's AAA is incomplete. Not all AAA activities approved before fiscal 2000 for the agriculture sector have been recorded in Bank databases. Data since then are better, but the compilations are still incomplete. For example, the Mali country study found that several relevant pieces of AAA were mentioned in CASs but were not available in the Bank's databases.

6. There are no outcome ratings for AAA products as there are for Bank projects.

7. IEG's 2007 Egypt CAE also found that AAA provided strong analytical underpinning for the Bank's engagement in the rural and irrigation sector.

8. The study reports 36 percent for Sub-Saharan Africa, 50 percent for Latin America and the Caribbean, 56 percent for the Middle East and North Africa, 59 percent for South Asia, 70 percent for Europe and Central Asia, and 83 percent for East Asia and the Pacific (IEG 2008n, p. 22).

9. This trend seems to continue based on estimates of 2009 commitments. However, this time it seems exacerbated by a slowdown in CAG commitments due to the recent financial crisis and to the ripple effects of the World Bank Group's moratorium on all palm oil–related investments due to environmental concerns.

10. The Africa Enterprise Fund was evaluated by IEG in 2004 (IEG-IFC 2004): "An Evaluation of IFC's Investments through the Africa Enterprise Fund." The performance of these projects was generally poor and the program has been phased out.

11. Estimates of 2009 point to Latin America and the Caribbean receiving 48.8 percent of commitments (33.1 percent by number of projects); Europe and Central Asia, 13.6 percent (15.4 percent by number); Sub-Saharan Africa, 11.4 percent (20 percent by number); and the Middle East and North Africa, 11.1 percent (16.2 percent by number). Therefore, there is an evident relative increase in the Sub-Saharan Africa share of IFC investments. In terms of WDR typology, urbanized and transforming economies received

81.5 percent of commitments (68.5 percent by number of projects), increasing the gap with agriculture-based economies.

12. Though this evaluation covers fiscal years 1998–2008, IEG-IFC has also assessed activities supported by IFC in the six months up to December 2008 because of the dynamic nature of the private sector development activities it supports.

13. These are loans for which IFC is lender of record (A-loans) and in which commercial banks or other financial institutions (the participants) acquire participations (B-loans). Participants share the risks with IFC. IFC originates loans for participants' accounts only when it makes a loan for its own account; participants' interest and capital in B-loans are always nonrecourse to IFC.

14. IFC's evaluation system for investment operations is based on self-evaluation. Investment staff prepare Expanded Project Supervision Reports (XPSRs) for a random, representative sample of projects. IEG-IFC then undertakes an independent review of the project's performance and the assigned ratings in the XPSR (and adjusts them if needed) to ensure that the prescribed evaluation guidelines and criteria are applied consistently.

15. It refers to the objectives defined in the document submitted by IFC to its Board, requesting the approval of each specific investment project.

16. Realization rates are the ratio of the number of projects that have attained additionality compared with the number of projects that specified that form of additionality at approval.

17. This increasing trend of approvals for advisory services appears to be continuing, according to estimates of 2009 commitments. However, this time the share of Sub-Saharan Africa has significantly increased, representing 32 percent of total approvals in the year.

18. IFC advisory services activities are organized in five business lines with multiple products. **Access to Finance** helps increase the availability and affordability of financial services to smaller businesses and lower-income people. **Business Enabling Environment** helps client countries improve their investment climate, enabling firms to grow, invest, and create jobs. **Environmental and Social Sustainability** develops and tests innovative environmental and social business models, including new ways to address climate change. **Infrastructure** helps improve access to basic services in transportation infrastructure, telecommunications, water and energy utilities, health, and education. **Corporate Advice** provides advisory services alongside investments in larger enterprises to help increase development impact.

19. IFC recently assigned a dedicated product specialist to run the agribusiness investment climate practice, with the expectation of growing its share of spending and projects in the overall investment climate portfolio.

20. Estimates of 2009 point to Corporate Advice and Environmental and Social Sustainability receiving the largest share of approvals (29 percent each), but this time followed by Business Enabling Environment, with 27 percent, and Access to Finance, with 13 percent. Therefore, it is evident that there was a relative increase in emphasis on Business Enabling Environment and Access to Finance over the year.

21. The 2009 estimates point to Sub-Saharan Africa receiving 32 percent of approvals; Europe and Central Asia, 16 percent; and East Asia and the Pacific, 13 percent. Therefore, it is also evident that there was a relative increase in the Sub-Saharan Africa share of IFC advisory services. In terms of WDR typology, urbanized and transforming economies received 32 percent of approvals, which is significantly lower than their share over the review period.

22. IEG has focused much of its effort to date on the evaluative substance of the Project Completion Reports (IEG–IFC 2009, p. 44), on the sufficiency of evidence, and on the correct application of the rating guidelines (supplemented with selective field validation).

23. There were 205 stand-alone advisory services projects over the review period. Of these, 81 projects were not evaluated because records were not systematically collected and stored centrally before 2006. Therefore, IEG evaluated 124 projects in the aggregate: 97 projects were evaluated for this specific agribusiness study; 27 projects had been previously evaluated by IEG in a pilot program across business lines.

24. These results were drawn from the Project Completion Report system, which was introduced in 2006. Before 2006, in IFC, advisory services records were not systematically collected and stored. As a result, information pertaining to a number of early advisory assignments was collected for this study on a best-effort basis, and evaluative judgments were based on all available data. IFC and IEG are planning to establish a more rigorous advisory self-evaluation system, validated by IEG, similar to the one used for investment projects.

25. The development effectiveness success rate in fiscal 2001–04 has not been considered in the analysis because it accounts for a very small number of evaluated advisory projects.

26. South Asia, the Middle East and North Africa, and Sub-Saharan Africa have accounted for small numbers of evaluated projects.

Chapter 3

1. IFC does not categorize its activities by these six areas, and analysis of Bank activities has been limited by shortcomings

in the coding system and the lack of availability of subsector ratings. For purposes of this evaluation, IEG developed measures of subsector performance.

2. Of the 60, 2 were cancelled before disbursement, and hence had a Note for Canceled Operation instead of a Completion Report. When the DPLs and the emergency and CDD-type interventions are excluded, 26 projects remain; their completion reports include results related to irrigation outcomes.

3. Funding for construction of new, large-scale irrigation systems has decreased, and emphasis on rehabilitation of existing systems has grown. Projects continue to support construction of small-scale irrigation. See IEG 2006e for a more complete discussion of this issue.

4. Although Project Completion Reports often discuss cost-recovery issues, quantifying the achievement of cost-recovery efforts is difficult because indicators are often not a part of the project's results framework. While improvement in cost recovery during the life of a project may be reported, in most cases it is also noted that overall cost recovery is still below irrigation system needs.

5. Insufficient funds for operation and maintenance was cited as a concern in 90 percent of the closed projects in which the irrigation investment was rated unlikely on sustainability.

6. CGSs attempt to mobilize resources for research (and extension) and make it demand-driven by involving clients in setting priorities and financing, executing, and evaluating research. More than 30 percent of projects supporting research activities featured CGSs. A recent IEG assessment of projects in four Latin America and the Caribbean countries (IEG 2009i) found that performance of CGSs depends on in-country capacity. The outcome of the project in Nicaragua, where capacity was the weakest, was unsatisfactory. Outcome was fully satisfactory in Brazil, the country with the strongest capacity of the four, and moderately satisfactory in Peru and Colombia. An assessment of the Armenia Agricultural Reform Support Project, fiscal 1998 (IEG forthcoming), found that the CGS program did not have sufficient focus, partly because of the inability of government agricultural scientists to devise solutions for the issues facing small-scale farmers in an evolving market economy.

7. However, research and extension activities are mostly found together in Bank interventions and there is considerable emphasis in projects on adapting research to meet local conditions and needs. The size of research and extension components in these Bank interventions has varied, though about 10 percent of the portfolio consists of stand-alone research and extension interventions, such as the Peru Agricultural Research and Extension Project (fiscal 2005).

8. Advice has mainly been for conventional rather than advanced technologies. Advice has been provided on improved irrigation and water conservation practices; technologies for land reclamation; soil fertility management, improved crop varieties, and livestock breeds; integrated pest management; technologies for promoting dairy development; improved aquaculture techniques and species; and control of diseases such as avian flu. The Azerbaijan country study found that the main knowledge transferred by the Agricultural Development and Credit Program (fiscal 1999) concerned conventional technologies such as high-yielding crop varieties and crop production techniques, including raised-bed planting and minimum tillage. The Egypt country study found that projects financed by the Bank supported improvements to pumping, drainage, and irrigation to optimize water use.

9. Some of the other Regions, such as the Middle East and North Africa and South Asia, also performed as poorly on extension as Sub-Saharan Africa, though the number of projects was smaller (5 for the Middle East and North Africa and 7 for South Asia).

10. The transition occurred between 1993 and 1997, at the time of the *Vision to Action* rural development strategy. The expectation was that efficient rural financial markets would provide access to finance for all rural population groups, including farmers. Recognizing the role that access to financial services can play in alleviating poverty, the rural finance approach has been broadly aligned with the Bank's financial systems strategy that applies also to micro and SME finance.

11. The latter was first documented by Yaron and others (1997) in their analysis of Bank Rakyat Indonesia, later substantiated by other Bank and non-Bank work. The Municipal Savings Banks of Peru, El Salvador's Procredit Bank, and Mexico's BANSEFI are more recent examples. See also CGAP 2005.

12. The tool is designed to help the government manage the financial impact of shortfalls in national maize production due to drought. The index-based weather derivative contract is designed to transfer to international markets the financial risk of severe and catastrophic national drought that adversely affects the government's budget. The Malawi Maize Index (MMI), as it is known, has been constructed using rainfall data from 23 weather stations throughout the country.

13. For example, IFC issued a letter of credit for $0.75 million whereby an agribusiness company in Bangladesh exported rice to Yemen. The Global Trade Finance Program has also helped to develop trade capacity in issuing banks through advisory work.

14. Previous IEG evaluations can inform IFC's agribusiness wholesaling and microfinance support efforts. The IEG evaluation of the African Enterprise Fund (IEG-IFC 2004) offers useful lessons on some of the challenges presented by working with indigenous entrepreneurs and financial intermedi-

aries. These challenges may be germane to IFC's renewed focus on Sub-Saharan Africa and other frontier markets. The evaluation recommended that IFC should: (i) become proactive in selectively building capacity in banks; (ii) emphasize screening for impact and creditworthiness in SME project selection with a view to attracting cofinancing from regional banks; (iii) apply SME loan pricing and instrument selection that aim to avoid distorting local markets; and (iv) develop and use effectively unit metrics and incentives that reinforce progress toward achieving the strategy's objective of expanding IFC's sustainable development reach.

15. It is a private investment and development company focused on small-scale agriculture whose shareholders include IFC, DEG (Kfw Bankengruppe), and private sector companies such as Monsanto, Unilever, Cargill, and John-Deere.

16. The focus of this review is on land and agricultural productivity; it does not cover issues such as land and governance. The findings reported here are based on the early work carried out for a separate IEG land study, including from fieldwork undertaken in four countries (Ghana, Kenya, Lao PDR, and Thailand), eight countries covered by project assessments, and an additional country (Malawi) covered by an impact study. See appendix C for details. The emerging findings have been triangulated with those in the literature.

17. In general, inequality in distribution in Sub-Saharan Africa is less than in Latin America and South Asia.

18. It is not possible to pin down a precise dollar amount for land activities in the component projects, because the Bank data systems do not have a separate code for land projects.

19. Examples of parallel land administration and support services projects are: the Kazakhstan Real Estate Registration Pilot Project and Agricultural Post-Privatization Assistance Project (both fiscal 1998) and Azerbaijan Real Estate Registration Project (fiscal 2007), and, for support services, the Agricultural Development and Credit Project (Phase II, fiscal 2006).

20. The Rural Access Index measures the number of rural people who live within 2 kilometers (typically equivalent to a walk of 20–25 minutes) of an all-season road as a proportion of the total rural population (Roberts, Shyam, and Rastogi 2006).

21. IEG's transport evaluation (IEG 2007a) found that roads and highways made up 61 percent of the transport portfolio between fiscal years 1995 and 2006. Ports, waterways, and shipping represented 5 percent; railways, 3 percent; and aviation, 1 percent.

22. Fan and Rao (2003) summarize findings from several econometric studies in China, India, Thailand, and Uganda. Rural roads were found to have among the highest social returns.

23. The outcomes of these advisory services could not be evaluated due to lack of information.

24. See Rios and others 2009 and Webber and Labaste 2010 for details of the challenges faced in Sub-Saharan Africa.

25. An illustrative "mainstream" agroenterprise project is the Philippines Diversified Farm Income and Market Development Project (fiscal 2004). It includes, for instance, a significant lending commitment to agribusiness that is designed to strengthen the safety and quality of agricultural products. More than $15 million, or close to 26 percent of the total project cost, is being allocated to support the Department of Agriculture's regulatory services, in particular to ensure that international standards for safety and quality are met.

26. According to IEG interviews, IFC also attempted to deliver an infamous, controversial butterfly ranching advisory services project.

27. For EBRD, this is already a normal business line.

28. Typically, two kinds of arrangements dominate the relationships between farmers and traders, processors, and retailers: (i) a vertical relationship linking processors and retailers to farmers and (ii) a horizontal relationship aggregating farmers in cooperatives. The single most important reason for conflicts in both types of arrangements is actual or perceived information asymmetry. This happens, for example, when one participant in the transaction has more market information than the other, especially on prices, and uses it to their advantage (Chowdhury, Negassa, and Torero 2005).

29. For example, projects in Sub-Saharan Africa require 1.8 investment officers per ten million dollars of commitments. That is roughly two or three times what is required in other Regions.

Chapter 4

1. Regression analysis found that projects implemented in a country where weak government or implementing agency capacity was identified as affecting project performance were less likely to have satisfactory borrower performance. The regression also found that projects implemented in countries where government commitment was low had a higher probability of unsatisfactory borrower performance. Good governance in a country was also positively associated with project performance (appendix table D.2).

2. "The protection rate is the outcome of various political decisions, including decisions on macroeconomic parameters and on other sectors. The implications of those decisions on agriculture are often unintended, at least partly, by political decision-makers. In contrast, the share of agriculture in the national budget is the most visible and direct measure on

which policy makers decide. Hence it is a useful variable for explaining the 'political will' [or commitment] to support agricultural development from a political economy perspective" (Palaniswamy and Birner 2006).

3. China's Ninth Five-Year Plan (1996–2000) placed sustained and stable growth in agriculture and the rural economy at the top of its agenda, at the same time acknowledging the challenges involved in achieving this goal. The Tenth Five-Year Plan (2000–05) follows the thrust of the previous plan by emphasizing the need to strengthen this sector and to increase farmers' income. The Eleventh Five-Year Plan (2006–10) includes increased agricultural productivity among its main objectives. In keeping with the country's priorities, during the evaluation period the World Bank supported agricultural productivity through a range of projects that supported irrigation, watershed development and soil conservation, fisheries and livestock, agricultural technology development and extension, and institutional reform.

4. See "Agricultural Sector Reform in Europe and Central Asia" (IEG 2010a), an IEG thematic overview covering the farm restructuring experience of five transition economies (Armenia, Azerbaijan, Georgia, Romania, and Tajikistan). The country study for Azerbaijan further elaborates how growth of agriculture and the agribusinesses sector, which employs 40 percent of the country's workforce, was considered key to the growth of the non-oil economy. Land privatization was achieved first, and the government then began making efforts to establish critical support services such as agricultural extension and credit, which had collapsed at the end of the Soviet period.

5. http://www.nepad-caadp.net/about-caadp.php#Vision.

6. The average size of a high DO/IO investment project was $22 million, while the average size of a low DO/IO project was $11 million. The average size of a high DO/IO project was $83 million, more than double the size of one with low DO/IO.

7. To examine project high-risk intensity at approval, IEG assesses whether eight high-risk factors were present at the time of project approval. These factors are: (i) sponsor quality: sponsor's experience, financial capacity, commitment to the project, and its business reputation; (ii) product market: distortions or no clear inherent competitive advantage add risk; (iii) debt service burden: burden of debt service in the year principal repayments start; (iv) project type: greenfield projects generally involve higher risks than expansions; (v) sector risk: sectors exposed to high price or supply volatility (such as agribusiness), or weather and safety conditions (such as tourism) are higher risk, as demonstrated in IFC's investment experience; (vi) country business climate at project approval: IEG uses the *Wall Street Journal*/Heritage Foundation Index of Economic Freedom (WSJ/Heritage) overall synthesis ratings as the primary indicator of a country's business climate quality; (vii) IFC review intensity: projects that do not go to the Credit Review Department (Credit Department) or the Corporate Investment Committee are considered to be higher risk; and (viii) nonrepeat project: IFC's first-time clients are generally assessed as higher risk.

8. Although the concept of additionality was introduced in 2002, IFC corporate strategies made only scant and random references to it until fiscal 2007 (IFC 2007). The definition of additionality was further refined the following year in a note sent to staff (IFC 2008). "IFC's Role and Additionality" has now become an integral element in every Board paper, and each project team is required to identify how IFC "adds value" to each project (also known as "role and contribution," "additionality," or "role and additionality"). IFC and IEG additionality definitions differ in their dimensions, although they are conceptually identical. IFC's definition of additionality has four dimensions (i) risk mitigation, (ii) knowledge and innovation, (iii) standard setting, and (iv) policy work (together with the World Bank). In contrast, IEG's definition of additionality has three dimensions (i) financial additionality (structuring, mobilization of funds, "halo" effects, countercyclical lending); (ii) operational additionality (project functioning, business strategy, operations management, business development, standards and regulations, business environments); and (iii) institutional additionality (corporate governance, knowledge and innovation, regulations, efficient public-private risk allocation). This evaluation follows IEG's dimensions.

9. IEG has regressed financial additionality (as a dependent variable) against the risk the factors discussed in this section (as independent variables).

10. IEG has measured realization rates as the ratio of the number of projects that have realized a certain form of additionality compared to the number of projects that specified that form of additionality at approval.

11. The average rating for indicators under the "public sector management and institutions" criterion of the Bank's Country Policy and Institutional Assessment was used as a measure of governance (appendix table D.1; also see IEG 2010g). The "transparency, accountability, and corruption in the public sector" indicator was used as a measure of corruption. (See appendix D for details.)

12. An IEG review of CDD interventions in the Sahel Region of Africa found that "although projects might allow for natural resource management and agriculture improvement activities, when communities are given limited resources and asked to prioritize, those without access to services such as schools or reliable sources of water will favor those investments over productive investments" (IEG 2003).

13. F&A investments linked to Corporate Advice advisory projects have traditionally dominated, and the ones linked to Sustainability advisory projects have recently increased. Investments linked with Corporate Advice and Sustainability have accounted for 57 percent and 42 percent, respectively, of the $574 million of advisory-linked F&A investment commitments—with ESS-linked investments accounting for the largest share since fiscal 2007.

14. For example, IFC no longer supports livestock slaughtering and meat processing in Argentina, in part because of taxation issues and export bans (Nogués 2008). However, four of the largest international groups in the sector have been acquiring slaughterhouses in Argentina, and local slaughterhouses lack access to financing (IPCVA 2008). At the same time, IFC has been heavily investing in the country's oilseed crushing sector, which is subject to unusually high export taxes (and to implied subsidies on soy meal through differential export taxes), and in modern retailers that face the same tax issues as the livestock and meat sectors.

15. Fiscal 2001 is the first year for which personnel information is available.

16. Five in Latin America, four in East Asia, three in Africa, two in India, and one in the Middle East.

17. Based on interviews with clients and IFC staff, there seems to be room for process improvements, in particular in business development and staff incentives.

18. The inadequate skills are illustrated by the complaints of some clients that Environment and Social Development Department staff often have little, if any, benefit-cost information about the impact of their environmental and social requirements. Therefore, IFC has not generally made the case for the potential economic benefits of its environmental and social requirements. For instance, a leading food processor in Peru has achieved the same environmental and social objective as requested by IFC, but it has done so by successfully reducing water usage instead of building the costly wastewater treatment plant prescribed by IFC. While some environmental and social elements should be considered public goods, in many situations explaining the relations between environmental and social improvements and the company's bottom line could help IFC's dialogue with its clients.

19. The Foreign Investment Advisory Service, a joint World Bank-IFC-MIGA unit that advises governments on business environment issues.

20. As measured by staff weeks (which typically represent over 80 percent of total departmental expenditures), CAG's resources fell from 3 percent to 2 percent of total IFC staff weeks from 2001 to 2007.

21. According to IEG interviews, CAG seldom resorts to hiring industry consultants.

22. CAG is presently working on some knowledge-sharing initiatives, such as AgriLessons, the Global Agribusiness Intranet Site, the "CAG kitchen," Global Agribusiness Practice Groups, and blending advisory services with investment.

23. Some of those clients had connections to the Washington, DC, area.

24. IFC's efforts to decentralize its operations and expedite decision making gained momentum in fiscal 2008 with the Global-Local Initiative. Senior investment officers have been placed in Regional hubs, and more decision-making authority has been transferred to Regions, with the intention of increasing client focus. Since fiscal 2009, the Industry Clustering Initiative has aimed to increase staff specialization in country offices, enhance career development opportunities, and increase levels of client service. CAG has been clustered with Global Manufacturing and Services and the Health and Education Department. These initiatives could help eliminate often artificial organizational delineations and encourage a more integrated approach to the F&A subsectors. Conversely, these initiatives may overstretch CAG's already limited industry expertise because they disperse CAG's limited knowledge among IFC's country offices and assign CAG responsibilities to staff lacking sector knowledge (for example, investment and portfolio staff, managers, and directors in other Regional or functional departments).

25. The degree of decentralization of CAG staff further increased after calendar year 2008. For example, by the end of fiscal 2009, CAG had 23 investment officers in headquarters, 20 investment officers in field offices, and 9 additional field investment-officer positions were well advanced in their hiring stage. In addition, a total of 25 investment officers hired by the IFC Regions were also providing support to CAG.

26. For example, the IFC investment officer supervising a soybean processor in Argentina was located first in Thailand and later in Turkey. Expertise probably prevailed over closeness to clients in this case. IFC staff also noted that project size and visibility really mattered; therefore, they felt pushed to deliver larger projects with existing clients.

27. IFC 2013 is a comprehensive effort to provide a foundation for expanding IFC's impact globally by enhancing its development impact, making life easier for staff, and improving its ability to deliver the best to IFC clients (see the IFC Web site).

28. For example, the borrower's request to use the experience of the Madhya Pradesh District Poverty Initiatives Project (fiscal 2001) in the Madhya Pradesh Water Sector Restructuring Project (fiscal 2005) remained unaddressed, most likely because of communication barriers between sector units.

29. The Sustainable Development Network was created by bringing together the Infrastructure and Environmentally

and Socially Sustainable Development Vice-Presidencies. The Network brings together key areas of development activity, such as energy, water supply and sanitation, transport, urban development, agriculture and rural development, environment, and social development with the objective of strengthening the institution's focus on sustainability. The Water Sector Board was also formed as a part of this reorganization, and all irrigation staff in the Bank were brought under its umbrella.

30. IEG found similar organizational issues across IFC departments in IEG 2009h.

31. For instance, EBRD has had an "Agribusiness Operations Policy" since May 2002 that uses the supply chain approach. However, the Bank's evaluation department has found that the EBRD has not always followed this approach. Furthermore, in cases of strong sponsors and repeat business, the backward linkages were left to the resources of the borrower.

32. Seven IFC departments target projects related to agribusiness (see appendix figure B.1). CAG focuses on seeds, farm production, and distribution projects. The six departments that work on other parts of the agribusiness supply chain are: Global Information and Communication Technologies; Infrastructure; Oil, Gas, Mining, and Chemicals; Private Equity and Investment Funds; Global Financial Markets; and Global Manufacturing and Services.

33. The five advisory services business lines are: Access to Finance, Business Enabling Environment, Corporate Advice, Sustainability, and Infrastructure.

34. However, it is beginning to partner with Global and Financial Markets and Private Equity and Investment Funds in order to address needs in other links of the supply chain, but there appears to be less systemic cooperation with Oil, Gas, Mining, and Chemicals; Global Manufacturing and Services; Infrastructure; Global Information and Communication Technologies; and the World Bank.

35. In the Bank, the *Vision to Action* document (World Bank 1997a) contains a four-page annex devoted to IFC agribusiness and, in a section titled "Interacting with IBRD," discussing complementarity: "Interaction is therefore a natural and desirable outcome of each institution's objective to leverage each other's work by sharing sectoral knowledge and operational experience, while each institution confines its operations to areas where it has a recognized comparative advantage." (World Bank 1997a, p. 149). *Reaching the Rural Poor* (World Bank 2003d) also discusses coordination between the two: "Donor Coordination Issues and Plans: We are committed to working with other partners, recognizing the enormous strengths and assets they contribute to our efforts. We have found, however,

that this is not always easy and their priorities, procedures (especially procurement, but also many others) and time horizons can be quite different. In our strategy, we explicitly recognize that partnerships, even with IFC, are not cost-free or easy, and we adjust our expectations accordingly. We will strive to maximize synergies with our partners, carefully balancing the costs and benefits of these relationships for our clients" (World Bank 2003d, p. 119). In IFC, the fiscal 2003 CAG strategy reported a few joint initiatives (for example, project reviews and the Mozambique investor conference). The fiscal 2006–08 strategies were silent about coordination with the World Bank, because they emphasized other priorities. Coordination with the World Bank was reintroduced in the fiscal 2009–11 strategy, which focused on knowledge and sector expertise objectives. It stressed that: (i) World Bank staff would participate in IFC industry practice groups; (ii) joint World Bank–IFC teams would identify risks and opportunities in rural wholesaling projects; and (iii) CAG would benefit from World Bank knowledge in agricultural water use efficiency, and IFC would provide an entry point for the World Bank to the private sector.

36. Project ID P081704, Agricultural Competitiveness and Diversification Project, World Bank, July 5, 2005.

37. "Investment Climate Reform Program in Mali," Phase 2, approved in December 2009 (#570427).

38. When they were visited by IEG, they had never met each other.

39. While IFC investments are made to the private sector only, IFC advisory services are delivered to the private sector and the government.

40. "There was to have been a follow-on RFIV [Rural Finance IV] Project. However, there was a dispute over 'turf' with IFC, and IBRD senior management chose to withdraw. While the guideline characterization of the need for policy dialogue signifying IBRD/IDA responsibility would seem to have been still a factor for RFIV, the late stage of resolution of this dispute, the tardy notification of the decision, and the fact that, in any case, IFC did not occupy the disputed 'turf' was clearly an unsatisfactory coordination episode" (IEG 2009l).

41. An earlier IEG report (IEG 2007c, pp. 57–64) found that coordination was more at the strategy rather than the country or project level and attributed this failure to incompatible project timelines and cultural differences. A more recent IEG report (IEG 2008i, pp. vii–viii) summarized factors that hindered World Bank-IFC coordination and pointed to "anti-cooperative," "anti-collaborative," and "pro-competitive" biases in the cultural and incentive systems of both institutions. The report listed cases where IFC-World Bank collaboration enhanced additionality. Joint projects across sectors other than

F&A indicate that IFC additionality can benefit through coordination with the World Bank (World Bank-IFC 2009).

42. The donors providing support for development of agriculture in client countries have varied. For example, the French have played a much more active role in Francophone Africa, the Inter-American Development Bank in Latin America and the Caribbean, and the EBRD in Europe and Central Asia.

43. The projects assessed were not randomly selected. Though they involved field visits, those visits may not have been able to catch minor environmental violations if they had not been picked up by the project M&E systems, a topic discussed later in this report.

44. As reported by an IEG project assessment of the China Hebei Agricultural Development Project (fiscal 1991) (IEG 2002).

45. In the Agro-Pastoral Export Promotion Project (fiscal 2000) in Niger, the PPAR (p. 35) stated "the project was designated as an environmental category B operation, subjected to a partial environmental assessment as well as an environmental analysis at project preparation. Nonetheless, the QER identified significant weaknesses in the analysis of potential environmental impacts, pointing out that the project's environmental assessment contained limited mitigation measures and inadequate guidance on responsibilities, scheduling, costs, and procedures for processing projects." In China's Tarim Basin II project (fiscal 1998) the PPAR (p. 25) stated that "Environmental assessment (OD 4.01) at appraisal categorized this project as 'B.' However, because the project included the new large dam at Xinir in a seismically active area and 75,350 ha of new irrigation on reclaimed land it should have been classified as a category 'A' project."

46. Vietnam Rural Finance Project (fiscal 1996), Tajikistan Farm Privatization (fiscal 1999), Azerbaijan Agricultural Development and Credit (fiscal 1999), and Bulgaria Agricultural Sector Adjustment Loan (fiscal 1999).

47. Because climate change has only recently become an important issue in Bank projects, this analysis is restricted to a population review of projects approved in the last three years of the evaluation period.

48. Only 26 percent of projects included "significant" adaptation or mitigation measures. Projects rated "significant" typically included three or more adaptation or mitigation measures and two or more contributing activities that constitute, together, an important part in the project. This IEG assessment surveyed the projects' intentions rather than their outcomes. An IEG study in fiscal 2012 will review the effectiveness of Bank Group support for adaptation.

49. Adaptation is understood to mean "Initiatives and measures to reduce the vulnerability of natural and human systems against actual or expected climate change effects" (IPCC 2007; IPCC Glossary Working Group III: 809). Examples of adaptation activities include measures to improve efficiency in water use on and off farm, improve soil conservation and prevent degradation, and other measures such as diversification of cropping patterns, introduction of heat-resistant crops, seed banks, and improved drought management. Mitigation denotes "Technological change and substitution that reduce resource inputs and emissions per unit of output" (IPCC 2007; IPCC Glossary Working Group III: 809). Examples of mitigation activities include measures to improve cropland management by promoting improved crop varieties, water conservation practices, and agroforestry, and actions to improve livestock management, especially by improving pasture quality and preventing its degradation and by increasing the efficiency and productivity in livestock production through breeding.

50. IFC's environmental and social policies have changed significantly over the review period. In April 2006, IFC's Board approved the Policy and Eight Performance Standards on Environmental and Social Sustainability, and IFC management approved the Environmental and Social Review Procedure. The framework in place previously was based on the nine World Bank Group safeguard policies (Operational Policies and Directives), IFC's policy statement on forced labor and harmful child labor, the guidelines in the World Bank Group *Pollution Prevention and Abatement Handbook* (World Bank, UNEP, and UNIDO 1999), the additional IFC industry-specific guidelines, and the 1998 Environmental and Social Review Procedure.

51. PS2: Labor & Working Conditions (Addressing the four core labor standards and promoting the safety and fair treatment of workers).

52. IEG visited a project in Nicaragua approved after the 2006 Performance Standards, where IFC interpreted its supply-chain requirements more broadly, and the Environmental and Social Action Plan required attention to environmental and social issues in the woodchip and cane supply chains at appraisal (not located in areas legally defined as protected). Subsequently, the project was found not to pose a threat upstream of the supply chain.

53. PS6: Biodiversity Conservation & Sustainable Natural Resource Management (Protecting biodiversity and managing natural resources sustainably).

54. The client is a large processor and merchandiser of palm and lauric oils with plantation companies in Indonesia and Malaysia. IFC's activities with the client included two investments in a trade facility to facilitate palm oil trading and two investments in a palm oil refinery in

Ukraine. In July 2007, NGOs, smallholders, and indigenous peoples' organizations in Indonesia filed a complaint with the compliance advisor and ombudsman. The advisor found that IFC's use of category C for the project and its approach to environmental and social due diligence was inconsistent with IFC's own analysis of this project's identified projected outcomes, including the sensitivity of the environmental and social issues inherent in the sector and country. This example of IFC failure to address sustainability issues in a visible agribusiness project, as well as other compliance advisor and ombudsman complaints in the agribusiness sector, emphasize the importance of proper assessments of supply chains in agribusiness projects. Another lesson drawn from IFC experience is that sponsors' commitment and skills to ensure sustainability of the supply chain are crucial in F&A projects operating close to regions with high tropical biodiversity.

55. Shifting to sustainable production techniques poses financial challenges to individual growers, processors, and sellers of important commodities such as soy, oil plants, and sugar. The product they offer the market is identical, irrespective of how it is grown or processed, making it difficult for individual growers to choose more sustainable—but also more costly—techniques if competitors do not do the same. The roundtables have emerged as a response to this challenge. Their logic is to engage all actors in the industry in agreeing on a set of standards for sustainable production. If everyone subscribes to those standards, they will lead to an across-the-board increase in costs, and it will be affordable for everyone to produce sustainably.

56. The Roundtable on Sustainable Palm Oil approved its principles and criteria in 2006 and has had an agreed-upon certifiable standard since July 2008. As of May 2010, about 2 million tons of Roundtable palm oil is produced annually. IFC expects the Better Cotton Initiative, the Roundtable on Responsible Soy, and the Better Sugarcane Initiative to approve their respective standards in 2010.

57. The requirement in Performance Standard 6 for an appropriate certification system applies only to renewable natural resources (such as forests and plantations), but not to commodities. However, IFC regards certification as good practice when available.

58. There is a difference in presentation of gender findings between IEG's recent gender evaluation and this study. The former presents findings by sector board, while the agriculture evaluation presents findings on agriculture by agricultural projects, which also fall under sector boards other than ARD. Examples include the Water, Environment, Finance, and Private Sector Development Sector Boards.

59. According to the Development Effectiveness Unit, CAG could improve coverage of the female employment indicator and provide additional indicators. Based on the industry departments' standard indicators, the Development Effectiveness Unit produces indicators that systematically capture key outcomes by client-company stakeholders. There currently are no established gender baselines; they will be defined after a complete dataset has been gathered. Coverage of 80 percent or above of the population for every indicator by the industry department is considered "good." CAG's coverage of female employment is currently 70 percent.

60. Operational Directive 10.70: Project Monitoring and Evaluation, November 1989.

61. This particular point was reported by an IEG project assessment for the China Second Loess Plateau Watershed Rehabilitation Project (fiscal 1999) (IEG 2007h).

Appendix A

1. Where these were not available, the closest document—such as President's Reports, Technical Annexes, Memoranda and Recommendations of the President, Program Documents, or Loan/Credit Agreements—were used.

2. Based on the WDR on agriculture (World Bank 2007b, p. 5), countries were categorized as agriculture-based, transforming, and urbanized based on the relationship between agriculture's contribution to growth (percent) over the period 1990–2005 and percentage of rural poor/total poor in 2002. (See also table 1.2 in chapter 1.) Countries that were not classified by the WDR on agriculture and the five regional projects in Sub-Saharan Africa, three of which involved an urbanized or transforming country, were included among the not-classified category in this evaluation. These five regional projects had total commitments of $404 million, which is 1 percent of all commitments to all projects in the evaluation portfolio. In total, the not-classified countries (including the five regional projects) had total commitments of $2,217 million, which is 5 percent of all commitments to projects in the evaluation portfolio.

3. See http://www.surveysystem.com/sscalc.htm and www.raosoft.com/samplesize.html for information on required sample size given a desired confidence level and margin of error.

4. To provide an accurate comparison between ratings of agriculture-focused projects approved in the later years (fiscal 2002–08) to ratings of agriculture-focused projects approved earlier, in fiscal 1998–2001, the ratings data were updated on May 5, 2010, from the World Bank database. All other analyses used ratings data that were downloaded on December 2, 2008.

5. The average rating of indicators in the public sector management and institutions cluster of the Country Policy and Institutional Assessment index was matched to projects in

the closed evaluation portfolio using the project's approval year. The income groups are: low income, $935 or less; lower-middle income, $936–$3,705; upper-middle income, $3,706–$11,455; and high income, $11,456 or more.

6. The client districts exhibit higher amounts of nonpoor nonwage than the counterfactual districts (making overestimation of the impact on that dimension possible).

Appendix B

1. The 48 percent excludes regional AAA that was global. When that is included, the percentage of Regional AAA to Sub-Saharan Africa is 36 percent. In both cases, Regional AAA was more likely to be done in Africa than in other Regions.

2. The study was on ESW for all sectors, not just agriculture.

3. This result indicates lower usefulness of AAA in Sub-Saharan Africa, which had relatively more Regional AAA (among the 1,110 AAA products) compared with other Regions.

4. Those with a sustainability rating of highly likely or likely or those with a risk to development outcome rating of moderate or negligible to low were given a sustainability rating of 1, those with a sustainability rating of unlikely or uncertain or highly unlikely or those with a risk to development outcome rating of significant or high were given a sustainability rating of 0.

Appendix D

1. These are probit models that provide marginal effects instead of coefficients. Marginal effects (DF/dx) is the change in probability due to a discrete change from 0 to 1 of the explanatory variable (evaluated at the mean) or due to a 1 percent change in the explanatory variable, if it is a continuous variable.

Bibliography

Abbott, Philip C., Christopher Hurt, and Wallace E. Tyner. 2008. *What's Driving Food Prices?* Farm Foundation Issue Report. http://www.farmfoundation.org/ news/ articlefiles/404-FINAL%20WDFP%20REPORT%20 7-28-08.pdf.

Abildtrup, J., and M. Gylling. 2001. *Climate Change and Regulation of Agricultural Land Use: A Literature Survey on Adaptation Options and Policy Measures.* Danish Institute of Agricultural and Fisheries Economics. Copenhagen: SJFI. http://www.foi.life.ku.dk/English/Publica tions/~/media/migration%20 folder/upload/foi/docs/ publikationer/working%20papers/2001/19.pdf.ashx.

Acker, Jenny C. 2008. "'Can You Hear Me Now?' How Cell Phones Are Transforming Markets in Sub-Saharan Africa." *CGD Notes.* Washington, DC: Center for Global Development. http:// mobileactive.org/files/file_uploads/ Aker_Cell_Phone_Niger.pdf

Adams, Martin. 2000. *Breaking Ground: Development Aid for Land Reform.* London: Overseas Development Institute.

ADB (Asian Development Bank). 2000. "Vietnam Agricultural Sector Program. Phase I Technical Report." Prepared for the ADB by ANZDEC Limited in association with IFPRI and Lincoln International.

Adger, W.N. 2003. "Social Capital, Collective Action and Adaptation to Climate Change." *Economic Geography* 79(4): 387–404.

Africa News Network. 2008. "Africa Lacks Political Will to Invest in Agriculture." http://www.africanagriculture-blog.com/2008/03/africa-lacks-political-will-to-invest .html.

AgCLIR (Agriculture Enabling Environment): Ghana. 2008. "Commercial Legal and Institutional Reform Diagnostic of Ghana's Agriculture Sector." USAID, BizCLIR project. http://bizclir.com/ galleries/country-assessments/ ghana. pdf.

Akroyd, S., and L. Smith. 2007. "Review of Public Spending to Agriculture. A Joint DFID/World Bank Study." Oxford Policy Management. http://www1.worldbank.org/public-sector/pe/pfma07/OPMReview.pdf

Alene, Arega D., and Ousmane Coulibaly. 2009. "The Impact of Agricultural Research on Productivity and Poverty." *Food Policy* 34(2): 198–209.

Alston, J.M., C-C Kang, M.C. Marra, P.G. Pardey, and T.J. Wyatt. 2000. *A Meta-Analysis of Rates of Return to Agricultural R&D: Ex Pede Herculem?* IFPRI Research Report No. 113. Washington, DC: IFPRI. http://books.google. com/books?hl=en&lr=&id=a9gjVt9cLEoC&oi=fnd&pg =PR4&dq=A+Meta-Analysis+of+Rates+ of+Return+to +Agricultural+R%26D:+Ex+Pede+Herculem&ots=6SK YLpWUe1&sig=7UmcPdGzYiL2bDfwOIDCP1wLJPs#v =onepage&q&f=false.

Alston, J.M., P.G. Pardey, and V.H. Smith, eds. 1999. *Paying for Agricultural Productivity.* Food Policy Statement 30. Baltimore: The Johns Hopkins University Press for IFPRI.

Altieri, Miguel A., and Clara I. Nicholls. 2008. "Scaling Up Agroecological Approaches for Food Sovereignty in Latin America." *Development* 51(4): 472–80.

Anderson, J.R. 2008. *Aligning Global Agricultural Research Investments with National Development Activities: The CGIAR Experience.* Washington, DC: CGIAR.

———. 2007. "Agricultural Advisory Services." A background paper for "Innovating through Science and Technology," chapter 7 of *World Development Report 2008.* http://econ. worldbank.org/WBSITE/EXTERNAL/EXTDEC/EX-TRESEARCH/EXTWDRS/EXTWDR2008/0,,contentM DK:21496980~menuPK:4304383~pagePK:64167689~pi PK:64167673~theSitePK:2795143,00.html

———. 1998. "Selected Policy Issues in International Agricultural Research: On Striving for International Public Goods in an Era of Donor Fatigue." *World Development* 26(6): 1149–64.

Anderson, J.R., and D.G. Dalrymple. 1999. "The World Bank, the Grant Program, and the CGIAR: A Retrospective Review." OED Working Paper Series No. 1, OED, Washington, DC.

Anderson, J.R., G. Feder, and S. Ganguly. 2006. "The Rise and Fall of Training and Visit Extension: An Asian Mini-Drama with an African Epilogue." In *Changing Roles of Agricultural Extension in Asian Nations,* ed. A.W. Van den Ban and R.K. Samanta. New Delhi: B.R. Publishing.

Anderson, J.R., R.W. Herdt, and G.M. Scobie. 1988. *Science and Food: The CGIAR and Its Partners.* Washington, DC: World Bank.

Anderson, Kym. 2008. "Fifty Years of Distortions in World Food Markets." World Bank and University of Adelaide. Paper for a Seminar Presented at IFPRI, Washington, DC.

———, ed. 2009. *Distortions to Agricultural Incentives. A Global Perspective, 1955–2007*. Washington, DC: Palgrave Macmillan and World Bank.

Anderson, Kym, and Will Martin. 2009. *Distortions to Agricultural Incentives in Asia*. Washington DC: World Bank.

Ariga, Joshua, T.S. Jayne, and J. Nyoro. 2006. "Factors Driving the Growth in Fertilizer Consumption in Kenya, 1990–2005: Sustaining the Momentum in Kenya and Lessons for Broader Replicability in Sub-Saharan Africa." Tegemeo Working Paper 24, Egerton University, Kenya.

Aune, Jens B., and Andre Bationo. 2008. "Agricultural Intensification in the Sahel—The Ladder Approach." *Agricultural Systems* 98(2): 119–125.

Badiane, Ousmane. 2008. "Sustaining and Accelerating Africa's Agricultural Growth Recovery in the Context of Changing Global Food Prices." *IFPRI Policy Brief 9*. Washington, DC: IFPRI.

Barrett, Christopher B., Michael R. Carter, and C. Peter Timmer. 2010. "A Century-Long Perspective on Agricultural Development." *American Journal of Agricultural Economics* 92 (2): 447–68.

Beintema, Nienke M., and Gert-jan Stads. 2008. "Measuring Agricultural Research Investments: A Revised Global Picture." *ASTI Background Note*. Washington, DC: IFPRI. http://www.egfar.org/egfar/digitalAssets/1329_Global_revision_final.pdf

Beintema, Nienke M., Philip G. Pardey, and Flavio Avila. 2006. "Brazil: Maintaining the Momentum." In *Agricultural R&D in the Developing World: Too Little, Too Late?* ed. Philip G. Pardey, Julian M. Alston, and Roley R. Piggott. Washington, DC: IFPRI.

Bill and Melinda Gates Foundation. 2008. *Working to Break the Cycle of Hunger and Poverty*. www.gatesfoundation.org.

Binswanger, Hans, Klaus Deininger, and Gershon Feder. 1993. "Agricultural Land Relations in the Developing World." *American Journal of Agricultural Economics* 75(5):1242–48.

Birner, R. 2007. "Improving Governance to Eradicate Hunger and Poverty." *2020 Focus Brief on the World's Poor and Hungry People*. Washington, DC: IFPRI.

Birner, R., and J.R. Anderson. 2009. "How to Make Agricultural Extension Demand-Driven? The Case of India's Agricultural Extension Policy." In *Changing Contours of Asian Agriculture: Policies, Performance and Challenges: Essays in Honour of Professor V.S. Vyas*, ed. V. Ratina Reddy and Surjit Singh. New Delhi: Academic Foundation.

———. 2007. "How to Make Agricultural Extension Demand-Driven?" Discussion Paper 00729, IFPRI, Washington, DC.

Birner, R., and Danielle Resnick. Forthcoming. "The Political Economy of Policies for Smallholder Agriculture." *World Development* (in press).

———. 2005. *Governance for Agricultural and Rural Development*. Washington, DC: IFPRI.

Birner, R., M. Cohen, and J. Ilukor. 2010. "Rebuilding Agricultural Livelihoods in Post-Conflict Situations: What Are the Governance Challenges? The Case of Northern Uganda." Unpublished project report, IFPRI, Washington, DC.

Birner, R., S. Gupta, and N. Sharma. 2009. *The Political Economy of Agricultural Policy Reform in India: The Case of Fertilizer Supply and Electricity Supply for Groundwater Irrigation*. Washington, DC: IFPRI.

Birner, R., K. Davis, J. Pender, E. Nkonya, P. Anandajayasekeram, J. Ekboir, A. Mbabu, D. Spielman, D. Horna, S. Benin, and M. Cohen. 2009. "From Best Practice to Best Fit: A Framework for Designing and Analyzing Pluralistic Agricultural Advisory Services Worldwide." *Journal of Agricultural Education and Extension* 15(4): 341–55.

Birthal, Pratap S., P.K. Joshi, and Ashok Gulati. 2005. "Vertical Coordination in High-Value Food Commodities: Implications for Smallholders." MTID Discussion Paper No. 85, IFPRI, Washington, DC.

Bonnen, J.T. 1998. "Agricultural Development: Transforming Human Capital, Technology, and Institutions." In *International Agricultural Development*, Third edition, ed. Carl K. Eicher and John M. Staatz. Baltimore: The Johns Hopkins University Press.

Brahmbhatt, Milan, and Albert Hu. 2007. "Ideas and Innovation in East Asia." Chief Economist Office, East Asia and Pacific Region. Policy Research Working Paper No. 4403, World Bank, Washington, DC.

Bruinsma, J. 2009. "The Resource Outlook to 2050: By How Much Do Land, Water and Crop Yields Need to Increase by 2050?" Prepared for How to Feed the World: High-Level Expert Forum, FAO, Rome, October 12–13, 2009. http://www.fao.org/wsfs/forum2050/wsfs-background-documents/wsfs-expert-papers/en/.

———. ed. 2003. "World Agriculture: Towards 2015/30, an FAO Perspective." London and Rome: Earthscan and FAO. http://www.fao.org/es/esd/gstudies.htm.

Byerlee, D., and G.E. Alex. 1999. *Competitive Research Grant Programs: Good Practice for Design and Management*. Washington, DC: World Bank. (Revisited in 2005 as an investment note for the *AgInvestment Sourcebook* on the Web; updated in 2006.)

———. 1998. *Strengthening National Agricultural Research Systems: Policy Issues and Good Practice*. Washington, DC: World Bank.

CGAP (Consultative Group to Assist the Poorest). 2005. "CGAP Case Studies in Agricultural Finance: An Overview." CGAP, Washington, DC.

CGD (Center for Global Development). 2009. "Coping with Rising Food Prices: Policy Dilemmas in the Developing World." Working paper No. 164, CGD, Washington, DC.

———. 2007. *The World Bank's Work in the Poorest Countries: Five Recommendations for a New IDA*. Report of the IDA 15 Working Group. Washington, DC: CGD.

CGIAR (Consultative Group on International Agricultural Research). 2008. *Bringing Together the Best of Science and the Best of Development. Independent Review of the CGIAR System*. Report to the Executive Council. Washington, DC: CGIAR.

CGIAR Science Council. 2006. *Evaluation and Impact of Training in the CGIAR*. Science Council Secretariat. Rome: FAO.

Chambers, R., and B.P. Ghildyal. 1985. "Agricultural Research for Resource Poor Farmers: The Farmer-First-and-Last Model." *Agricultural Administration* 20(1): 1–30.

Chambers, R., A. Pacey, and L.A. Thrupp. 1989. *Farmer First: Farmer Innovation and Agricultural Research*. London: IT Publications. http://www.ntd.co.uk/idsbookshop/details.asp?id=243.

Chowdhury, Shyamal, Asfaw Negassa, and Maximo Torero. 2005. "Market Institutions: Enhancing the Value of Rural-Urban Links." Washington, DC: IFPRI.

Christiaensen, Luc, and Lionel Demery. 2007. *Down to Earth Agriculture and Poverty Reduction in Africa*. Directions in Development. Washington, DC: World Bank.

Christy, R., E. Mabaya, N. Wilson, E. Mutambatsere, and N. Mhlanga. 2009. "Enabling Environments for Competitive Agro-industries." In *Agro-industries for Development,* ed. C.A. Da Silva, D. Baker, A.W. Shepherd, S.M. da Cruz, and C. Jenane. London: CABI International.

Cline, William. 2007. *Global Warming and Agriculture Impact Estimates by Country*. Washington, DC: Center for Global Development.

Collinson, M. ed. 2000. *A History of Farming Systems Research*. Wallingford, UK: FAO and CABI.

Commission for Africa 2005. *Our Common Interest: Report of the Commission for Africa*. http://allafrica.com/sustainable/resources/view/00010595.pdf.

Conning, Jonathan, and Christopher Udry. 2007. "Rural Financial Markets in the Developing Countries." In the *Handbook of Agricultural Economics,* Volume 3, *Agricultural Development: Farmers, Farm Production, and Farm Markets,* ed. R. E. Evenson, P. Pingali, and T.P. Schultz. Amsterdam: North-Holland.

Constantin, A.L. 2008. "Turning High Prices into an Opportunity: What is Needed?" Minneapolis, MN: IATP (Institute for Agriculture and Trade Policy).

Cotula, L., S. Vermeulen, R. Leonard, and J. Keeley. 2009. *Land Grab or Development Opportunity? Agricultural Investment and International Land Deals in Africa*. London/Rome: FAO, IIED, and IFAD.

Coulter, J. 2007. "Farmer Groups Enterprises and the Marketing of Staple Food Commodities in Africa." Working Paper No. 72, prepared for CAPRI (Collective Action and Property Rights), IFPRI, Washington, DC.

Crawford, E.W., T. S. Jayne, and V.A. Kelly. 2006. "Alternative Approaches for Promoting Fertilizer Use in Africa." ARD Discussion Paper 22, World Bank, Washington, DC.

de Haan, Cornelis, Tjaart Schillhorn van Veen, Brian Brandenburg, Jérôme Gauthier, François Le Gall, Robin Mearns, and Michael Siméon. 2001. *Livestock Development: Implications for Rural Poverty, the Environment, and Global Food Security*. Washington, DC: World Bank.

Dehejia, R. H., and S. Wahba. 2002. "Propensity Score Matching Methods for Nonexperimental Causal Studies." Discussion Paper 0102-14, Columbia University, Department of Economics, New York, New York.

Deininger, K., and others. 2010. "The Impact of Demand-Driven Extension in Uganda." World Bank, Washington, DC.

de Janvry, Alain, and Elisabeth Sadoulet. 2010. "Agricultural Growth and Poverty Reduction: Additional Evidence." *World Bank Research Observer* 25(1):1–20.

Delgado, C., M. Rosegrant, H. Steinfeld, S. Ehui, and C. Courbois. 1999. "Livestock to 2020: The Next Food Revolution." Food, Agriculture, and the Environment Discussion Paper 28, IFPRI, Washington, DC.

DFID (Department for International Development, U.K.). 2004. "Official Development Assistance to Agriculture." Paper produced by the Agriculture and Natural Resources Team of DFID, London.

Diouf, J. 2003. "Agriculture, Food Security and Water: Towards a Blue Revolution." *OECD Observer* No. 236, March. http://www.oecdobserver.org/news/fullstory.php/aid/942/Agriculture,_food_security_and_water_:_Towards_a_blue_revolution.html.

Dixon, John, and Aidan Gulliver, with David Gibbon. 2001. *Farming Systems and Poverty: Improving Farmers' Livelihoods in a Changing World*. Rome and Washington, DC: FAO and World Bank.

Djurfeldt, G., H. Holmén, and M. Jirström. 2006. *Addressing Food Crisis in Africa: What Can Sub-Saharan Africa Learn From Asian Experiences in Addressing Its Food Crisis*? Stockholm: SIDA.

Djurfeldt, G., H. Holmén, M. Jirström, and R. Larsson, eds.

2005. *The African Food Crisis: Lessons from the Asian Green Revolution.* Wallingford, UK: CABI.

Dorward, Andrew, Jonathan Kyd, Jamie Morrison, and Ian Urey. 2004. "A Policy Agenda for Pro-Poor Agricultural Growth." *World Development* 32(1): 73–89.

EBRD (European Bank for Reconstruction and Development). 2008. *Agribusiness Operations.* Special Study, Oper No: PE07-378S, Evaluation Department. London: EBRD.

EC (European Commission). 2008. *Sector Approaches in Agriculture and Rural Development.* Tools and Methods Series, Reference Document 5. Luxemburg: EC.

ECG (Evaluation Cooperation Group). 2010. "Synthesis of the Agriculture and Agribusiness Literature: MDB Lessons Learned." ECG mimeo.

Egypt, Arab Republic of. 2009. *Agriculture Sustainable Development Strategy.* Dokki: Ministry of Agriculture and Land Reclamation.

Eicher, Carl K. 1999. "Institutions and the African Farmer." Third Distinguished Economist Lecture, Mexico City, CIMMYT Economic Program, January 22, *Issues in Agriculture* 14. Mexico D.F. Mexico.

Elliott, Kimberly. 2008. "Biofuels and the Food Price Crisis: A Survey of the Issues." Working Paper No. 151, CGD, Washington, DC.

Elliott, K.A., and M. Hoffman. 2010. *Pulling Agricultural Innovation into the Market.* Washington, DC: CGD.

Ellis, F. 1992. *Agricultural Policies in Developing Countries.* Cambridge, U.K.: Cambridge University Press.

Ellsworth, Lynn. 2004. *A Place in the World: A Review of the Global Debate on Tenure Security.* New York, NY: Ford Foundation.

Evans, A. 2009. "The Feeding of the Nine Billion, Global Food Security for the 21st Century." London: Royal Institute of International Affairs. http://www.chatham house.org.uk/files/13179_r0109food.pdf.

———. 2008. "Rising Food Prices, Drivers and Implications for Development." London: Royal Institute of International Affairs. http://www.chathamhouse.org.uk/files/11422_bp0408food.pdf.

Evenson, R.E. 2003. "Production Impacts of Crop Genetic Improvement." In *Crop Variety Improvement and Its Effect on Productivity: The Impact of International Agricultural Research*, ed. R.E. Evenson and D. Gollin. Wallingford, UK: CABI.

Evenson, R.E., and D. Gollin. 2003. "Assessing the Impact of the Green Revolution, 1960 to 2000." *Science* 300(5620): 758–62.

Evenson, Robert, Carl Pray, and Mark Rosegrant. 1999. *Agricultural Research and Productivity Growth in India.* IFPRI Research Report 109. Washington, DC: IFPRI.

Fan, Shenggen. 2008a. "Public Expenditures, Growth and Poverty. Lessons from Developing Countries." *IFPRI Issues Brief* 51. Washington, DC: IFPRI.

———. 2008b. *Public Expenditures, Growth, and Poverty.* Baltimore: The Johns Hopkins University Press for IFPRI.

Fan, Shenggen, and Connie Chan-Kang. 2009. "Regional Road Development, Rural and Urban Poverty: Evidence from China." *Transport Policy* 15(5): 305–14.

Fan, Shenggen, and Peter Hazell 1999. "Are Returns to Public Investment Lower in Less-Favored Rural Areas? An Empirical Analysis." Environment and Production Technology Division, EPTD Discussion Paper No. 43, IFPRI, Washington, DC.

Fan, Shenggen, and Neetha Rao. 2003. "Public Spending in Developing Countries: Trends, Determination and Impact." EPTD Discussion Paper No. 99, IFPRI, Washington, DC.

Fan, Shenggen, and M.W. Rosegrant. 2008. "Investing in Agriculture to Overcome the World Food Crisis and Reduce Poverty and Hunger." *IFPRI Policy Brief* 3. IFPRI, Washington, DC.

Fan, Shenggen, and Sukhadeo K. Thorat. 2007. "Public Investment, Growth, Poverty Reduction: A Comparative Analysis of India and China." In *The Dragon and the Elephant. Agricultural and Rural Reforms in China and India*, ed. Gulati Ashok and Shenggen Fan. Baltimore: The Johns Hopkins University Press.

Fan, Shenggen, Peter Hazell, and Sukhadeo K. Thorat. 1999. "Linkages between Government Spending, Growth, and Poverty in Rural India." Research Report No. 110, IFPRI, Washington, DC.

Fan, Shenggen, T. Mogues, and S. Benin. 2009. "Setting Priorities for Public Spending for Agricultural and Rural Development in Africa." *Policy Brief* 12, IFPRI, Washington, DC.

Fan, Shenggen, Keming Quian, and X.B. Zhang. 2006. "China: An Unfinished Reform Agenda." In *Agricultural R&D in the Developing World: Too Little, Too Late?*, ed. P.G. Pardey, J.M. Alston, and R.R. Piggott. Baltimore: The Johns Hopkins University Press for IFPRI.

Fan, Shenggen, L. Zhang, and X. Zhang. 2002. *Growth, Inequality, and Poverty in Rural China: The Role of Public Investments.* IFPRI Research Report 125. Washington, DC: IFPRI.

FAO (Food and Agriculture Organization). 2010a. "Crop Prospects and Food Situation" No. 1, February. http://www.fao.org/giews/english/cpfs/index.htm

———. 2010b. "FAO Initiative on Soaring Food Prices." http://www.fao.org/isfp/about/en/

———. 2010c. "Policies and Institutions to Support Smallholder Agriculture." Committee on Agriculture, Twenty-Second Session, Rome, June 16–19.

———. 2009a. "Capital Requirements of Developing Countries' Agriculture to 2050." Paper Presented at How to Feed the World in 2050 Expert Meeting. ftp://ftp.fao.org/docrep/fao/012/ak974e/ak974e00.pdf

———. 2009b. "The Resource Outlook to 2050: By How Much do Land, Water and Crop Yields Need to Increase by 2050?" Paper Presented at How to Feed the World in 2050 Expert Meeting, 24–26 June 2009. ftp://ftp.fao.org/docrep/fao/012/ak971e/ak971e00.pdf

———. 2009c. "The Special Challenge for Sub-Saharan Africa." How to Feed the World 2050, High-Level Export Forum, October 12–13. http://www.fao.org/fileadmin/templates/wsfs/docs/Issues_papers/HLEF2050_Africa.pdf

———. 2009d. *The State of Food Insecurity in the World Economic Crises—Impacts and Lessons Learned*. Rome: FAO.

———. 2009e. "The Technology Challenge." How to Feed the World 2050, High-Level Export Forum, October 12–13. http://www.fao.org/fileadmin/templates/wsfs/docs/Issues_papers/HLEF2050_Technology.pdf

———. 2008a. "Crop Prospects and Food Situation." Rome. http://www.fao.org/docrep/010/ai465e/ai465e00.htm

———. 2008b. "Food Outlook: Global Markets Analysis." Rome. http://www.fao.org/docrep/010/ai466e/ai466e00.HTM

———. 2008c. "Investing in Sustainable Agricultural Intensification, The Role of Conservation Agriculture, A Framework for Action." FAO, Rome.

———. 2008d. *Soaring Food Prices: Facts, Perspectives, Impacts and Actions Required. High-Level Conference on World Food Security: The Challenges of Climate Change and Bio-energy, 3–5 June 2008, Rome*. Rome: FAO.

———. 2006a. *Agricultural Commodity Markets and Trade: New Approaches to Analyzing Market Structure and Instability*, ed. Alexander Sarris and David Hallam. Cheltenham Gloucester, UK: Edward Elgar.

———. 2006b. *Livestock's Long Shadow: Environmental Issues and Options*. FAO: Rome.

———. 2006c. *The State of Food Insecurity in the World. Eradicating World Hunger—Taking Stock Ten Years After the World Food Summit*. FAO: Rome.

———. 2006d. *World Agriculture: Towards 2030/2050—Interim Report: Prospects for Food, Nutrition, Agriculture, and Major Commodity Groups*. FAO: Rome.

———. 2004. *Water Charging in Irrigated Agriculture: An Analysis of International Experience*. FAO: Rome.

———. 2003a. *Term Financing in Agriculture: A Review of Relevant Experience*. FAO: Rome.

———. 2003b. *Unlocking the Water Potential of Agriculture*. FAO: Rome.

FAO and World Bank. 2000. "Agricultural Knowledge and Information System for Rural Development (AKIS/RD): Strategic Vision and Guiding Principles." Food and Agriculture Organization of the United Nations and the AKIS Thematic Group of the World Bank, FAO and World Bank, Rome and Washington, DC.

Feder, G., and S. Savastano. 2006. "The Role of Opinion Leaders in the Diffusion of New Knowledge: The Case of Integrated Pest Management." *World Development* 34(7): 1287–300.

Feder, Gershon, Jock Anderson, Regina Birner, and Klaus Deininger. 2010. "Promises and Realities of Community-Based Agricultural Extension." IFPRI Discussion Paper 959, IFPRI, Washington, DC.

Feder, Gershon, Lawrence J. Lau, and Justin Y. LinLuo Xiaopeng. 1989. "Agricultural Credit and Farm Performance in China." *Journal of Comparative Economics* 13(4): 508–26.

Feder, Gershon, R. Murgai, and J.B. Quizon. 2003. "Sending Farmers Back to School: The Impact of Farmer Field Schools in Indonesia." *Review of Agricultural Economics* 26(1): 45–62.

Felloni, F., T. Wahl, P. Wandschneider, and J. Gilbert. 2001. "Infrastructure and Agricultural Production: Cross-Country Evidence and Implications for China." TW-2001-103, Washington, State University, Pullman.

FIAS (Foreign Investment Advisory Service), IFC. 2008. "Supporting Agribusiness Investment in Mali—Opportunities for Investment in the Mango, Potato, Tomato, and Onion Sub-sectors." August 22, 2008, Washington, DC.

Friis-Hansen, E., ed. 2000. *Agricultural Policy in Africa after Adjustment*. CDR Policy Paper. Copenhagen: Centre for Development Research.

Friis-Hansen, E., C. Aben, and M. Kidoid. 2004. "Smallholder Agricultural Technology Development in Soroti District: Synergy between NAADS [National Agricultural Advisory Services] and Farmer Field Schools." *Ugandan Journal of Agricultural Sciences* 9(1), 250–57.

Fuglie, K.O., and D.E. Schimmelpfennig, eds. 2000. *Public-Private Collaboration in Agricultural Research: New Institutional Arrangements and Economic Implications*. Ames, IA: Iowa State University Press.

Gamba, Paul, Caroline Ngugi, Hugo Verkuijl, Wilfred Mwangi, and Frank Kiriswa. 2003. "Wheat Farmers' Seed Management and Varietal Adoption in Kenya." KARI CIMMYT, Egerton University.

Gardner, Bruce L. 2005. "Causes of Rural Economic Development." *Agricultural Economics* 32(1): 21–41.

GDPRD (Global Donor Platform for Rural Development). 2009. *Joint Donor Principles for Agriculture and Rural Development Programmes: Incentives for Change.* Bonn: GDPRD.

GDPRD, World Bank, and FAO. 2008. *Tracking Results in Agriculture and Rural Development in Less-than-Ideal Conditions. A Sourcebook of Indicators for Monitoring and Evaluation.* Bonn, Rome, and Washington, DC: GDPRD, FAO, and the World Bank.

Goetz, L., and H. Grethe 2009. "The E[uropean] U[nion] Entry System for Fresh Fruits and Vegetables—Paper Tiger or Powerful Market Barrier?" *Food Policy* 34(1): 81–93.

Govereh, Jones, and T.S. Jayne. 2003. "Cash Cropping and Food Crop Productivity: Synergies or Trade-offs?" *Agricultural Economics* 28(1): 39–50.

Gowing, J.W., and M. Palmer. 2008. "Sustainable Agricultural Development in Sub-Saharan Africa: The Case for a Paradigm Shift in Land Husbandry." *Soil Use and Management* 24(1): 92–99.

Gulati, Ashok, and Shenggen Fan, eds. 2007. *The Dragon and the Elephant. Agricultural and Rural Reforms in China and India.* Baltimore: The Johns Hopkins University Press.

Gulati, A., P.K. Joshi, and R. Cummings, Jr. 2007. "The Way Forward: Towards Accelerated Agricultural Diversification and Greater Participation of Smallholders." In *Agricultural Diversification and Smallholders in South Asia,* ed. P.K. Joshi, A. Gulati, and R. Cummings, Jr. New Delhi: Academic Foundation.

Harrigan, Jane. 2008. "Food Insecurity, Poverty and the Malawian Starter Pack: Fresh Start or False Start?" *Food Policy* 33(3): 237–49.

Hartemink, Alfred E. 2008. "Soils Are Back on the Global Agenda." *Soil Use and Management* 24(4): 327–30.

Hartmann, P. 2004. *An Approach to Hunger and Poverty Reduction for Sub-Saharan Africa.* Ibadan, Nigeria: International Institute of Topical Agriculture.

Hartwich, Frank, Carolina Gonzalez, and Luis-Fernando Vieira. 2005. "Public-Private Partnerships for Innovation-Led Growth in Agrichains: A Useful Tool for Development in Latin America?" ISNAR Discussion Paper 1, IFPRI, Washington, DC.

Hazell, Peter, and Joachim von Braun 2006. "Aid to Agriculture, Growth and Poverty Reduction." *EuroChoices* 5(1): 6–13.

Heckman, J. J., H. Ichimura, and P. Todd. 1998. "Matching as an Econometric Evaluation Estimator." *Review of Economic Studies* 65: 261–94

Heisey, Paul W., and George W. Norton. 2007. "Fertilizers and Other Farm Chemicals." In *Handbook of Agricultural Economics, Volume 3, Agricultural Development: Farmers,* *Farm Production and Farm Markets,* ed. Robert Evenson and Prabhu Pingali. Amsterdam: North-Holland.

Hout, Wil. 2002. "Good Governance and Aid: Selectivity Criteria in Development Assistance." *Development and Change* 33(3): 511–27.

Howden, S. M., J. F. Soussana, F. N. Tubiello, N. Chhetri, M. Dunlop, and H. Meinke. 2007. "Adapting Agriculture to Climate Change." *Proceedings of the National Academy of Sciences* 104(50): 19691–96.

Huang, Jikun, Scott Rozelle, Will Martin, and Yu Liu. 2009. "China in Distortions to Agricultural Incentives in Asia." Agricultural Distortions Working Paper, World Bank, Washington, DC.

Hudson Institute, Center for Global Prosperity. 2009. *The Index of Global Philanthropy and Remittances.* Washington, DC: Hudson Institute.

Huffman, W., and R.E. Evenson. 2006. "Do Formula or Competitive Grant Funds Have Greater Impacts on State Agricultural Productivity?" *American Journal of Agricultural Economics* 88(4): 783–98.

———. 2003. "New Econometric Evidence on Agricultural Total Factor Productivity Determinants: Impact of Funding Sources." Department of Economics Working Paper # 03029, Iowa State University, Ames, IA.

Hyman, Glenn, Sam Fujisaka, Peter Jones, Stanley Wood, M. Carmen de Vicente, and John Dixon. 2008. "Strategic Approaches to Targeting Technology Generation: Assessing the Coincidence of Poverty and Drought-Prone Crop Production." *Agricultural Systems* 98(1): 50–61.

IAASTD (International Assessment of Agricultural Knowledge Science and Technology for Development). 2009. *Summary for Decision Makers of the Global Report.* Washington, DC: IAASTD.

———. 2008a. "Business as Usual is Not an Option: Trade and Markets." *Issues in Brief.* IAASTD, Washington, DC.

———. 2008b. "Food Security in a Volatile World." *Issues in Brief.* IAASTD, Washington, DC.

IDB (Inter-American Development Bank). 1999. "Strategy for Agricultural Development in Latin America and the Caribbean." Sustainable Development Department, IDB, Washington, DC.

IEG (Independent Evaluation Group, World Bank Group). Forthcoming. "IEG Assessment of Agriculture and Rural Development AAA. Pilot Study on Agriculture and Rural Development." IEG, Washington, DC.

———. 2010a. "Agricultural Sector Reform in Europe and Central Asia: An IEG Review of the Performance of Seven Projects." Report No. 55258, World Bank, Washington, DC.

———. 2010b. *Gender and Development: An Evaluation of*

World Bank Support, 2002–08. Washington, DC: World Bank.

———. 2010c. *Impact Evaluations in Agriculture. An Assessment of the Evidence.* Washington, DC: World Bank.

———. 2010d. "Kyrgyz Republic: Land and Real Estate Registration Project (Credit 3370)." Project Performance Assessment Report, IEG, Washington, DC.

———. 2010e. "Slovenia: Real Estate Registration Modernization Project (L-44980)." Project Performance Assessment Report, IEG, Washington, DC.

———. 2010f. *Water and Development: An Evaluation of World Bank Support, 1997–2007.* Washington, DC: World Bank.

———. 2010g. *The World Bank's Country Policy and Institutional Assessment: An Evaluation.* Washington, DC: World Bank.

———. 2010h. "World Bank Support to Land Administration and Land Redistribution in Central America." An IEG Performance Assessment of Three Projects: El Salvador, Land Administration Project (L-3982), Guatemala, Land Administration Project (L-4415), Guatemala, Land Fund Project (L-4432), IEG, Washington, DC.

———. 2009a. "Armenia Agricultural Reform Support Project." Project Performance Assessment Report, IEG, Washington, DC.

———. 2009b. *Bangladesh Country Assistance Evaluation.* Washington, DC: World Bank.

———. 2009c. *Climate Change and the World Bank Group Phase I: An Evaluation of World Bank Win-Win Energy Policy Reforms.* Washington, DC: World Bank.

———. 2009d. "Cluster Assessment: Rural Finance." IEG, Washington, DC.

———. 2009e. "Georgia: Agricultural Development Project." Project Performance Assessment Report, IEG, Washington, DC.

———. 2009f. *An Impact Evaluation of a Multicomponent Irrigation Project on Farm Households in Peru.* Washington, DC: World Bank.

———. 2009g. "Impact Study of Community-Based Land Access Project in Malawi." IEG, Washington, DC.

———. 2009h. *Improving Effectiveness and Outcomes for the Poor in Health, Nutrition, and Population, An Evaluation of World Bank Group Support since 1997.* Washington, DC: World Bank.

———. 2009i. "Latin America and the Caribbean Region: Agricultural Research and Competitive Grant Schemes." Project Performance Assessment Report, IEG, Washington, DC.

———. 2009j. "Morocco: Water Resources Management Project." Project Performance Assessment Report, IEG, Washington, DC.

———. 2009k. *Nepal Country Assistance Evaluation.* Washington, DC: World Bank.

———. 2009l. "Philippines: Third Rural Finance Project." Project Performance Assessment Report, IEG, Washington, DC.

———. 2008a. "Azerbaijan: Farm Privatization Project and Agricultural Development and Credit Project." Project Performance Assessment Report, IEG, Washington, DC.

———. 2008b. *Environmental Sustainability: An Evaluation of World Bank Group Support.* Washington, DC: World Bank.

———. 2008c. *Ethiopia Country Assistance Evaluation.* Washington, DC: World Bank.

———. 2008d. *Georgia Country Assistance Evaluation.* Washington, DC: World Bank.

———. 2008e. *An Impact Evaluation of India's Second and Third Andhra Pradesh Irrigation Projects: A Case of Poverty Reduction with Low Economic Returns.* Washington, DC: World Bank.

———. 2008f. "The International Land Coalition." *Global Program Review* 2(4). Washington, DC: World Bank.

———. 2008g. *Nepal Country Assistance Evaluation.* Washington, DC: World Bank.

———. 2008h. "Nepal: Irrigation Sector Project." Project Performance Assessment Report, IEG, Washington, DC.

———. 2008i. "Niger: Pilot Private Irrigation Project, Natural Resources Management Project, Agro-Pastoral Export Promotion Project." Project Performance Assessment Report, IEG, Washington, DC.

———. 2008j. *Nigeria Country Assistance Evaluation.* Washington, DC: World Bank.

———. 2008k. *Public Sector Reform: What Works Where and Why? An Evaluation of World Bank Support.* Washington, DC: World Bank.

———. 2008l. "Republic of Tajikistan Farm Privatization Support Project PPFI-Q1080 & Credit 32400 & 32401." Project Performance Assessment Report, IEG, Washington, DC.

———. 2008m. "Romania: General Cadastre and Land Registration Project and Agricultural Support Services Project." Project Performance Assessment Report, IEG, Washington, DC.

———. 2008n. *Using Knowledge to Improve Development Effectiveness. An Evaluation of World Bank Economic and Sector Work and Technical Assistance 2000–2006.* Washington, DC: World Bank.

———. 2008o. *Using Training to Build Capacity for Development: An Evaluation of the World Bank's Project-Based and WBI Training.* Washington, DC: World Bank.

———. 2008p. "The World Bank Group Collaboration: Evidence and Lessons from IEG Evaluations," November 18, 2008. Washington, DC.

———. 2007a. *A Decade of Action in Transport: An Evaluation of World Bank Assistance to the Transport Sector, 1995–2005*. Washington, DC: World Bank.

———. 2007b. *The Development Potential of Regional Programs. An Evaluation of World Bank Support for Multicountry Operations*. Washington, DC: World Bank.

———. 2007c. *Development Results in Middle-Income Countries*. Washington, DC: World Bank.

———. 2007d. "Ethiopia: Seed System Development Project (Credit 2741) National Fertilizer Sector Project (Credit 27400 and 27401)." Project Performance Assessment Report, IEG, Washington, DC.

———. 2007e. "Ghana Country Assistance Strategy Completion Report Review." World Bank, Washington, DC.

———. 2007f. *Mali Country Assistance Evaluation*. Washington, DC: World Bank.

———. 2007g. "Mali: National Agricultural Research Project, Agricultural Trading and Processing Promotion Pilot Project, and Pilot Private Irrigation Promotion Project." Project Performance Assessment Report, IEG, Washington, DC.

———. 2007h. "People's Republic of China: Second Loess Plateau Watershed Rehabilitation Project, Xialangdi Multipurpose Projects I&II, and Tarim Basin II Project." Project Performance Assessment Report, IEG, Washington, DC.

———. 2007i. "United Republic of Tanzania: Agricultural Sector Management Project, Second Agricultural Research Project, National Agricultural Extension Project II." Project Performance Assessment Report and Sector Overview, IEG, Washington, DC.

———. 2007j. *World Bank Assistance to Agriculture in Sub-Saharan Africa: An IEG Review*. Washington, DC: World Bank.

———. 2006a. *Annual Review of Development Effectiveness: Getting Results*. Washington, DC: World Bank.

———. 2006b. *Improving Investment Climates*. Washington, DC: World Bank.

———. 2006c. *Malawi Country Assistance Evaluation*. Washington, DC: World Bank.

———. 2006d. *Madagascar Country Assistance Evaluation*. Washington, DC: World Bank.

———. 2006e. *Water Management in Agriculture: Ten Years of World Bank Assistance, 1994–2004*. Washington, DC: World Bank.

———. 2005a. *Country Assistance Evaluation Retrospective. An OED Self-Evaluation*. Washington, DC: World Bank.

———. 2005b. *Evaluating a Decade of World Bank Gender Policy: 1990–1999*. Washington, DC: World Bank.

———. 2005c. "Mexico: Irrigation and Drainage Sector Project, on-Farm and Minor Irrigation Networks Improvement Project and Agricultural Productivity Improvement Project." Project Performance Assessment Report, IEG, Washington, DC.

———. 2004a. *Addressing Challenges of Globalization: An Independent Evaluation of the World Bank's Approach to Global Programs*. Washington, DC: World Bank.

———. 2004b. *The CGIAR at 31: An Independent Meta-Evaluation of the Consultative Group on International Agricultural Research*. Washington, DC: World Bank.

———. 2004c. *Improving Investment Climates: An Evaluation of World Bank Group Assistance, Overview Report*. Washington, DC: World Bank.

———. 2004d. *The Poverty Reduction Strategy Initiative—An Independent Evaluation of the World Bank's Support Through 2003*. Washington, DC: World Bank.

———. 2003. *Community-Driven Development: Lessons from the Sahel—An Analytical Review*. Washington, DC: World Bank.

———. 2002. "China: A Review of Development Challenges Across Selected Sectors and Performance Assessment Reports: Hebei Agricultural Development Project, Henan Agricultural Development Project, National Afforestation Project, Rural Health Workers Development Project, Basic Education in Poor and Minority Areas Project, Third Basic Education Project, Henan Provincial Transport Project, Hebei/Hena Highway Project." Project Performance Assessment Report, IEG, Washington, DC.

———. 2001a. "Bulgaria: (First) Agriculture Sector Adjustment Loan." Performance Audit Report, IEG, Washington, DC.

———. 2001b. *The Drive to Partnership: Aid Coordination and the World Bank*. Washington, DC: World Bank.

———. 1998. *India: The Dairy Revolution*. Washington, DC: World Bank.

———. 1997. *Agricultural Extension Research: Achievements and Problems in National Systems*. Washington, DC: World Bank.

———. 1996. "A Review of Bank Lending for Agricultural Credit and Rural Finance (1948–1992): A Follow Up." Report No. 15221, World Bank, Washington, DC.

IEG-IFC (Independent Evaluation Group, International Finance Corporation). 2009. "Independent Evaluation of IFC's Development Results 2009: Knowledge for Private Sector Development—Enhancing the Performance of IFC's Advisory Services." IEG-IFC, Washington, DC.

———. 2008a. "Enhancing Monitoring and Evaluation for Better Results, Biennial Report on Operations Evaluation in IFC 2008." October 1, 2008. IFC, Washington, DC.

———. 2008b. "IFC in Ukraine: An Independent Country Impact Review." *IEG Findings* No. 10. IEG-IFC, Washington, DC.

———. 2008c. "Independent Evaluation of IFC's Development Results 2008: IFC's Additionality in Supporting Private Sector Development." IFC/R2008-0020, February 15, 2008. IEG-IFC, Washington, DC.

———. 2007. "Financing Micro, Small, and Medium Enterprises in Frontier Countries through Financial Intermediaries—An Independent Evaluation of IFC's Experience." CODE2007-0051, June 29, 2007. IEG-IFC, Washington, DC.

———. 2004. "An Evaluation of IFC's Investment through the Africa Enterprise Fund." IEG-IFC, Washington, DC.

———. 2003. *Toward Country-Led Development. A Multi-Partner Evaluation of the Comprehensive Development Framework*. Washington, DC: World Bank.

———. 2000. "An Evaluation of IFC's Investments through the Africa Enterprise Fund." Operations Evaluation Group, IFC, Washington, DC.

IFAD (International Fund for Agricultural Development). 2005. *Achieving the Millennium Development Goals: Rural Investment and Enabling Policy*. Panel Discussion Paper, IFAD Governing Council—Twenty-Eighth Session. Rome: IFAD.

———. 2004. *Livestock Services and the Poor: A Global Initiative—Collecting, Coordinating and Sharing Experiences*. Rome: IFAD.

IFC (International Finance Corporation). 2008. "IFC's Role and Additionality: A Primer," IFC, February 11, 2008, Washington, DC.

———. 2007. "Road Map, IFC, 2007," IFC, Washington, DC.

IFDC (International Fertilizer Development Center). 2008. "Agricultural Development and Long-Term Solutions to the Food Crisis." Statement of Amit H. Roy, President, and Chief Executive Officer, Before the House Hunger Caucus, June 5. 2008, IFDC, Muscle Shoals, Alabama.

IFPRI (International Food Policy Research Institute). 2009. "Agriculture and Climate Change: An Agenda for Negotiation in Copenhagen." *Focus 16 Brief* 1, March, IFPRI, Washington, DC.

———. 2008. "High Food Price: The What, Who, and How of Proposed Policy Actions." *Policy Brief* (May), IFPRI, Washington, DC.

———. 2004. "Investing in Sub-Saharan African Agricultural Research: Recent Trends." *2020 Africa Conference Brief* 8, IFPRI, Washington, DC.

———. 2003. "Will Supermarkets Be Super for Small Farmers?" *IFPRI Forum,* December. Washington, DC: IFPRI.

InSTePP (Ubterbatuibak Science and Technology Practice and Policy). 2007. *Science Technology and Skills: International Science and Technology Practice and Policy Report*. October. Department of Applied Economics, University of Minnesota, and Science Council, CGIAR.

IPCC (Intergovernmental Panel on Climate Change). 2007. *Climate Change 2007: Mitigation,* ed. Bert Metz, Ogunlade Davidson, Peter Bosch, Rutu Dave, and Leo Myer. Cambridge, U.K.: Cambridge University Press.

IPCVA (Instituto de Promoción de la Carne Vacuna). 2008. "Estructura de la Oferta de Carnes Bovinas en la Argentina, Actualidad y Evolución reciente." Cuadernillo Técnico No. 6, IPCVA, Buenos Aires.

Ivanic, Maros, and Will Martin. 2008. "Implications of Higher Global Food Prices for Poverty in Low-Income Countries." Policy Research Working Paper 4594, World Bank, Washington, DC.

Jaffee, S. 2003. "From Challenge to Opportunity: Transforming Kenya's Fresh Vegetable Trade in the Context of Emerging Food Safety and Other Standards in Europe." Agricultural and Rural Development Discussion Paper, World Bank, Washington, DC.

Jaffee, S., and S. Henson. 2005. "Agro-food Exports from Developing Countries: the Challenges Posed by Standards." In *Global Agricultural Trade and Developing Countries*, ed. M.A. Aksoy and J.C. Beghin. Washington, DC: World Bank.

Jaffee, S., and J. Morton. 1995. *Marketing Africa's High-Value Foods: Comparative Experiences of an Emergent Private Sector*. Dubuque, Iowa: Kendall/Hunt.

Johnson, D.G. 1995. "The Limited But Essential Role of Government in Agriculture and Rural Life." In *Agricultural Competitiveness: Market Forces and Policy Choice*, ed. G.H. Peters and D.D. Hedley. Proceedings of the Twenty-Second Conference of Agricultural Economists, IAAE, Aldershot, 8–21. London: Ashgate Publishing.

Josling, Timothy, and Stefan Tangermann. 1998. "The Agriculture and Food Sectors: The Role of Foreign Direct Investment in the Creation of an Integrated European Agriculture." In *Enlarging Europe: The Industrial Foundations of New Political Reality,* ed. John Zysman and Andrew Schwartz. Research Series, University of California International and Area Studies Digital Collection, Edited Volume No. 99. Berkeley, CA: University of California Press.

Keeley, J., and I. Scoones. 2003. *Understanding Environmental Policy Processes: Cases from Africa*. London: Earthscan.

Kloeppinger-Tood, R., and Jonathan Agwe 2008. "Pilot Innovations Could Reignite Anemic Rural Finance." *Development Outreach* 10(3): 27–30.

Kristjanson, P.M., P.K.Thornton, R.L. Kruska, R.S. Reid, N. Henninger, T.O. Williams, S.A. Tarawali, J. Niezen, and P.

Hiernaux. 2004. "Mapping Livestock Systems and Changes to 2050: Implications for West Africa." In *Sustainable Crop–Livestock Production for Improved Livelihoods and Natural Resource Management in West Africa*, ed. T.O. Williams, S.A. Tarawali, P. Hiernaux, and S. Fernández-Rivera. Proceedings of an international conference held at the International Institute of Tropical Agriculture (IITA), Ibadan, Nigeria, 19–22 November 2001. CTA (Technical Centre for Agricultural and Rural Cooperation), ACP-EC, Wageningen, The Netherlands and ILRI (International Livestock Research Institute), Nairobi, Kenya.

Kurukulasuriya, P., and S. Rosenthal. 2003. "Climate Change and Agriculture: A Review of Impacts and Adaptations." Climate Change Series 91, Environment Department Papers, World Bank, Washington, DC.

Labaste, P., C. Poulton, and D. Tschirley. 2009. "Conclusions." In *Organization and Performance of Cotton Sectors in Africa*, ed. D. Tschirley, C. Poulton, and P. Labaste. Washington, DC: ARD, World Bank.

Lal, S. 2006. "Can Good Economics Ever Be Good Politics? Case Study of India's Power Sector." Working Paper No. 83, World Bank, Washington, DC.

Langenkamp, Christoph. 2008. Presentation Delivered at the Brussels Rural Development Briefing Session Number 6: "New Drivers, New Players in ACP Rural Development." http://brusselsbriefings.net/2008/07/22/new-drivers-new-players-in-acp-rural-development-audience-reactions/

Lee, David R., Christopher B. Barrett, and John G. McPeak. 2006. "Policy, Technology and Management Strategies for Achieving Sustainable Agricultural Intensification." *Agricultural Economics* 34(2): 123–27.

Leksmono, C., J. Young, N. Hooton, H. Muriuki, and D. Romney. 2006. "Informal Traders Lock Horns with the Formal Milk Industry: The Role of Research in Pro-Poor Dairy Policy Shift in Kenya." ODI Working Paper 266, Overseas Development Institute and ILRI, London and Nairobi. http://www.odi.org.uk/resources/download/135.pdf

Lele, Uma, and Arthur A. Goldsmith. 1989. "The Development of National Agricultural Research Capacity: India's Experience with the Rockefeller Foundation and Its Significance for Africa." *Economic Development and Cultural Change* 37(2): 305–43.

Leles, C., and D. Zylbersztajn. 2007. "Pacta Sunt Servanda Versus the Social Role of Contracts: The Case of Brazilian Agriculture Contracts." Paper presented at the Conference of the Latin American Law and Economics Association, Brasilia, 2007

Liberia, Ministry of Agriculture. 2007. *Comprehensive Assessment of the Agriculture Sector in Liberia. Volume 1, Synthesis Report*. Rome: Ministry of Agriculture (Republic of Liberia), IFAD, the World Bank, and FAO.

Lin, Justin Yifu. 2008. *Economic Development and Transition: Thought, Strategy, and Viability*. Marshall Lectures, Cambridge University. Cambridge, U.K.: Cambridge University Press.

Losch, Bruno, Sandrine Freguin-Gresh, and Thierry Giordano. 2008. "Structural Dimensions of Liberalization on Agriculture and Rural Development Background, Positioning and Results of the First Phase," RuralStruc Program, World Bank, Washington, DC.

Maertens, M., and J.F.M. Swinnen. 2009. "Trade, Standards, and Poverty: Evidence from Senegal." *World Development* 37(1), 161–78.

Mafeje, Archibald Boyce. 2003. *The Agrarian Question: Access to Land, and Peasant Responses in Sub-Saharan Africa*. Geneva: United Nations Research Institute for Social Development (UNRISD).

Majid, Nomaan. 2004. "Reaching Millennium Goals: How Well Does Agricultural Productivity Growth Reduce Poverty?" Employment Analysis Unit Employment Strategy Papers, ILO, Geneva.

Maredia, Mywish K., and David A. Raitzer. 2006. *CGIAR and NARS Partner Research in Africa. Evidence of Impact to Date*. Rome: CGIAR Science Council Secretariat.

Matthews, A. 2005. "Development Assistance to Agriculture: Can the Decline be Reversed?" *EuroChoices* 4(1): 24–25.

McCalla, A.F. 1998. "Agriculture and Food Needs to 2025." In *International Agricultural Development*, 3rd edition, ed. C.K. Eicher and J.M. Staatz. Baltimore: The Johns Hopkins University Press.

McCalla, A.F., and Cesar L. Revoredo. 2001. "Prospects for Global Food Security: A Critical Appraisal of Past Projections and Predictions." Food, Agriculture, and the Environment Discussion Paper 35, IFPRI, Washington, DC.

McCarthy, N., C. Dutilly-Diane, B. Drabo, A. Kamara, and J-P. Vanderlinden. 2004. *Managing Resources in Erratic Environments: An Analysis of Pastoralist Systems in Ethiopia, Niger and Burkina Faso*. Research Report 135. Washington, DC: IFPRI.

McKinsey and Company. 2009. "Charting Our Water Future: Economic Framework to Inform Decision Making." http://www.mckinsey.com/App_Media/Reports/Water/Charting_Our_Water_Future_Full_Report_001.pdf

Mellor, John W. 1998. "Foreign Aid and Agricultural–Led Development." In *International Agricultural Development*, ed. Carl K. Eicher and John Staatz. Baltimore: The Johns Hopkins University Press.

Mitchell, Donald. 2008. "A Note on Rising Food Prices." Policy Research Working Paper 4682, World Bank, Washington, DC.

Mitchell, D.O., M.D. Ingco, and R.C. Duncan. 1997. *The World Food Outlook*. Cambridge, U.K.: Cambridge University Press.

Mooij, J. 2005. *The Politics of Economic Reforms in India*. New Delhi: Sage.

Morris, Michael, Loraine Ronchi, and David Rorbach. 2009. "Building Sustainable Fertilizer Markets in Africa." Presentation for Towards Priority Actions for Market Development for African Farmers, May 13–15, 2009, Nairobi, Kenya.

Moss, Todd, and Sarah Rose. 2006. "China ExIm Bank and Africa: New Lending, New Challenges." *CGD Notes*. Washington, DC: Center for Global Development. http://www.eldis.org/vfile/upload/1/document/0708/DOC22802.pdf.

Narrod, Clare, Devesh Roy, Julius Okello, Belem Avendano, Karl Rich, and Amit Thorat. 2009. "Public-Private Partnership and Collective Action in High Value Fruit." *Food Policy* 34(1): 8–15.

Naylor, Rosamond L., Adam J. Liska, Marshall B. Burke, Walter P. Falcon, Joanne C. Gaskell, Scott D. Rozelle, and Kenneth G. Cassman. 2007. "The Ripple Effect: Biofuels, Food Security, and the Environment." *Environment* 49(9): 30–43.

Nin Pratt, A., B. Yu, and S. Fan. 2009. "Total Factor Productivity in Chinese and Indian Agriculture: Measures and Determinants." *China Agricultural Economic Review* 1(1): 9–12.

Nkamleu, Guy Blaise. 2004. "Productivity Growth, Technical Progress and Efficiency Change in African Agriculture." *African Development Review* 16(1): 203–22.

Nogueira, Roberto Martinez. 2006. "New Roles of the Public Sector for an Agriculture for Development Agenda." Latin American Center for Rural Development (RIMISP), Santiago, Chile.

Nogués, J.J. 2008. "The Domestic Impact of Export Restrictions: The Case of Argentina." International Food & Agricultural Trade Policy Council (IPC) Position Paper—Agricultural and Rural Development Policy Series, July 2008, Rome.

Nottenburg, C., P.G. Pardey, and B.D. Wright. 2003. "Biotechnology and Genetic Resource Policies: Accessing Other People's Technology." Brief 4. Washington, DC: IFPRI.

ODI (Overseas Development Institute). 2008a. "The Political Economy of Pro-Poor Growth." Briefing Paper 35, January, London.

———. 2008b. "Supporting Pro-Poor Growth Processes: Implications for Donors." Briefing Paper 34, January, London.

———. 2006. "Governance, Development and Aid Effectiveness: A Quick Guide to Complex Relationships." Briefing Paper, March, London.

———. 1995. "Land Reform: New Seeds on Old Ground?" *ODI Natural Resource Perspective* Number 6. London.

OECD (Organisation for Economic Co-operation and Development). 2009. *Agricultural Policies in Emerging Economies: Monitoring and Evaluation*. Paris: OECD.

———. 2006. *Development Aid at a Glance: Statistics by Region*. 2006 Edition. Paris: OECD.

———. 1999. *Agricultural Policies in Emerging and Transition Economies*. OECD Center for Cooperation with Non-Members. Paris: OECD.

Paarlberg, R.L. 2002. "Governance and Food Security in an Age of Globalization: Food, Agriculture, and the Environment." Discussion Paper 36, IFPRI, Washington, DC.

Palaniswamy, Nethra, and Regina Birner. 2006. "Financing Agricultural Development: The Political Economy of Public Spending on Agriculture in Sub-Saharan Africa." In *Proceedings of the German Development Economics Conference*. Berlin, No. 4.

Pardey, P. G., J.M. Alston, and R.R. Piggott, eds. 2006. *Agricultural R&D in the Developing World: Too Little, Too Late?* Washington, DC: IFPRI.

Pardey, P.G., N. Beintema, S. Dehmer, and S. Wood. 2006. *Agricultural Research: A Growing Global Divide?* Agricultural Science and Technology Indicators Initiative. Washington, DC: IFPRI.

Parkinson, S. 2008. "Learning Participation in Rural Development: A Study of Uganda's National Agricultural Advisory Services." University of Guelph.

Parris, K., and W. Legg. 2006. "Water and Farms: Towards Sustainable Use." *OECD Observer* No. 254. March. http://www.oecdobserver.org/news/fullstory.php/aid/1801/Water_and_farms:_Towards_sustainable_use.html

Parthasarthy Rao, P., P.S. Birthal, and P.K. Joshi. 2006. "Sustaining Growth in High-Value Food Commodities: Role of Urbanization and Infrastructure." *Strategic Assessments and Development Pathways for Agriculture in the Semi-Arid Tropics Policy Brief* 9. International Crops Research Institute for the Semi-Arid Tropics, Andhra Pradesh, India.

Peacock, Christie, Andrew Jowett, Andrew Dorward, Colin Poulton, and Ian Urey. 2004. *Reaching the Poor: A Call to Action. Investment in Smallholder Agriculture in Sub-Saharan Africa*. London: FARM-Africa.

Peacock, Tony, Christopher Ward, and Gretel Gambarelli. 2007. "Investment in Agricultural Water for Poverty Reduction and Economic Growth in Sub-Saharan Africa. Synthesis Report." World Bank, Washington, DC.

Pingali, Prabhu, and Tim Kelley. 2007. "The Role of International Agricultural Research in Contributing to Global

Food Security and Poverty Alleviation: The Case of the CGIAR." In *Handbook of Agricultural Economics*, Volume 3, *Agricultural Development: Farmers, Farm Production and Farm Markets*. Amsterdam: North-Holland.

Pinstrup-Andersen, P., and R. Pandya-Lorch. 1994. "Alleviating Poverty, Intensifying Agriculture and Effectively Managing Natural Resources, Food, Agriculture, and Environment." Discussion Paper, IFPRI, Washington, DC.

Porter, M.E. 1985. *Competitive Advantage, Crating and Sustaining Superior Performance*. New York: The Free Press.

Poulton, Colin, Geoff Tyler, Peter Hazell, Andrew Dorward, Jonathan Kydd, and Mike Stockbridge. 2008. "All-Africa Review of Experiences with Commercial Agriculture." Background paper for the Competitive Commercial Agriculture in Sub-Saharan Africa (CCAA) Study, World Bank, Washington, DC.

Pray, C.E., K. Fuglie, and D.K.N. Johnson. 2007. "Private Sector Research." In *Handbook of Agricultural Economics*, Volume 3, *Agricultural Development: Farmers, Farm Production and Farm Markets*, ed. R.E. Evenson, P. Pingali, and T. Paul Schultz. Amsterdam: North-Holland.

Pray, C.E., S. Ribeiro, R.A.E. Muller, and P. Parthsarathy Rao. 1991. "Private Research and Public Benefit: The Private Seed Industry for Sorghum and Pearl Millet in India." *Research Policy* 20(4): 315–24.

Pretty, Jules. 2006. "Agroecological Approaches to Agricultural Development." Latin American Center for Rural Development (RIMISP), Santiago, Chile.

Pursell, Garry, Ashok Gulati, and Kanupriya Gupta. 2009. "India." In *Distortions to Agricultural Incentives in Asia*, ed. J. Anderson and K. Martin. Washington, DC: World Bank.

QAG (Quality Assurance Group, World Bank). 2004. "Cross–Country ARD Sector AAA Assessment." World Bank, Washington, DC.

Quan, J. 2002. "Better Livelihoods for Poor People: The Role of Land Policy." Discussion draft, Department for International Development (DFID), London.

Rabobank International. 2008. "Watering Scarcity: Private Investment Opportunities in Agricultural Water Use Efficiency." http://pdf.wri.org/watering_scarcity.pdf.

Raitzer, D.A. 2003. "Benefit-Cost Meta-Analysis of Investment in the International Agricultural Research Centers of the CGIAR." CGIAR Science Council Secretariat (www.cgiar.org/pdf/bcmeta.pdf), Rome.

Ravallion, Martin, and Shaohua Chen. 2007. "China's (Uneven) Progress against Poverty." *Journal of Development Economics* 82(1): 1–42.

Reardon, T., and J.A. Berdegué. 2006. "The Retail-led Transformation of Agrifood Systems and Its Implications for Development Policies." Latin American Center for Rural Development (RIMISP), Santiago, Chile.

Reardon, T., and A. Gulati. 2008. "The Supermarket Revolution in Developing Countries. Policies for 'Competitiveness with Inclusiveness.'" *Policy Brief* 2, June, IFPRI, Washington, DC.

Renkow, Mitch, and Derek Byerlee. Forthcoming. "The Impacts of CGIAR Research: A Review of Recent Evidence." *Food Policy*.

Restuccia, D., D.T. Yang, and X. Zhu. 2007. "Agriculture and Aggregate Productivity: A Quantitative Cross-Country Analysis." *Journal of Monetary Economics* 55(2): 234–50.

Rios, L.D., S. Jaffee, S. Henson, and J. Mugisha. 2009. *Not Yet up to Standard: The Legacy of Two Decades of Private, Government and Donor Efforts to Promote Ugandan Horticultural Exports*. Joint Organizational Discussion Paper Issue 1. Washington, DC: World Bank.

Roberts, Peter, KC Shyam, and Cordula Rastogi. 2006. "Rural Access Index: A Key Development Indicator." Transport Papers No. 10, Transport Sector Board, World Bank, Washington, DC.

Rohrbach, David, and Kizito Mazvimavi. 2006. "Do Seed Fairs Improve Food Security and Strengthen Rural Markets?" *Briefing Note* No. 3, ICRISAT-Bulawayo.

Romstad, E. 2007. "What Is So Special About Agriculture?" *EuroChoices* 6(3): 4–5.

Ruttan, Vernon 2002. "Productivity Growth in World Agriculture: Sources and Constraints." *Journal of Economic Perspectives* 16(4): 161–84.

Schultz, T.W. 1953. *The Economic Organization of Agriculture*. New York: McGraw-Hill.

———. 1998. "Investing in People." In *International Agricultural Development*, 3rd ed. Baltimore: The Johns Hopkins University Press.

Scoones, I. 2008. "Policy Frameworks for Increasing Soil Fertility in Africa: Debating the Alternatives a Future Agricultures Consortium Debate." www.future-agricultures.org/pdf%20files/soilfert.pdf

Scoones, I., and J. Thompson. 2009. *Farmer First Revisited: Innovation for Agricultural Research and Development*. Oxford: ITDG Publishing.

Senthikumar, K., P.S. Bindraban, T.M. Thiyagarajan, N. de Ridder, and K.E. Giller. 2008. "Modified Rice Cultivation in Tamil Nadu, India: Yield Gains and Farmers." *Agricultural Systems* 98(2): 82–94.

Sharma, R.P., and J.R. Anderson. 1985. "Nepal and the CGIAR Centers: A Study of Their Collaboration in Agricultural Research." CGIAR Study Paper No. 7, World Bank, Washington, DC.

Simmonds, N.W. 1985. "Farming Systems Research: A Review." World Bank Technical Paper No. 43, Washington, DC.

Singh, J.P., B.E. Swanson, and K.M. Singh. 2006. "Developing a Decentralized, Market-Driven Extension System in India: The ATMA Model." In *Changing Roles of Agricultural Extension in Asian Nations*, ed. A.W. Van den Ban and R.K. Samanta. New Delhi: B.R. Publishing.

Smale, M., M.J. Cohen, and L. Nagarajan. 2009. "Local Markets, Local Varieties, Rising Food Prices and Small Farmers' Access to Seed." *IFPRI Issue Brief* 59, IFPRI, Washington, DC.

Smit, B., and M. W. Skinner. 2002. "Adaptation Options in Agriculture to Climate Change: A Typology." *Mitigation and Adaptation Strategies for Global Change* 7: 85–114.

Smith, L., and I. Urey. 2002. "Institutions and Economic Policies for Pro-Poor Agricultural Growth: India Literature Review." Working Paper, *Institutions and Economic Policies for Pro-Poor Agricultural Growth*, Imperial College, London.

Speelman, Stijn, Marijke D'Haese, Jeroen Buysse, and Luc D'Haese. 2008. "A Measure for the Efficiency of Water Use and its Determinants: A Case Study of Small-Scale Irrigation Schemes in North-West Province, South Africa." *Agricultural Systems* 98: 31–39.

Spielman, David J., Javier Ekboir, Kristin Davis, and Cosmas M.O. Ochieng. 2008. "An Innovation Systems Perspective on Strengthening Agricultural Education and Training in Sub-Saharan Africa." *Agricultural Systems* 98: 1–9.

Staatz, John M., and Carl K. Eicher 1998. "Agricultural Development Ideas in Historical Perspective." In *International Agricultural Development*, ed. Carl K. Eicher and John M. Staatz. Baltimore: The Johns Hopkins University Press.

Stads, Gert-Jan, and Nienke M. Bientema. 2009. *Public Agricultural Research in Latin America and the Caribbean. ASTI Synthesis Report,* March. Washington, DC: ASTI, IFPRI, and IDB.

Steinfeld, Henning, Pierre Gerber, Tom Wassenaar, Vincent Castel, Mauricio Rosales, and Cees de Haan. 2006. *Livestock's Long Shadow: Environmental Issues and Options.* Rome: FAO and LEAD.

Stern, N. 2007. *The Economics of Climate Change: The Stern Review.* Cambridge, U.K.: Cambridge University Press.

Stevens, R.D., and C. L. Jabara. 1988. *Agricultural Development Principles: Economic Theory and Empirical Evidence.* Baltimore: The Johns Hopkins University Press

Stiglitz, J.E. 1998. "Markets, Market Failures, and Development." In *International Agricultural Development*, 3rd ed., ed. C.K. Eicher and J.M. Staatz. Baltimore: The Johns Hopkins University Press.

Subramaniam, C. 1995. *Hand of Destiny.- Volume 2: The Green Revolution.* Bombay: Bharatiya Vidya Bhavan.

Swanson, B. E. 2008. *Global Review of Good Agricultural Extension and Advisory Service Practices.* Rome: Food and Agriculture Organization of the United Nations.

Swanson, B., and R. Rajalahti. 2010. *Strengthening Agricultural Extension and Advisory Systems: Procedures for Addressing, Transforming and Evaluating Extension Systems.* Washington, DC: World Bank.

Swinnen, J.F.M., ed. 2007. *Global Supply Chains, Standards and the Poor: How the Globalization of Food Systems and Standards Affects Rural Development and Poverty.* Wallingford: CABI Publishing.

Swinnen, J.F.M., and Maertens, M. 2007. "Globalization, Privatization, and Vertical Coordination in Food Value Chains in Developing and Transition Countries." In *Contributions of Agricultural Economics to Critical Policy Issues: Proceedings of the Twenty-Sixth Conference of the International Association of Agricultural Economists,* ed. K. Otsuka and K. Kalirajan. Malden, MA: Blackwell.

Thirtle, C., and J. Piesse. 2007. "Governance, Agricultural Productivity and Poverty Reduction in Africa, Asia and Latin America." *Irrigation and Drainage* 56(2-3): 165–77.

Thirtle, C., L. Lin, and J. Piesse. 2003. "The Impact of Research-Led Agricultural Productivity Growth on Poverty Reduction in Africa, Asia and Latin America." *World Development* 31 (12): 1959–75.

Thomas, N., M. Demment, C. Lessard, W. Masters, J. Sutherland, E. Terry, and A. Youdeowei. 2007. *The Forum for Agricultural Research in Africa: Joint External Evaluation.* London: DFID.

Timmer, C. Peter 2007. *A World Without Agriculture The Structural Transformation in Historical Perspective.* Washington, DC: The AEI Press.

———. 2005a. "Agriculture and Pro-Poor Growth: An Asian Perspective." Working Paper Number 63. July. Center for Global Development, Washington, DC.

———. 2005b. "Food Aid: Doing Well by Doing Good." *CGD Notes,* Center for Global Development, Washington, DC.

———. 1998. "The Role of Agriculture in Indonesia's Development." In *International Agricultural Development*, 3rd ed., ed. Carl K. Eicher and John M. Staatz. Baltimore: The Johns Hopkins University Press.

———. 1997. "Farmers and Markets: The Political Economy of New Paradigms." *American Journal of Agricultural Economics* 79(2): 621–27.

———. 1991. "The Role of the State in Agricultural Development." In *Agriculture and the State: Growth, Employment, and Poverty in Developing Countries*, ed. C. Peter Timmer. . Ithaca, NY: Cornell University Press.

Timmer, C.P., W. P. Falcon, and S. R. Pearson. 1983. *Food*

Policy Analysis. Baltimore: The Johns Hopkins University Press for the World Bank.

Torero, Maximo, and Joachim von Braun, eds. 2006. *Information and Communication Technologies for Development and Poverty Reduction: The Potential of Telecommunications.* Baltimore, MD: The Johns Hopkins University Press for IFPRI.

Tschirley, David, Colin Poulton, and Patrick Labaste, eds. 2009. *Organization and Performance of Cotton Sectors in Africa: Learning from Reform Experience.* Agriculture and Rural Development. Washington, DC: World Bank.

Tsumagari, Maki 2008. "A Review of 15 Years of World Bank Lending from 1996–2006." Transport Unit, World Bank, Washington, DC.

Tripp, R., M. Wijeratne, and V.H. Piyadasa. 2005. "What Should We Expect from Farmer Field Schools? A Sri Lanka Case Study." *World Development* 33(10): 1705–20.

Umali-Deininger, D., and M. Sur. 2007. "Food Safety in a Globalizing World: Opportunities and Challenges for India." In *Contributions of Agricultural Economics to Critical Policy Issues: Proceedings of the Twenty-Sixth Conference of the International Association of Agricultural Economists,* ed. K. Otsuka and K. Kalirajan. Malden, MA: Blackwell.

UNCTAD (United Nations Conference on Trade and Development). 2009. *World Investment Report (WIR), Transnational Corporations, Agricultural Production, and Development.* Geneva: United Nations.

UNEP (United Nations Environment Programme). 2008. "Governance and Agriculture." Prepared for One Nature—One World—Our Future, the 9th UN Conference of the Parties to the Convention on Biological Diversity, Bonn, Germany, May 19-30.

United Nations. 2008. *The Millennium Development Goals Report.* New York, NY: United Nations.

———. 2002. "A Framework for Action on Agriculture. "WEHAB Working Group, World Summit on Sustainable Development, Johannesburg, August 26—September 4.

Uphoff, Norman, ed. 2002. *Agroecological Innovations: Increasing Food Production with Participatory Development.* London and Sterling, VA: Earthscan.

van Arkadie, Brian, and Do Duc Dinh. 2004. "Economic Reform in Tanzania and Vietnam: A Comparative Commentary." William Davidson Institute Working Paper No. 706, University of Michigan, Ann Arbor.

van den Berg, H., and J. Jiggins. 2007. "The Impacts of Farmer Field Schools in Relation to Integrated Pest Management." *World Development* 35(4): 663–86.

van Koppen, Barbara. 2009. "Gender, Resource Rights, and Wetland Rice Productivity in Burkina Faso." In *Institutional Economics: Perspectives on African Agricultural Development,* ed. Johann F Kirsten, Andrew R Dorward, Colin Poulton, and Nick Vink. Washington, DC: IFPRI.

Van Steenbergen, Frank, Gerz Cornish, and Chris Perry. 2007. *Charging for Irrigation Services: Guidelines for Practitioners.* London: IWA Publishing.

von Braun, J. 2008. *Food and Financial Crises: Implications for Agriculture and the Poor.* Washington, DC: IFPRI.

———. 2007. *The World Food Situation: New Driving Forces and Required Actions.* Washington, DC: IFPRI.

———. 2005. "The World Food Situation: An Overview." IFPRI Policy Brief, Washington, DC.

von Braun, Joachim, and Nurul Islam. 2008. "Toward a New Global Governance System for Agriculture, Food, and Nutrition: What are the Options?" *IFPRI Forum,* March.

von Braun, J., and Ruth Meinzen-Dick. 2009. "'Land Grabbing' by Foreign Investors in Developing Countries: Risks and Opportunities." *IFPRI Policy Brief* 13, Washington, DC.

von Braun, J., M.S. Swaminathan, and M.W. Rosegrant. 2004. "Agriculture, Food Security, Nutrition and the Millennium Development Goals." IFPRI Essay, Washington, DC.

Vyas, V.S., and Bingsheng Ke. 2004. "Market Reforms in China and India—Approach, Impact and Lessons Learned." Revised version of a paper presented at the Chinese Academy of Agricultural Sciences (CAAS), International Food Policy Research Institute (IFPRI) International Conference of the Dragon and the Elephant, Beijing, November 11–12, 2003.

Wang, Jinxia, Robert Mendelsohn, Ariel Dinar, Jikun Huang, Scott Rozelle, and Lijuan Zhang 2007. "Can China Continue Feeding Itself? The Impact of Climate Change on Agriculture." Sustainable Rural and Urban Development Team Development Research Group, Policy Research Working Paper No. 4470, World Bank, Washington, DC.

Weatherspoon, Dave, and Anthony Ross. 2008. "Designing the Last Mile of the Supply Chain in Africa: Firm Expansion and Managerial Inferences from a Grocer Model of Location Decisions." *International Food and Agribusiness Management Review* 11(1).

Webber, C. M., and P. Labaste. 2010. *Building Competitiveness in Africa's Agriculture; A Guide to Value Chain Concepts and Applications.* Washington, DC: World Bank.

Wily, L. A. 2006. *Land Rights Reform and Governance in Africa: How to Make It Work in the 21st Century?* Discussion Paper. Drylands Development Centre and Oslo Governance Centre, UNDP, Nairobi, and Oslo. New York: UNDP.

World Bank. 2010a. "Fiscal 09 Review of Lending to Agriculture and Related Sectors," Draft. World Bank, Washington, DC.

———. 2010b. "Agricultural Water Management in Rainfed Areas and Climate Change: Insights from a Portfolio Review." Presentation for Adapting Agricultural Water Management to Climate Change. SDN Forum 2010, January 21, World Bank, Washington, DC.

———. 2009a. "Arab Republic of Egypt—Linking Funding to Outputs: Expenditures of the Ministry of Agriculture and Land Reclamation." Public Expenditure Review, Report No. 47547-EG, Sustainable Department Middle East and North Africa Region, Washington, DC, World Bank.

———. 2009b. *Awakening Africa's Sleeping Giant: Prospects for Commercial Agriculture in the Guinea Savannah Zone and Beyond.* Directions in Development, Agriculture and Rural Development. Washington, DC: World Bank.

———. 2009c. *The Changing Face of Rural Space. Agriculture and Rural Development in the Western Balkans.* Directions in Development, Agriculture and Rural Development. Washington, DC: World Bank.

———. 2009d. "Country Assistance Strategies: Retrospective and Future Directions." Draft, OPCS. http://siteresources.worldbank.org/PROJECTS/Resources/40940-1258057670156/ContentsandExecutiveSummary.pdf

———. 2009e. *Implementing Agriculture for Development: World Bank Group Agriculture Action Plan: Fiscal 2010–2012.* Washington, DC: World Bank.

———. 2009f. *Low-Carbon Development: Latin American Responses to Climate Change,* ed. Augusto de la Torre, Pablo Fajnzylber, and John Nash. Washington, DC: World Bank.

———. 2009g. *Minding the Stock: Bringing Public Policy to Bear on Livestock Sector Development.* Report No. 44010-GLB. Washington, DC: World Bank.

———. 2009h. "Review of the Fiscal Year 2008 Rural Portfolio." World Bank, Washington, DC.

———. 2009i. "Rising Food Prices: Policy Options and World Bank Response." Background Note for the Development Committee. http://siteresources.worldbank.org/NEWS/Resources/risingfoodprices_backgroundnote_apr08.pdf

———. 2009j. "Strengthening Agricultural Extension and Advisory Systems: Procedures for Assessing, Transforming, and Evaluating Extension Systems." Agriculture and Rural Development Discussion Paper 44, World Bank, Washington, DC.

———. 2009k. *Trade and Transit Facilitation for Landlocked Developing Countries.* International Trade Department. Washington, DC: World Bank.

———. 2008a. "Agriculture, an Engine for Growth and Poverty Reduction: IDA at Work." Sustainable Development Network, World Bank, Washington, DC. http://siteresources.worldbank.org/IDA/Resources/IDA-Agriculture.pdf

———. 2008b. "Agricultural Innovation Systems: From Diagnostics Towards Operational Practices." Agriculture and Rural Development Discussion Paper No. 38, World Bank, Washington, DC.

———. 2008c. "From Agriculture to Nutrition: Pathways, Synergies and Outcomes." *Agricultural and Rural Development Notes* Issue 40, World Bank, Washington, DC.

———. 2008d. *Climate Change Adaptation and Mitigation in Development Programs: A Practical Guide.* Washington, DC: World Bank.

———. 2008e. "Double Jeopardy: Responding to High Food and Fuel Prices." Prepared for the G8 Hokkaido-Tokyo Summit, July 2. World Bank, Washington, DC.

———. 2008f. "Implementing Low-Cost Rural Land Certification: The Case of Ethiopia." *Agriculture and Rural Development Notes* Issue 34, World Bank, Washington, DC.

———. 2008g. *Land in Transition. Reform and Poverty in Rural Vietnam.* Washington, DC: World Bank.

———. 2008h. "Livestock Externalities: Public Policy and Investment Needs." Report No. 44010-GLB, World Bank, Washington, DC.

———. 2008i. "A New Model for Public-Private Partnership for Land Access and Rural Enterprise Formation." *Agricultural & Rural Development Notes on Land Policy and Administration* 42693. World Bank, Washington, DC.

———. 2008j. "Response to the Food Crisis: IDA at Work." Sustainable Development Network, World Bank, Washington, DC.

———. 2008k. "The Role of Mobile Phones in Sustainable Rural Poverty Reduction." ICT Policy Division, Global Information and Communications Department, World Bank, Washington, DC.

———. 2008l. *The Rural Investment Climate, Analysis and Findings.* Agriculture and Rural Development Department. Washington, DC: World Bank.

———. 2008m. "Utter Pradesh Sodic Lands Reclamation Project Implementation Completion and Results Report." Report No. ICR0000653. World Bank, Washington, DC.

———. 2008n. *World Bank Research Digest* 3(1).

———. 2007a. "Africa Region: Irrigation Business Plan." Revised Draft October 23, 2007, World Bank, Washington, DC.

———. 2007b. *Agriculture for Development: World Development Report 2008.* Washington, DC: World Bank.

———. 2007c. "Aid Architecture: An Overview of the Main Trends in Official Development Assistance Flows." IDA Resource Mobilization, World Bank Group, Washington, DC.

———. 2007d. "Community-based Financial Organizations: A Solution to Access in Remote Rural Areas?" Agriculture and Rural Development Discussion Paper 34, World Bank, Washington, DC.

———. 2007e. "Cultivating Knowledge and Skills to Grow African Agriculture." *Agricultural and Rural Development Notes,* Issue 29, World Bank, Washington, DC.

———. 2007f. *Cultivating Knowledge and Skills to Grow African Agriculture A Synthesis of an Institutional, Regional, and International Review.* Agriculture and Rural Development Department, World Bank. Washington, DC: World Bank.

———. 2007g. "Emerging Public-Private Partnerships in Irrigation Development and Management." Water Sector Board Discussion Paper No. 10, World Bank, Washington, DC.

———. 2007h. "More and Better Investment in Agriculture." *Agriculture for Development Policy Brief, World Development Report 2008.* World Bank, Washington, DC.

———. 2007i. "The Role of Technology and Institutions in the Cost Recovery of Irrigation and Drainage Projects." Agriculture and Rural Development Discussion Paper 33, World Bank, Washington, DC.

———. 2007j. "Social and Environmental Sustainability of Agriculture and Rural Development Investments: A Monitoring and Evaluation Toolkit." Agriculture and Rural Development Discussion Paper 31, World Bank, Washington, DC.

———. 2007k. "Strengthening Governance to Support Agriculture." *Agriculture for Development Policy Brief, World Development Report 2008*, World Bank, Washington, DC.

———. 2007l. "World Bank Support to the Livestock Sector: A Retrospective." World Bank, Washington, DC.

———. 2006a. *Agriculture Investment Sourcebook.* Washington, DC: World Bank.

———. 2006b. "Economic and Sector Work (ESW) in Agriculture and Rural Development (ARD): A Review of the Fiscal 2006 Experience." World Bank, Washington, DC.

———. 2006c. "India: Taking Agriculture to the Market." Agriculture and Rural Development Sector Unit, South Asia Region, Report No. 35953-INH, World Bank, Washington, DC.

———. 2006d. *Intellectual Property Rights: Designing Regimes to Support Plant Breeding in Developing Countries.* Report No. 35517-GLB. Washington, DC: World Bank.

———. 2006e. *Reengaging in Agricultural Water Management: Challenges and Options.* Directions in Development. Washington, DC: World Bank.

———. 2006f. *The Rural Investment Climate: It Differs and It Matters*, Agriculture and Rural Development Department. Washington, DC: World Bank.

———. 2006g. "Scenario Planning to Guide Long-Term In-

vestments in Agricultural Science and Technology: Theory and Practice from a Case Study on India." Agriculture and Rural Development Discussion Paper 29, World Bank, Washington, DC .

———. 2005a. *Agricultural Growth for the Poor: An Agenda for Development.* Directions in Development. Washington, DC: World Bank.

———. 2005b. "Agriculture, Rural Development and Pro-Poor Growth. Country Experiences in the Post-Reform Era." Agriculture and Rural Development Discussion Paper 21, World Bank, Washington, DC.

———. 2005c. "Conversations with Country Directors on the Agriculture and Rural Development Agenda." ARD Customer Satisfaction Survey. World Bank, Washington, DC.

———. 2005d. "Cost Recovery and Water Pricing for Irrigation and Drainage Projects." Agriculture and Rural Development Discussion Paper 26, World Bank, Washington, DC.

———. 2005e. *India: Re-Energizing the Agricultural Sector to Sustain Growth and Reduce Poverty.* New Delhi: Oxford University Press for the World Bank.

———. 2005f. "Meeting Development Challenges. Renewed Approaches to Rural Finance." Agriculture and Rural Development Department, World Bank, Washington, DC.

———. 2005g. "PACTA: Rural Development in Honduras Through Access to Land and the Development of Productive Enterprises." *En Breve* No. 75. Latin America and Caribbean Region, World Bank, Washington, DC.

———. 2005h. *Shaping the Future of Water for Agriculture. A Sourcebook for Investment in Agricultural Water Management.* Washington, D.C.: World Bank.

———. 2005i. "Investments in Rural Finance for Agriculture." In *World Bank Agricultural Investment Sourcebook*, Module 8. Washington, DC: World Bank.

———. 2004a. *Agriculture Investment Sourcebook.* Washington, DC: World Bank.

———. 2004b. *World Development Report 2005: A Better Investment Climate for Everyone.* Washington, DC: World Bank.

———. 2003a. "Agricultural Research and Extension, Implementation Completion Report (IDA-29770) Project." Report No. 25624-NEP, March 24, 2003, World Bank, Washington, DC.

———. 2003b. *Land Policies for Growth and Poverty Reduction.* World Bank Policy Research Report. Washington, DC: World Bank.

———. 2003c. "Promoting Agro-Enterprise and Agro-Food Systems Development in Developing and Transition Countries: Towards an Operational Strategy for the World

Bank Group." Agriculture & Rural Development Family, Report No. 26032, World Bank, Washington, DC.

———. 2003d. *Reaching the Rural Poor: A Renewed Strategy for Rural Development*. Washington, DC: World Bank.

———. 2002. "Adaptable Lending: Third Review of Experience." Operations Policy and Country Services. World Bank, Washington, DC.

———. 2001. "India Power Supply to Agriculture." World Bank, Washington, DC.

———. 1998. "India-Water Resources Management." Sector Review Report on the Irrigation Sector, Rural Development Unit, South Asia Region, World Bank, in Cooperation with Ministry of Water Resources Government of India, World Bank, Washington, DC.

———. 1997a. *Rural Development: From Vision to Action*. Washington, DC: World Bank.

———. 1997b. *The State in a Changing World. World Development Report 1997*. Washington, DC: World Bank.

———. 1986. *Trade and Pricing Policies in World Agriculture. World Development Report 1986*. Washington, DC: World Bank.

———. 1982. *World Development Report 1982*. New York, NY: Oxford University Press for the World Bank.

World Bank-IFC 2009. "Models of Collaboration, Working Across the World Bank Group Boundaries," September 2009. World Bank, Washington, DC.

World Bank and IFPRI. 2010. *Gender and Governance in Rural Services: Insights from India, Ethiopia and Ghana*. Washington, DC: World Bank.

———. 2006. "Agriculture and Achieving the Millennium Development Goals." World Bank, Washington, DC.

World Bank, FAO, and IFAD. 2009a. *Improving Food Security in Arab Countries*. Washington, DC: World Bank.

———. 2009b. *Gender in Agriculture Sourcebook*. Washington, DC: World Bank.

World Bank Group, UNEP, and UNIDO. 1999. *Pollution Prevention and Abatement Handbook 1998: Toward Cleaner Production*. Washington, DC: World Bank.

Wright, B.D., and P.G. Pardey. 2006. "Changing Intellectual Property Regimes: Implications for Developing Country Agriculture." *International Journal of Technology and Globalisation* 2(1/2), 93–114.

Wright, B. D, Philip Pardey, Carol Nottenburg, and Bonwoo Koo. 2007. "Agricultural Innovation: Investments and Incentives." In *Handbook of Agricultural Economics*, Volume 3, ed. R.E. Evenson and P. Pingali. Amsterdam: North-Holland.

Yadav, R.P. 1987. "Agricultural Research in Nepal: Resource Allocation, Structure, and Incentives." Research Report No. 62, IFPRI, Washington, DC.

Yaron, J., M. Benjamin, and G. Piprek. 1997. *Rural Finance: Issues, Design and Best Practices*. ESSD Monograph Series No. 14. Washington, DC: World Bank.

Photographs